Roxio® Easy Media Creator™ For Dummies®

Cheat Sheet

W9-BZW-061

Roxio Easy Media Creator 7 Home

Home is the starting point for all the digital media projects you create with Easy Media Creator. From Home, you can launch any Easy Media Creator application or tool and edit any media project that you've created recently.

Tasks   Recent projects   Applications   Tools

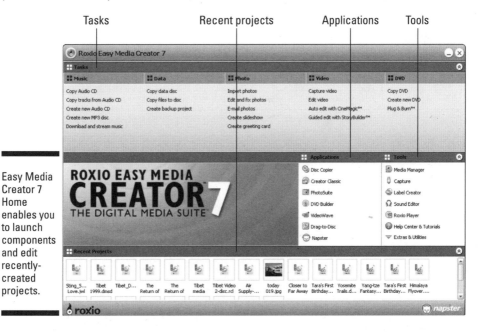

Easy Media Creator 7 Home enables you to launch components and edit recently-created projects.

Roxio® Easy Media Creator™ For Dummies®

Selecting the Right Easy Media Creator Component to Use

Use	To Do This	Chapter Reference
Roxio Disc Copier	To make duplicate copies of CD or DVD discs	3 & 8
Creator Classic	Compile and burn audio CD	8
	Copy tracks from audio CD	8
	Compile and burn MP3 disc	8
	Compile and burn data backup CD or DVD disc	3
	Schedule regular data backups	3
	Create Enhanced data and audio CD	8
	Create Mixed-mode CD	8
Drag-to-Disc	Compile and burn data backup CD or DVD disc	3
Label Creator	Design and print CD and DVD disc labels and case inserts	9
Capture	Acquire digital audio, photos, and video from connected analog and digital devices	10
Sound Editor	Record audio played on external devices and with internal playback software	5
	Edit audio recordings saved on disk	5
	Convert from one audio file format to another	5
Media Manager	Collect and organize all types of digital media files	4
	Tag and annotate digital media file for search	4
	Search folders and collections for specific media	4
PhotoSuite	Fix and edit digital photos	7
	Create collages, calendars, and the like with photos	7
	Create panoramas from individual panned shots	7
VideoWave	Design video productions and output them as movies for playback on various devices	11
DVD Builder	Design DVD projects and burn them to CD or DVD disc	12
	Burn videotape direct to CD or DVD disc	12
	Edit rewritable and unfinished DVD discs	12

Copyright © 2004 Wiley Publishing, Inc.
All rights reserved.

Item 7131-1.

For more information about Wiley Publishing,
call 1-800-762-2974.

For Dummies: Bestselling Book Series for Beginners

Roxio® Easy Media Creator™ FOR DUMMIES®

by Greg Harvey

WILEY

Wiley Publishing, Inc.

Roxio® Easy Media Creator™ For Dummies®

Published by
Wiley Publishing, Inc.
111 River Street
Hoboken, NJ 07030-5774

For general information on our other products and services or to obtain technical support, please contact our Customer Care Department within the U.S. at 800-762-2974, outside the U.S. at 317-572-3993, or fax 317-572-4002.

Wiley also publishes its books in a variety of electronic formats. Some content that appears in print may not be available in electronic books.

Library of Congress Control Number: 2004102601

ISBN: 0-7645-7131-1

Manufactured in the United States of America

10 9 8 7 6 5 4 3 2 1

1B/RR/QW/QU/IN

About the Author

Greg Harvey has authored tons of computer books, the most recent being *Excel 2003 For Dummies* and *Adobe Acrobat 6 PDF For Dummies*. He started out training business users on how to use IBM personal computers and their attendant computer software in the rough and tumble days of DOS, WordStar, and Lotus 1-2-3 in the mid-80s of the last century. After working for a number of independent training firms, he went on to teach semester-long courses in spreadsheet and database management software at Golden Gate University in San Francisco.

His love of teaching has translated into an equal love of writing. *For Dummies* books are, of course, his all-time favorites to write because they enable him to write to his favorite audience, the beginner. They also enable him to use humor (a key element to success in the training room) and, most delightful of all, to express an opinion or two about the subject matter at hand.

Dedication

To Chris — my partner and helpmate in all aspects of my life

Author's Acknowledgments

I'm always very grateful to the many people who work so hard to bring my book projects into being, and this one is no exception. This time, preliminary thanks are in order to Andy Cummings and Tiffany Franklin for giving me this opportunity to write about Roxio's great new suite of media creation programs.

Next, I want to express great thanks to my project editor, Christine Berman (a better person to work with you'll never find), and to my partner in crime, Christopher Aiken (I really appreciate all your editing, additions, and comments on this one). Thanks also go to Mark Chambers for the great technical edit, Adrienne Martinez for coordinating its production, and everybody at Wiley Publishing and TECHBOOKS Production Services for proofreading and indexing.

Special thanks to Chris Taylor, Product Market Manager at Roxio, for all his personal help and encouragement as well as to his staff and support personnel for their speedy responses to my few questions about this great version of their most versatile software.

Publisher's Acknowledgments

We're proud of this book; please send us your comments through our online registration form located at www.dummies.com/register/.

Some of the people who helped bring this book to market include the following:

Acquisitions, Editorial, and Media Development

Project Editor: Christine Berman

Acquisitions Editor: Tiffany Franklin

Copy Editor: Christine Berman

Technical Editor: Mark Chambers

Editorial Manager: Carol Sheehan

Media Development Manager: Laura VanWinkle

Media Development Supervisor: Richard Graves

Editorial Assistant: Amanda Foxworth

Cartoons: Rich Tennant (www.the5thwave.com)

Production

Project Coordinator: Adrienne Martinez

Layout and Graphics: Amanda Carter, Andrea Dahl, Lynsey Osborn, Heather Ryan

Proofreaders: David Faust, Andy Hollandbeck, Carl William Pierce, TECHBOOKS Production Services

Indexer: TECHBOOKS Production Services

Special Help
Melanee Prendergast

Publishing and Editorial for Technology Dummies

    Richard Swadley, Vice President and Executive Group Publisher

    Andy Cummings, Vice President and Publisher

    Mary C. Corder, Editorial Director

Publishing for Consumer Dummies

    Diane Graves Steele, Vice President and Publisher

    Joyce Pepple, Acquisitions Director

Composition Services

    Gerry Fahey, Vice President of Production Services

    Debbie Stailey, Director of Composition Services

Contents at a Glance

Table of Contents

Foreword

*W*ith *Roxio Easy Media Creator For Dummies*, Greg Harvey has put together a comprehensive overview of our software. In true *For Dummies* style, the book is written in plain language, logically arranged, and has an upbeat, entertaining tone that I believe you will enjoy.

Maybe you bought Creator 7 to accompany your new DVD burner, digital camera, or DV camcorder. Or perhaps you picked it up because you have a special project to complete such as archiving treasured family photos to CD, creating an engaging slideshow of your daughter's wedding, or producing an MP3 disc of your favorite Liberace tunes. Regardless of your endeavor, what you will quickly discover — if you haven't already — is that Creator 7 can perform, and perform well, any and all media tasks you throw at it.

What you've purchased represents the realization of Roxio's vision to bring together its complete line of next generation, uncompromised photo, video, music, burning, and authoring applications to deliver the first and only comprehensive, integrated digital media suite for the PC. Seamlessly combining the improved burning suite of **Easy CD & DVD Creator™**, with best-of-breed **PhotoSuite® 7 Platinum**, **VideoWave® 7 Professional**, and online music service **Napster®**, Roxio Easy Media Creator 7 will enable you to take full command of your digital life.

On behalf of the staff of Roxio who worked so diligently to deliver Easy Media Creator 7, I'd like to wish you well as you begin to fully explore the wonderful world of digital media.

Chris Taylor

Product Marketing Manager, Roxio

Introduction

*T*he good news is that Roxio Easy Media Creator 7 really lives up to its name by being genuinely easy to use. The bad news, if there is any, is that because of its nature as a collection or suite of different applications and tools, you may initially find it a bit confusing as to which part to turn to get a particular job done. This is where *Roxio Easy Media Creator For Dummies* comes in. This book is designed to make you familiar with Roxio Easy Media Creator's many capabilities and get you up and running and comfortable with its many features as quickly as possible.

If I had to choose just one word to characterize Easy Media Creator 7, it would have to be versatility because this baby can do almost anything you might want to do with the audio, photo, and video media that you collect. With Easy Media Creator, you can go from capturing original digital media to editing it and then using it in a wide array of different projects that you can then output to disc in a very short time. Because the program's emphasis is always on making these processes as easy as can be, you don't have to worry if you don't have any background in working with digital media and have limited or even no experience with multimedia editing and design.

I just hope that you find using Easy Media Creator to design, build, and burn your own media projects half as much fun I found writing about them in this book. I want to congratulate the Roxio engineers for providing all of us with a truly outstanding set of tools with which to transform the sounds and images of the world around us into memories that we can share with friends and family alike.

About This Book

Roxio Easy Media Creator For Dummies is meant to be a simple reference to the major components and features that its many components offer. I have, however, endeavored as much as possible to arrange this reference material according to the task you want to get done rather than according to the module that you use in performing it (as you sometimes use the same module to accomplish multiple tasks). This means that although the chapters in each part are laid in a logical order, each stands on its own, ready for you to dig into the information at any point.

Whenever I could, I have also tried to make the topics within each chapter stand on their own as well. When there's just no way around relying upon some information that's discussed elsewhere, I include a cross-reference that gives you the chapter and verse (actually the chapter and section) for where you can find that related information if you're of a mind to.

Use the Contents at a Glance along with the full Table of Contents and Index to look up the topic of the hour and find out exactly where it is in this compilation of Easy Media Creator information. You'll find that although most topics are introduced in a conversational manner, I don't waste much time cutting to the chase by laying down the main principles at work (usually in bulleted form) followed by the hard reality of how you do the deed (as numbered steps).

Foolish Assumptions

I'm going to make only one foolish assumption about you and that is that you have the means to acquire some sort of digital media (be that audio, photos, or video) and you now want to be able to something with that media (be that burn the audio into CDs, use the photos in collages, or create video productions that you can view in your DVD player). I'm not assuming that you have any experience in creating any of the kinds of projects you'd like to create with your digital media, so you don't have to be concerned about your level of multimedia expertise (or the lack thereof).

As far as your computer hardware and software goes, I'm assuming only that you have a computer that is robust enough to meet the rather stringent memory and storage requirements for Easy Media Creator 7and that this machine is running Windows 2000 or XP and is equipped with a CD-recordable or, hopefully, a DVD-recordable drive. I am not, however, assuming that you have access to the other peripherals such as a digital still camera, camcorder, scanner, DVD recorder, and the like that I describe in the text. If you do have all these goodies, so much the better, as this enables you to use all of Easy Media Creator's wonderful features. If not, you can still use the parts of the program that pertain to kind of system you have.

How This Book Is Organized

Roxio Easy Media Creator For Dummies is divided into five parts (giving rise to five of Rich Tennant's great cartoons). Each part is organized around a central topic (getting to know Easy Media Creator and digital media, making data backup discs, audio discs and photo projects, DVD projects, and the like). All the chapters in each part are then related to some aspect of performing the central task. In case you're the least bit curious, here's the low-down on each of the parts and their chapters and what you can expect to find there.

Part I: A Bit about Easy Media Creator and Digital Media

This part provides you with an orientation to Easy Media Creator 7's components and capabilities, along with an introduction to the sometimes confusing world of digital media.

Chapter 1 is your place to go to find out just what exactly is included in the Easy Media Creator suite. It also introduces you to the Easy Media Creator Home, the central bridge from which you can access all the other applications and tools in the suite.

Chapter 2 is not to be missed, even by those of you who do not consider yourselves beginners by any stretch of the imagination. This chapter covers the world of digital media, including the essential difference between analog and digital media, the many different types of CD and DVD media and media formats out there, as well as the different types of digital gear that Easy Media Creator supports. The chapter ends with Greg's advice on the proper treatment of CD and DVD discs.

Part II: Creating Data Discs

Part II focuses on the important tasks of backing up and organizing your media files. Chapter 3 takes up the call on how to use the Creator Classic module to compile and burn data backup discs. This chapter also includes information on how to use Creator Classic to schedule backups so that you're never at risk for losing invaluable data due to some computer malfunction.

Chapter 4 covers how to use the Media Manager module to organize, manage, and backup all the different types of media files (audio, still images, and video) that you use in your Easy Media Creator media projects. It covers tagging and annotating media files for quick retrieval later using Media Manager's Search capability and concludes with instructions on how to back up media files by burning them onto CD and DVD discs.

Part III: Creating Audio CDs and Photo Projects

This part takes an in-depth look at two of the most popular types of digital media out there: digital audio and photos. Chapter 5 covers recording and editing digital audio with Easy Media Creator's powerful Sound Editor.

Chapter 6 turns to the subject of digital photos and how you can use the PhotoSuite module not only to fix, edit, and enhance them but also to use them in all sorts of great photo projects including slideshows, photo collages, calendars, and the like. It concludes by giving you the lowdown on printing your digital photos as well as sharing them electronically with friends and family.

Chapters 7 and 8 give you the blow-by-blow for compiling and burning audio CDs and MP3 discs with Creator Classic and then using Label Creator to design and print labels for the discs and inserts for their jewel cases.

Part IV: Creating Projects for DVDs

Part IV is devoted to the subject of DVD projects. Chapter 9 concentrates on how to use the Capture tool to acquire all the types of digital media (audio, photo, and video) that you need for your DVD projects.

Chapter 10 then covers the use of Easy Media Creator's powerful VideoWave module to design video productions to be used as titles for your DVD projects. Chapter 11 fills out the part by giving you the lowdown on using the DVD Builder module to construct the titles for your DVD project complete with interactive menus and then burn the finished project to CD or DVD disc.

Part V: The Part of Tens

Part V contains chapters that make up the Part of Tens. Chapter 12 is the place to consult for a concise description of what each major application and tool in the Easy Media Creator suite can do for you. This chapter also gives cross references to the appropriate chapters in the book that give you in-depth information on the use of a particular module.

Chapter 13 highlights what I consider to be the top ten coolest features in the entire Easy Media Creator suite (and, of course, that's saying a lot when you have as many features to choose from as you do with this baby).

Icons Used in This Book

The following icons are strategically placed in the margins throughout all the chapters in this book. Their purpose is to get your attention and each has its own way of doing that.

This icon denotes some really cool information (in my humble opinion) that if you pay particular attention to will pay off by making your work just a lot more enjoyable or productive (or both).

This icon denotes a tidbit that you ought to pay extra attention to; otherwise, you may end up taking a detour that wastes valuable time.

This icon denotes a tidbit that you ought to pay extra attention to; otherwise, you'll be sorry.

This icon denotes a tidbit that makes free use of (oh no!) technical jargon. You may want to skip these sections (or, at least, read them when no one else is around).

Where to Go from Here

The question of where to go from here couldn't be simpler — why off to read the great Rich Tennant cartoons at the beginning of each of the four parts, of course. Which chapter you go to after that is a matter of personal interest and need. Just go for the gold and don't forget to have some fun while you're digging!

Part I

A Bit about Easy Media Creator and Digital Media

The 5th Wave   By Rich Tennant

Dating requirements have definitely changed. Today you've got to have a good job, a nice car, and at least one CD/DVD burner.

In this part . . .

*E*asy Media Creator, as you discover in this part, is not one single program but a collection or suite of several different application programs and tools that you can use to create a wide variety of audio, photo, and video projects. In Chapter 1 of this part, you get introduced to each of the programs and tools you'll be using and what they can do for you. Chapter 2 then presents essential information about the surplus of digital media and media file formats that you come in contact with as you create your various media projects. This chapter then concludes by giving you a rundown of the various pieces of cool digital gear you can use to play all the great projects you come up with in Easy Media Creator, and guidelines on the proper care of CDs and DVDs.

Chapter 1

Getting Acquainted with Easy Media Creator 7

*F*irst things first: Before you can use your newly installed Roxio Easy Media Creator 7 to go off and create a copy of your favorite Norah Jones audio CD or to burn a DVD of the family's most recent outing in the Adirondacks, you're going to need to know your way around the program. As you're about to discover, there's very little that Roxio Easy Media Creator 7 can't do when it comes to dealing with all the many types of digital media that are apt to come your way.

Better yet, not only is this baby versatile but it's as good as its name. The Roxio Easy Media Creator 7 offers you consistently easy ways to complete all of your media projects — from ripping, arranging, and burning your own copies of your favorite CDs to finally organizing and tagging those gazillions of digital photos you've dumped into nondescript folders all over your computer's hard disk.

The only catch (oh, there's always a catch) is that in order for the Easy Media Creator to be as multitalented as it is, the good engineers at Roxio had to carve the program up into dozens of different little specialized programs and utilities that taken in at once can be a bit overwhelming (to say the least). This is where Chapter 1 comes in: Here you not only get a much needed overview of the many individual and specialized components now at your fingertips but a good feel for the Easy Media Creator Home that ties them all together. Once you get your bearings in this all important hub, you're ready to see what this program can really do by looking at each of the individual components.

Welcome to the Easy Media Creator Home

 At the time you install the Roxio Easy Media Creator 7 on your computer's hard disk, the Windows Installer automatically puts a Roxio Easy Media Creator Home shortcut on the Windows desktop. To open the Easy Media Creator Home, you simply locate this shortcut icon (shown in the left margin of this paragraph) and double-click it.

Figure 1-1 shows the Easy Media Creator Home window that appears after you double-click this desktop shortcut. As you can see in this figure, the Home window that forms the hub of the Roxio Easy Media Creator 7 is divided into four distinct areas, each of which is labeled. Here's the lowdown on each of these areas:

- **Tasks:** This area, divided into the subsections: Music, Data, Photo, Video, and DVD, enables you to launch a particular Easy Media Creator program or tool by clicking the task you want to accomplish such as Copy Audio CD or Capture Video

- **Applications:** Lists all the programs that you can launch to accomplish the many things listed in the Tasks section

- **Tools:** Lists all the special tools and utilities that are available to you in the Easy Media Creator 7 suite

- **Recent Projects:** Contains a chronological list of any of the audio or video projects that you've been working on (this area is blank when you first open the Easy Media Creator Home window)

Note that you can condense parts of the Easy Media Creator Home window by hiding the display of any of its three horizontal bands (the Applications and Tools sections are lumped together as part of the horizontal band that contains the full product name: Roxio Easy Media Creator 7, The Digital Media Suite). You do this by clicking the any of the three buttons with the two upward-pointing arrowheads (one on top of the other) that appear at the far right of each band. When you click one of these buttons, the detailed information beneath its band is hidden and the button changes to one with two downward-pointing arrowheads (which you can click to expand the section and redisplay its details).

 If you really want to make it easy to open the Easy Media Creator Home, you can add this Home shortcut to the Windows Quick Launch toolbar by dragging its icon to this bar and dropping it at the place on this toolbar that immediately follows the Start button on the Windows taskbar.

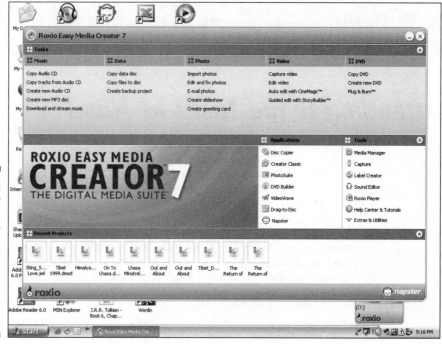

Figure 1-1:
The Easy
Media
Creator
Home offers
a hub tying
together the
program's
many com-
ponents.

If you're like me and are apt to become a really serious user of Easy Media Creator, you may also want to fix the Easy Media Creator Home option on the Windows Start menu. To do this, you follow these steps:

1. **Double-click the Easy Media Creator Home shortcut on the desktop.**

   If you don't have an Easy Media Creator Home shortcut on your desktop, you can click the Start button on the Windows taskbar, mouse over the All Programs option on the Start menu, the Roxio option on the All Programs menu, and then click Roxio Easy Media Creator Home option on the Roxio submenu.

   The Roxio Easy Media Creator 7 Home shown in Figure 1-1 then opens.

2. **Click the Start button on the Windows taskbar to open the Start menu.**

   The Roxio Easy Media Creator Home option now appears on the left side of the Windows Start menu.

3. **Right-click the Roxio Easy Media Creator Home option to open its short-cut menu and then click the Pin to Start Menu option on this menu.**

As soon as you click the Pin to Start Menu option, Windows moves the Roxio Easy Media Creator Home option to the upper area of the left side of the Start menu (under such Start menu stalwarts as the Internet Explorer and Outlook Express). If you later decide that you don't need this option to be a permanent part of the Start menu, you can remove it by right-clicking the option and then clicking the Unpin from Start Menu option on its shortcut menu.

Attending to the Tasks at Hand

The Tasks section at the top of the Roxio Easy Media Creator Home window (see Figure 1-1) divides the many things that you routinely want to accomplish with the program into five distinct task areas: Music, Data, Photo, Video, and DVD. Each task area contains a list of the most common tasks associated with that area and each task listing is a hyperlink (just on a Web page).

Clicking the link associated with a particular task opens the appropriate application for accomplishing that task. The beauty of the Tasks section in the Home window is that you don't have to give a second thought as to which Easy Media Creator application to use in order to get done the project you have in mind.

The only problem is that the tasks displayed in each of the five task areas represent only the most common things that you can do with Roxio Easy Media Creator 7. Although you can rely on the Tasks section for most of your media projects, be aware that not everything that you may need to do with the program is listed here. Therefore, you will not want to ignore totally the options listed in the Application and Tools areas.

My suggestion is that when you first start using the program, concentrate on using the items listed in the Tasks section of the Easy Media Creator Home window to get your work done. That way, as your experience with the program grows, you'll naturally become familiar with which applications are associated with which types of media tasks. In no time at all, especially with the help of the information in this book, you'll pick up on which application or tool to launch in order to complete a particular media project.

Acclimating to the Many Applications

The applications listed in the Application area of the Easy Media Creator Home window form the core of the Roxio Easy Media Creator 7 program. As you see in the center section of the window shown in Figure 1-1, this list includes these seven: Disc Copier, Creator Classic, PhotoSuite, DVD Builder, VideoWave, Drag-to-Disc, and Napster. Although this area of the window refers to them as applications (a technical term for a program that enables the user to create certain types of documents saved in individual file formats), you will find that the program and documentation also refers to these guys as "components" because they are just parts of the whole Media Suite. A good example of this is when you click an Applications link such as Creator Classic, an alert box appears with the following message: "Please wait . . . Loading component."

The following seven sections give you a brief introduction to each of the components that you can load by clicking its Applications link in the Easy Media Creator Home. Use this information to get a quick overview of the capabilities and functions of each of Roxio Easy Media Creator 7 applications.

Copying discs with Disc Copier

As the name says, Disc Copier is the application you use when you need to make a copy of an unprotected CD or DVD. When you click the Disc Copier link in the Applications area in the Easy Media Creator Home window, the program opens the window shown in Figure 1-2. Or, I should say, this window opens after you dismiss an alert dialog box reminding you that you should use the Disc Copier component only to make copies of digital media for which you have the clear legal right to make copies. Knowing that none of you would ever do anything like that, you can click the Don't Show Me This Again check box before you click OK to close this alert dialog box (for once and all).

Figure 1-2:
Disc Copier
makes it
easy to copy
audio or
data CDs
and DVDs.

You can use Disc Copier to copy an audio or data CD or DVD (usually one that you've created with Roxio's DVD Builder, since almost every single commercial movie on DVD that you rent or purchase is copy-protected and can't be copied with Disc Copier). As you can see in Figure 1-2, all you need to do to copy one of these discs is to specify the source and destination drive. The great thing is, if your situation is like mine and you have only one CD or DVD drive on your computer system, you can still use Disc Copier to copy your audio, data, or video discs (refer to Chapters 3 and 5 for steps with concrete examples of how you use Disc Copier to copy audio and data CDs).

The comforts of Creator Classic

Creator Classic is the application you use primarily to assemble and burn your audio and data CDs. Figure 1-3 shows you the window that opens when you click the Creator Classic link in the Applications area of the Easy Media Creator Home. As you can see in this figure, the Creator Classic window is divided into three major areas:

- **Tasks** where you select the type of disc to burn to CD (Data Disc, Audio, or MP3 Disc) and where you can indicate what type of CD to create (Enhanced, Mixed-Mode, or Bootable)

- **Select Source** where you locate and select the files you want to copy to data or audio CD

- **Data Disc Project** which displays the name of your project as well as all the files you've added for burning onto the CD

Whereas you can use Disc Copier to make a copy of an existing audio or data CD or DVD, you use Creator Classic to actually put together and burn your own audio CDs or data CDs or DVDs. You use Creator Classic when you want to make backups or archive data files on your disk. You can also use Creator Classic to burn audio CDs that you can play in your computer's CD or DVD drive or in any standard CD player that you have handy. If you have audio tracks saved on your hard disk in the more-and-more popular MP3 audio file format, you can also burn them as an MP3 disc that you can play in most CD computer drives. See Chapters 3, 5, and 6 for specific information and examples on using Creator Classic to assemble and burn audio and data CDs.

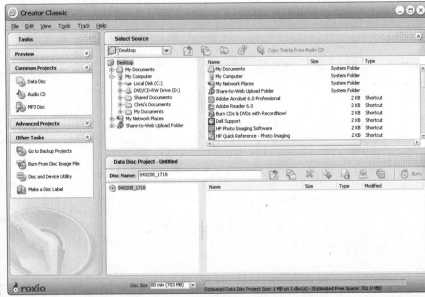

Figure 1-3:
Use Creator Classic to backup or archive data on CD or assemble and burn your own audio CDs.

Picture it in PhotoSuite

PhotoSuite is the application that you use to organize, edit, and share the digital photos that you take. You can use this component to enhance the photos, organize them into albums, use them in creating projects like greeting cards and calendars, as well as easily share them with friends and family. Figure 1-4 shows you the basic PhotoSuite window that appears when you click the PhotoSuite link in Applications area in the Easy Media Creator Home.

Figure 1-4:
Use
PhotoSuite
to correct
and
enhance
digital
photos as
well as
share them
with family
and friends.

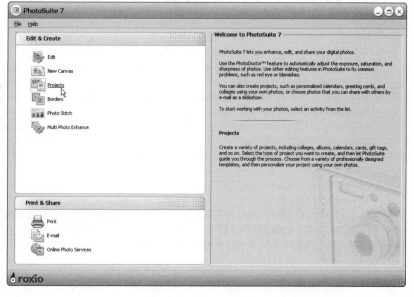

As you can see in this figure, the startup window for PhotoSuite is divided into two panes on the left: Edit & Create and Print & Share. The upper Edit & Create pane contains the common options for editing your digital photos and starting new photo projects. The lower Print & Share pane contains a Print option for printing digital photos that you've saved on your hard disk, an E-mail option for sending photos either as an attachment to an e-mail or right inside the body of the e-mail message. The last option in this pane, Online Photo Services, enables you to post your digital photos to a Web site where others can view them with their Web browsers or to have them printed by a professional photo finisher.

Note that the pane on the right side of the initial PhotoSuite window gives you general information about PhotoSuite 7. This area can also give you a quick description of any option in the Edit & Create and Print & Share panes that you might want to select. To display this descriptive information in the pane on the right, simply position the mouse pointer somewhere over option in the panes on the left (when you do, not only does this descriptive information appear on the right, but the option becomes underlined, indicating that it contains a link). To initiate a particular option, you simply click its link. When you do so, the layout and menu options in the PhotoSuite window change to suit the task you've selected. See Chapter 8 for detailed information on using all the PhotoSuite options.

Easy multimedia projects thanks to DVD Builder

The DVD Builder is the application that you use to assemble and burn multimedia projects on DVD. Multimedia projects are those that can combine more than one type of media, including video clips, still photo images, text, and audio tracks. You can use DVD Builder to quickly and easily convert your digital home movies into menu-driven productions that you can play on a computer DVD drive or a standalone DVD player attached to your TV. You can also use DVD Builder to assemble your digital photo collections into slideshows that once burned onto a DVD disc can be played in the selfsame computer DVD drives or standalone DVD players.

Figure 1-5 shows the DVD Builder window that first opens after you click the DVD Builder link in the Applications area in the Easy Media Creator Home (and have indicated what type of DVD project to create). The DVD Builder window is the most complicated of those that you'll run into in Roxio Easy Media Creator 7. As you can see in Figure 1-5, this window is divided into five panes:

- ✔ **Add Content** where you capture video for your DVD project from a video camera attached to your computer or import it from clips or collections already stored on your hard disk

- ✔ **DVD Menu Settings** where you can specify a visual theme for the project's menu screens (including layout and labeling of the menu buttons), select a photo or video to use as the background of all menu screens, or add music or sound effects to play whenever the project's menu screens are displayed on the screen

- ✔ **On-Disc Options** where you can choose to burn your DVD project onto disc or to edit a multimedia presentation previously saved on a DVD disc

- ✔ **Menu Editor** where you can customize the menu buttons or background graphic

- ✔ **Production Editor** where you can edit the content of any one or all of the *titles* (preassembled collections of photos or productions containing video clips, still images, and audio) you've added to the DVD project, including marking *chapters* (points in the title that you can jump to in playback) and selecting transitions between individual video clips and still images

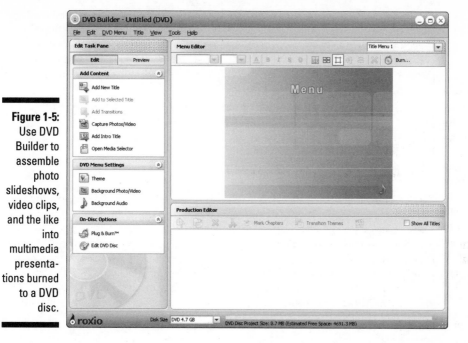

Figure 1-5:
Use DVD
Builder to
assemble
photo
slideshows,
video clips,
and the like
into
multimedia
presenta-
tions burned
to a DVD
disc.

DVD Builder is possibly the most versatile application in the entire Easy Media Creator suite. Because you can combine all types of media (video, still images, text, and audio) as you want, this is the place where you can be really creative. In no time, you'll be creating personalized and professional-looking multimedia projects that you can share with all your friends and family who have access to either a DVD drive in their computers or a standalone DVD player. See Chapters 9, 10, and 11 for details on using the DVD Builder to create your own DVD projects.

Riding the VideoWave

VideoWave is the application that you use to assemble and edit video projects (referred to in the Roxio documentation as *productions*) that can include video clips, still images, and audio. After assembling and editing a production in VideoWave, you can either add it to a DVD project that you're making in DVD Builder or use DVD Builder to burn it onto a DVD disc (see "Easy multimedia projects thanks to DVD Builder" that immediately precedes this section).

Figure 1-6 shows you the VideoWave 7 window that appears when you click the VideoWave link in the Applications list in the Easy Media Creator Home. When you first open the VideoWave window, it is divided into the three major panes shown in this figure:

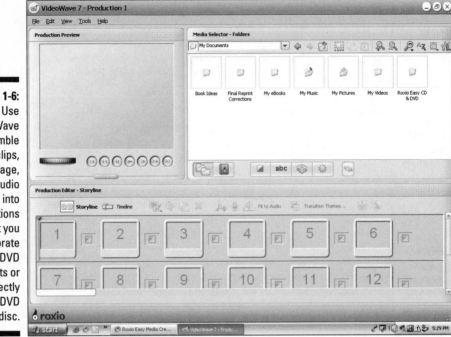

Figure 1-6:
Use
VideoWave
to assemble
video clips,
still image,
and audio
into
productions
that you
incorporate
into DVD
projects or
burn directly
onto DVD
disc.

✔ **Production Preview** where you can preview how your production will play as you create and edit it

✔ **Media Selector - Folders** displaying file folders on your hard disk or network with the media files (audio, video, or still) that you want to add to the production (this pane can also display preassembled media collections, transitions, text styles, overlays, or effects that you can add to a production)

✔ **Production Editor - Storyline** displaying a storyboard view of the video production, showing all the individual video clips and stills with any in-between transitions in the order in which they will play in the final production (this pane can also display the production in a Timeline view which shows the timing of each element in the production along with any audio or narration track that you've added)

Personally, I find that VideoWave interface is one of the easiest and most straightforward for editing video that I've run across. I'm sure that with just a little experience using this beauty, you're going to *love* video editing. If, however, you're a complete newbie to video editing and are the least bit intimidated about producing your own videos, you'll be glad to know that VideoWave includes two new components designed to make video editing nearly foolproof:

✔ **CineMagic** which automatically edits your video production by trimming your video clips and adjusting the tempo of the audio to fit the flow and transitions you use (perfect for making MTV-type videos)

✔ **StoryBuilder** which uses a Wizard-type interface, providing step-by-step guidance through assembling the various elements in your video production

Starting your video-editing career with CineMagic and StoryBuilder is a perfect way to become familiar with the VideoWave interface and its capabilities. From there, you can quickly move on to video editing on your own right using the Storyline and Timeline views. See Chapter 11 for complete details on using all aspects of VideoWave.

You launch VideoWave from the Easy Media Creator Home to create new video productions. You also launch VideoWave directly from within the DVD Builder application when you need to do some advanced editing on a video production created earlier with VideoWave that you've imported into the Video Project you're currently working on or to do similar editing to the contents of a new title that you added to DVD project. Suffice it to say that knowing how to use VideoWave goes a long way in mastering the video end of the Easy Media Creator suite.

Instant data copying thanks to Drag-to-Disc

Drag-to-Disc is one of the neatest yet simplest applications in the Easy Media Creator suite. You can use this nifty program to make CD or DVD backups or archives of data files on your hard disk or network simply by dragging their folder or file icons on the Windows desktop and dropping them on the Drag-to-Disc icon (shown in Figure 1-7). The Drag-to-Disc application is great because it automatically does any formatting for the data CD or DVD as needed to accommodate the files that you add.

To open the Drag-to-Disc icon, you can either click the Drag-to-Disc link in the Applications area of the Easy Media Creator Home or click the Drag-to-Disc icon (shown in the left margin of this paragraph) that appears in the Systems Tray on the right side of the Windows taskbar immediately to the left of the clock. If you click the Drag-to-Disc link when the Drag-to-Disc icon is already displayed on your computer's desktop (something that automatically happens when you first start your computer after installing Roxio Easy Media Creator 7), the Easy Media Creator Home window is automatically minimized to a button on Windows taskbar, displaying the Drag-to-Disc icon on your desktop. For details on making quick data backups and archives with Drag-to-Disc, see Chapter 3.

Listening to the rap on Napster

Napster renown as *the* place to go on the Internet to download some cool tracks is back, this time as one of the most complete online music stores available. Napster enables you to search for, organize, and sample music tracks in seemingly all genres of music, from Pop, Rock, Jazz, Metal, Hip-Hop, R&B, Soul, Classical, Opera, to my personal favorite, Disco. Once you've found the album or track you can't live without, you can purchase it (99 cents a track and $9.95 for an entire album — much less than half the price you'd pay for the album in a typical music store). You can then burn the tracks you've purchased to an audio CD for playback in computer CD or DVD drive or standalone CD player or transfer them directly to a standalone MP3 player (such as the Samsung - Napster 20 GB Digital Audio Player so prominently advertised on the Napster Home page).

The Easy Media Creator Home window contains two Napster buttons, one at the bottom of the Applications area with a link labeled Napster and the other in the lower-right corner of the Easy Media Creator Home window labeled *napster* (in lowercase italic letters). You need Internet access in order to use either one of these buttons. If you've never installed Napster on your computer, you click the *napster* button at the bottom of the Easy Media Creator Home window and sign up. After you've installed Napster on your computer, you can click the Napster link at the bottom of the Applications area to launch Napster (which, in turn, connects you to the Napster Web site).

Figure 1-8 shows you the Napster window as it opens when I click the Napster link at the bottom of the Applications area on the Easy Media Creator Home window (your Napster window won't be quite as elaborate until you've started using it to find and sample the music that turns you on). As you can see from this figure, the main pane in the Napster window contains three buttons (Home, Browse, and Library) with the Home button automatically selected. You can also see that Home area contains four tabs (Music, Radio, Magazine, and Message Boards) with Music automatically selected and its options displayed in the main viewing area below. To the immediate right of the main pane with the Music tab information displayed is a Now Playing pane (your Napster window will lack this pane until you start playing around with the Napster radio).

The Napster Home screen enables you to quickly display all sorts of artists and albums for different music presets (Alternative, Classical, Country, Dance, Hip-Hop, and so on) when the Music tab is selected, play a whole playlist of tunes assembled into "radio" stations when the Radio tab is selected, peruse issues of an online music magazine when the Magazine tab is selected, and participate in online threaded chats about various music-related subjects.

You must subscribe to the Napster Premium service in order to have access to the Radio, Magazine, and Message Boards tabs on the Napster Home screen. This subscription service costs $9.99 a month and also entitles you to completely sample and download most of the music available on the entire Napster sites (some artists insist that you purchase their music before you can play their entire track). Just be aware that if you don't opt for joining this Premium service, all of your music sampling on Napster is restricted to 30 seconds of any track!

Figure 1-8:
Napster's back and you can use it to listen to and purchase your favorite tunes by launching it directly from the Easy Media Creator Home.

The Napster Browse screen (displayed by clicking the Browse button at the top of the Napster window) enables you to browse through the Napster catalog for the artists and albums that you want to sample and potentially purchase. The Napster Library button (displayed by clicking the Library button) organizes the music that you sample and purchase into convenient folders. From this screen, you can play a track, send it to someone by e-mail, or even burn it directly to an audio CD.

Tools for Every Need

The Tools area of the Easy Media Creator Home window (see Figure 1-1) contains a list of links to five tools (Media Manager, Capture, Label Creator, Sound Editor, and Roxio Player), along with a link to the entire suite's Help Center and Tutorials. At the bottom of the this list, you find a pop-up button labeled Extras & Utilities, which when clicked displays a menu of seven services and utilities that you can access in using Roxio Easy Media Creator 7.

Clicking any of the five tool links launches a smaller program that performs a specialized function that helps in creating various CD and DVD projects with the applications discussed earlier in this chapter. The Help Center & Tutorial link opens a Help Center window that you can access when you need guidance in using any of the Easy Media Creator Applications and Tools. The remaining sections of this chapter acquaint you with the primary function of each of the program's Tools, the Help Center, and the services and utilities collected on the Extras & Utilities pop-up menu.

Media Manager at your service

You use the Media Manager to organize the many types of media files (video clips, still images, audio, and video projects) that you use in the CD and DVD projects you create. This handy-dandy little program enables you to keep tabs on particular media files through the use of *collections*, special Easy Media Creator files that associate selected media files together regardless of where these files are actually physically located on your computer system. Because collections reference to the media files you want to associate as a group, you don't have to go through all the trouble of copying or moving the files into a single folder. You can also use the Media Manager to peruse your media files, tag them with keywords for easy searching, as well as backing these files up by burning them onto CD or DVD discs.

Figure 1-9 shows the Media Manager window that appears when you click the Media Manager link in the Tools area of the Easy Media Creator Home window. Deceptively simple at first glance, this window is made up of only two panes:

a pane named Folders on the left that enables you to select any drive or folder on your system and a pane with the name of the selected drive or folder on the right that displays all the folders and files that that drive or folder contains. You do the rest of the organizing magic with the buttons at both the top of the Media Manager window and these panes (see Chapter 4 for details).

Figure 1-9:
Use the
Media
Manager
tool to
organize,
view, and
search the
many types
of media
files you use
in your CD
and DVD
projects.

Catching up with Capture

As the name suggests, you use the Capture utility to import media files from various devices such as a digital photo camera, video camera, scanner, and microphone that's connected to your computer system. You can also use Capture to import media files from CD or DVD discs (which aren't copy protected and to which you have the right to make copies) loaded into the CD or DVD drive built into your computer.

Figure 1-10 shows the Capture window as it appears when I click the Capture link in the Tools area of the Easy Media Creator Home window (your Capture window may differ depending upon the actual devices you have connected to your computer). As you can see, this window shows you all the devices from which you can import media that are currently connected to your computer system in the Detected Devices pane on the left. It then displays descriptive general help information at the top of the Welcome to Capture pane on the right, along with specific help about any of the connected devices when you position the mouse pointer on its link in the Detected Devices pane.

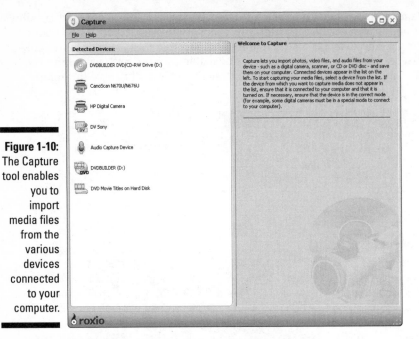

Figure 1-10:
The Capture tool enables you to import media files from the various devices connected to your computer.

To import media from any of the devices connected to your computer system, you simply click the link associated with the device link in the Detected Devices pane. The layout and the options in the Capture window then change to suit the type of device and the type of media file it supports (see Chapter 10 for details on using Capture to import various types of media files).

Lauding the Label Creator

You use the Label Creator tool to design and print labels for the CD and DVD discs that you burn with the other Roxio Easy Media Creator applications. The Label Creator makes quick work of designing both disc labels and the inserts for their jewel cases. Figure 1-11 shows the Roxio Label Creator window as it first opens. Note that you open this window not only by clicking the Label Creator link in the Tools area of the Easy Media Creator Home window but also by clicking a Create Label button in the final dialog box when burning CD and DVD discs (see Chapters 5 and 12 for details).

The Label Creator window is divided into two panes: Tasks on the left and Layout on the Right. The Tasks pane contains all of the tools you commonly need to do the layout and add the content for your disc labels and jewel case inserts. The Layout pane previews the contents of your disc label or jewel case insert (the front and back printed cards that go inside the clear plastic case that holds the disc), while at the same time enabling you to edit these contents. For detailed information on using the Roxio Label Creator to design and print labels for any of your CD or DVD discs, see Chapter 9.

Saying Hello to Sound Editor

You can use the Sound Editor tool to record audio from audio devices connected to your computer (including analog sources such as cassettes and LP records). You can then use its features to edit or enhance the audio recording and convert to any of the supported digital audio file formats, including MP3, WAV, OGG, and WMA (see Chapter 2 to find out what in the world all these acronyms stand for).

Figure 1-12 shows you the Sound Editor window that appears when you click the Sound Editor link in the Tools area of the Easy Media Creator Home window after opening an MP3 audio file for editing. As you can see in this figure, the Sound Editor interface represents the audio file graphically with a sort of waveform readout (reminiscent of a snapshot of an oscilloscope display). This waveform displays the relative amplitude of the sound for the left and right channels (marked L and R) of the audio file.

Figure 1-11: Label Creator enables you to design and print disc labels and jewel case inserts for all the CD and DVD projects you create.

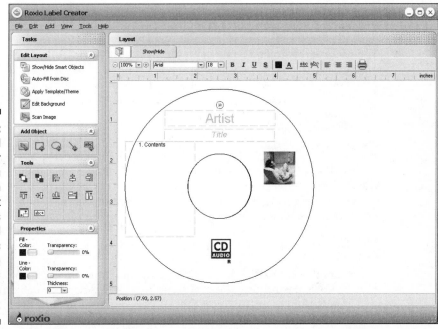

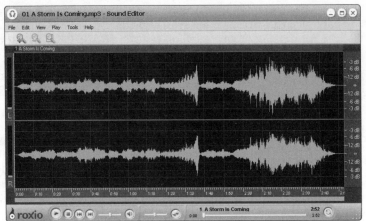

Figure 1-12:
Use Sound
Editor to
record and
edit audio
for the CD
and DVD
projects you
create.

You can then use the controls at the bottom of the Sound Editor to playback all of or any part of the audio track. You can also use the zoom controls located immediately above the waveform display to magnify portions of the audio's waveform display or zoom out on it so that more of the entire track is shown in the Sound Editor. See Chapter 5 for details on using the Sound Editor to record and edit the audio files that you burn to CD or use in your DVD projects.

Playback with the Roxio Player

You can use the Roxio Player to playback video CDs or DVDs discs that you create with the Roxio Easy Media Creator suite or video projects that you've saved on your hard disk. This tool is particularly useful for previewing a video CD or DVD disc that you've burned with your equipment before distributing it to others for viewing on their equipment.

Figure 1-13 shows you the Roxio Player window after launching it by clicking the Roxio Player link in the Tools area of the Easy Media Creator Home window and loading a DVD movie that I created with the Roxio DVD Builder application. Note that this simple window is composed of two parts: a display area above where the video plays and a band at the bottom that contains all the controls for playing the video.

To play a video CD or DVD that you've created, you follow these steps:

1. **Start the Roxio Player by clicking the Start button on the Windows taskbar, positioning the mouse pointer over All Programs on the Start menu, then over Roxio on the All Programs Menu, and then click Roxio Player on the Roxio submenu.**

   You can also start the Roxio Player from the Easy Media Creator Home window by clicking the Roxio Player link in the Tools area.

LCD Display

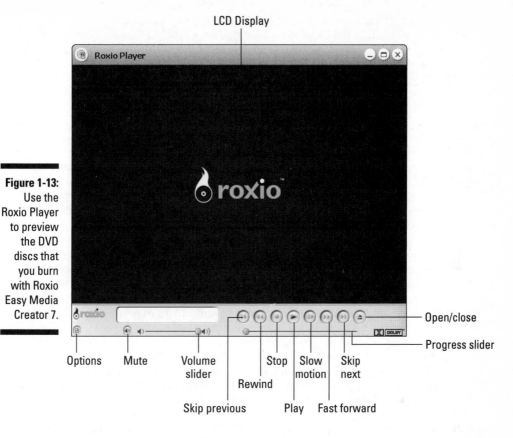

Figure 1-13:
Use the
Roxio Player
to preview
the DVD
discs that
you burn
with Roxio
Easy Media
Creator 7.

Open/close

Progress slider

Options   Mute   Volume   Stop   Slow   Skip
                     slider   motion next

                              Rewind

         Skip previous   Play   Fast forward

2. **Place the disc with the video CD or DVD you want to play in the Roxio Player in your computer's CD or DVD drive.**

   Wait a few seconds before performing Step 3 so that your CD or DVD drive can wind up and the Roxio Player can find the disc.

3. **Click the Play button in the middle of the Player controls at the bottom of the Roxio Player window (see Figure 1-13).**

   If your computer is equipped with both a CD and DVD drive, you may have to specify which drive contains the disc you want to play. To do this, click the Options button in the lower-left corner of the Roxio Player window and then click Change Selected Drive. Use the drop-down Drive Letter menu in the Change Selected Drive dialog box to select the correct drive before you click OK.

As soon as you click the Play button in the Player controls, the video CD or DVD begins playing. If you're playing a DVD and it has an Intro title, this introduction title begins playing. If your video CD or DVD has an opening menu screen, this screen appears, waiting for you to select the menu option for the title you want to play.

If the menu screen offers several titles, each represented by its own menu button, each of the titles is represented by a labeled button. You can play a particular title by positioning the mouse pointer over the button to highlight it and then clicking its button (when playing the disc in a standalone DVD player, you would do this by pressing the arrow keys on the DVD controller to highlight the button for the title you want to view and then pressing the controller's Enter key).

When playing a video CD or DVD, you can toggle back and forth between full-screen video viewing and viewing the video within your normal Roxio Player window by pressing the "F" key on your keyboard or double-clicking the video display area. If you need access to the video controls after switching to full screen, click the screen (it doesn't matter where the mouse pointer is when you do this). To make the video controls disappear, just click the screen another time.

If after viewing part of a particular DVD title, you want to return to the main menu screen to select another title to view, click the Menu button on the Player controls. If the title you're viewing in the Roxio player has chapters (specific jump points in the video), you can jump to the next chapter by clicking the Skip Next button. If you want to jump to an earlier chapter in the title, you click the Skip Previous button instead.

To pause the playing of a video CD or DVD, click the Pause button in the Player controls. When you finish playing the disc, you can either stop the play by clicking the Stop button or simply eject the disc from its CD or DVD drive by clicking the Eject button in the Player controls.

You can't use the Roxio Player to play DVDs that you haven't created and burned with the Roxio Easy Media Creator suite such as commercial DVD movies that you've rented or purchased. To play these DVDs on your computer, you need to use another player capable of playing DVDs such as the Windows Media Player.

Help is on the way!

The Help Center & Tutorials link near the very bottom of the Tools area of the Easy Media Creator window is your ticket to complete online help with using any and all aspects of the Roxio Easy Media Creator 7 suite. Figure 1-14 shows you the Easy Media Creator Home Help Center window that opens when you click this link in the Home window.

In getting program help from this window, you have a choice between help topics that give you an overview of using the various applications and tools included in the suite (sort of like this chapter gives you) or getting specific help on a particular application or tool. To seek out general program help, use the Contents, Index, Search, and Favorites tabs in the pane on the left (this pane presents its help topics on the standard tabs in the manner common to all Windows programs).

To get application- or tool-specific help, locate the name of the application or tool in the larger Welcome to Roxio Easy Media Creator 7 pane on the right side of the Home Help Center window. For a great many of the applications and tools shown in this pane, you can choose between seeing an animated tutorial and perusing the user guide for that application or tool.

If you've never opened a particular application or tool and are curious about what it can do, you should definitely start by clicking the application's or tool's Tutorial link. When you do this, the Help Center opens a separate window in which the tutorial plays. Each animated tutorial has a sound track and subtitles that explain the screens and animated actions shown in each scene in the tutorial. To pause the playing of a tutorial, click the Pause button (the second button) in the controls at the very bottom of the Tutorial window. To resume playing the tutorial, click the Play button (the very first control). To advance to a particular scene in the tutorial, drag the slider button in the slider at the bottom or click the Skip Next (the button with the two arrowheads pointing to the right) or the Skip Previous (the button with the two arrowheads pointing to the left). When you finish playing the tutorial, click its window's Close box (the upper-right corner of the window) to close the window.

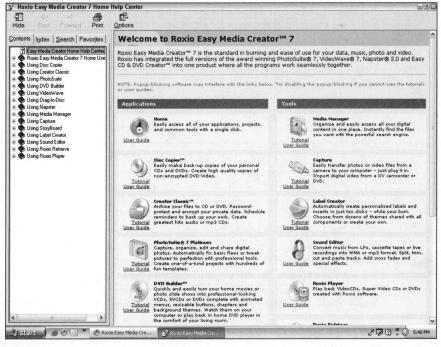

Figure 1-14:
The Easy Media Creator Home Help Center is the place to go when you need help using any of the program's components.

Open an application's or tool's user guide when you need a printed copy of the guide for using that particular application or tool. When you click the User Guide link for an application or tool, the Help Center launches your Web browser and Adobe Acrobat Reader (which appears inside the browser). The opening page of the user guide (which is saved as PDF file) then appears in browser window along with the Adobe Reader controls.

To print a copy of the entire user guide, click the Print button on the very first toolbar displayed at the top of your browser's window and then click OK in the Print dialog box. To print a particular help topic, use the bookmarks in the Bookmarks Navigation pane on the left to determine its page numbers; then click the Print button and fill in the appropriate start and stop page numbers in the Pages From and To text boxes in the Print dialog box before you click OK.

To copy a particular help topic or step-by-step instructions into a document in another Windows program, click the Select Text Tool (labeled Select Text); then use the I-beam pointer to drag through and select all the text you want to copy. Then press Ctrl+C to copy the selected text to the Windows Clipboard, switch to the document in the other program, click the insertion point at the place where you want the help text copied, and then press Ctrl+V to insert the help text into the document at the insertion point.

When perusing the help information in an application or tool user guide, you can use the Zoom controls or the Actual Size, Fit Page, and Fit Width buttons to resize the text in the Document pane on the right side of the browser window. Click Fit Page to resize the text so that each page is fully displayed in Document pane. Click Fit Width to resize the text so that it fills out the width of the Document pane. Click Actual Size to resize the text with the 100% setting so that it represents more-or-less the size at which the text prints.

You can also use the Zoom Out and Zoom In buttons to decrease and increase the magnification of the text in set increments. To select a particular magnification, click the Magnification drop-down button and click a preset or click the Insertion Point in the Magnification text box and replace the current setting with one of your own (by selecting the current setting and then typing in a new one). When you finish printing or viewing the help information in the user guide, you can close it, Adobe Acrobat Reader, and your Internet Browser by clicking the Browser window's Close button in its upper-right corner.

Because each of the application and tool user guides are saved in the Adobe PDF file format, you must have the Adobe Acrobat Reader (simply called the Adobe Reader in version 6) or a full-fledged version of Adobe Acrobat installed on your computer in order to view and print these guides. If you don't yet have Adobe Reader installed on your computer, you can download and install a free copy by going on the Internet and visiting the following Web page:

`www.adobe.com/products/acrobat/readerstep2/html`.

Exploring the Extras and Utilities

The last item in the Tools area of the Easy Media Creator Home window is an Extras & Utilities pop-up button. When you click this button, a pop-up menu with the following options appears:

- ✔ **Disc and Device Utility** to display a Disc and Device Utility dialog box where you can view all of the drives and external devices that are connected to your computer system

- ✔ **Roxio Retrieve** to open the Roxio Retrieve utility that enables you to get files from multi-disc data discs, backup data discs, and encrypted data discs that you created with the Creator Classic application (see Chapter 3 for information on using Roxio Retrieve to restore media files stored across multiple CD or DVD discs)

- ✔ **Roxio Updater** to go online to the Roxio Web site to check for updates to your Roxio Easy Media Creator 7 suite that you can download and install

- ✔ **Audible Manager** to go online to the Audible.com Web site where you can register and purchase audio books for playing on your computer or your MP3 player (see Chapter 6)

- ✔ **Digital Media Services** to go online to the Roxio.com Web site where you get information about all the online services available for processing the digital media you use in your CD and DVD projects

- ✔ **Roxio Registration** to register your copy of the Roxio Easy Media Creator 7 suite online at the Roxio.com Web site (you have to do this only if you didn't register the program when you installed it)

- ✔ **About Roxio Easy Media Creator 7** to display the About Roxio Easy Media Creator 7 dialog box that contains a bunch of technical and legal information (spread out on four tabs: General, Details, Legal, and System Information) about your copy of Roxio Easy Media Creator 7 and your computer system

To open a particular utility dialog box or window on this menu, you simply click its name in the pop-up menu. Remember, however, that you must have Internet access in order to use the Roxio Updater, Audible Manager, Digital Media Services, and Roxio Registration options.

The Disc and Device Utility and About Roxio Easy Media Creator 7 options are most helpful when you're having technical trouble getting some part of the program to run properly. Your system information combined with the information on the various devices connected to your computer system can be most helpful to a Roxio support technician trying to diagnose and help you fix the problem.

Chapter 2

The Ins and Outs of Digital Media and Gear

In This Chapter

▶ Getting familiar with the wide range of digital media file formats

▶ Converting analog media to digital

▶ Selecting your digital camera and camcorder

▶ Selecting your DVD and MP3 player

▶ The proper care and handling of your CD and DVD discs

*T*he many tools the Roxio Easy Media Creator 7 suite puts at your disposal certainly make it easy to create your own audio and video projects. This ease of use, however, is not quite matched when it comes to making heads or tails of the many and sundry media formats and equipment you can use in recording and saving these projects.

To help dispel potential confusion over your choices of media formats for the particular audio and video gear you're using, this chapter begins by examining the relationship of media formats to digital recording and playback equipment. It then goes on to introduce you to the essential difference between analog and digital media, why you want to get on the digital bandwagon, and some of the devices you can use to convert your analog media to digital for use with the Easy Media Creator.

Finally, this chapter looks at some of your options in terms of digital recording and playback paraphernalia, including digital still cameras, video cameras, and audio recorders, not to mention CD and DVD drives, and CD, MP3, and DVD players. It ends with a few important pointers on the care and feeding (I mean, handling) of the CD and DVD discs you use for saving and recording your Easy Media Creator projects.

Feeling at Home in the Digital Media Menagerie

Before I can clear up any perplexity that you might have about the different types of media that are available to you as you start working with the Easy Media Creator, you need to be clear about the relationship between the digital media formats and the kinds of recorders and playback gear you have.

The standard media formats for both CD and DVD discs come in several flavors (see the sidebar that follows for the essential difference between CD and DVD discs). As you see in Table 2-1, by and large these formats differ according to how much data they hold, their recording speed, and whether or not they enable you to record data on them only once or erase and rerecord data multiple times (referred to by the term *rewritable*).

Table 2-1	Digital Media and Data Capacity		
Media Types	*Maximum Capacity*	*Record Once*	*Rewritable*
CD-R	210 MB, 650 MB, or 700 MB	✓	
CD-RW	210 MB, 650 MB, or 700 MB		✓
DVD-R, DVD+R	4.7 GB	✓	
DVD-RW, DVD+RW	4.7 GB		✓
DVD-RAM	from 2.6 GB up to 9.4 GB		✓

When shopping for discs to use for your various Easy Media Creator projects, you need to match the capacities of your recording and playback hardware with the proper media. Be sure to check the boxes of media for the following pieces of information:

- CD or DVD indicating whether the discs are formatted for recording and playback of CDs or DVDs
- Maximum data capacity expressed in megabytes (MB) or gigabytes (GB)
- Recording speed, anywhere from 1x (times) up to about 8x for DVDs and anywhere up 52x for CDs
- R or RW indicating whether the discs can be recorded once or are rewritable

What separates the CDs from the DVDs

CD stands for Compact Disc and comes in two very familiar forms: audio CDs that play in all standard CD players and CD-ROMs that play in your computer's CD or DVD drive. DVD stands for Digital Versatile Disc (although some replace the *Versatile* with *Video*) and is most familiar in the form of movies on DVD disc that you rent or purchase.

Both CDs and DVDs rely on laser technology to decode their sequence of binary (0 and 1) data. The big difference between CDs and DVDs is their data capacity. Because DVDs use smaller tracks than CDs (0.74 microns wide as opposed to 1.6 microns), they can store much more digital data on the same size disc (both CD and DVD are the same diameter and often the same thickness), about two hours of video or about 4.7 GB (gigabytes or one billion bytes!) of digital data compared to about 74 minutes of audio or about 700 MB (megabytes or one million bytes) of digital data or less. Because DVDs use smaller tracks to fit more data on the same-size disc, they also require special computer drives for recording and playing their discs. Fortunately, DVD drives can also record and play back CDs (although CD drives cannot record and play back DVD discs).

You may be scratching your head wondering about what's up with the DVD-R and DVD+R and the DVD-RW and DVD+RW formats listed in Table 2-1. Basically, the minus and plus indicate two slightly different single and multi-session DVD recording formats. The -R and -RW formats were the first DVD recording formats that were compatible with standalone DVD players (the ones you connect to your TV). The +R and +RW formats are newer and boast some improvements in recording (newer DVD-ROM computer drives tend to be DVD+RW compatible drives).

DVD-R and DVD+R are the non-rewritable formats that are compatible with almost all DVD players and DVD-ROM drives. DVD-RW and DVD+RW are the rewritable formats and are compatible with about 75 percent of the DVD players and almost all DVD-ROM drives.

Note that the DVD+RW format supports both a single-side 4.7 GB disc (known as DVD-5) and a double-side 9.2 GB disc (known as DVD-10). The DVD-RAM has the best recording features but it is not compatible with most DVD-ROM drives and standalone DVD-video players (you need to check to make sure that your recorder and player can deal with DVD-RAM discs).

In terms of selecting new hardware for your computer, keep in mind the following distinctions among drives:

- **CD-ROM** drives can only read CD discs

- **DVD-ROM** drives can only read CD and DVD discs

- **CD-RW/DVD** combo drives can read and write CD discs but only read DVD discs

- **DVD-R and DVD+R** drives can read and write CD discs but only read DVD discs

- **DVD-RW and DVD+RW** drives can read and write both CD and DVD discs

If you're in a position of selecting among the different types of drives for a new computer system, go with a DVD+RW drive if you can possibly afford it. By selecting a DVD+RW drive, you get the benefits of all the other three types of drives as well as the ability to back up data and video on your own DVD discs. This means that you get to play your favorite music CDs and movies and videos on your computer while at same time being able to take full advantage of the Roxio Easy Media Creator software to create and burn your own CD and DVD creations (including data and audio CDs and data and multimedia DVDs).

Let's hear it for the Video and Super Video CD formats

In addition to the regular CD-R format used to record standard data and audio CDs, you need to be aware of two other CD formats, both of which can incorporate both audio and video like a DVD:

- **Video CD (VCD)** which can hold up to 74/80 minutes of video on a 650/700 MB CD and can be played in most of the new standalone DVD players

- **Super Video CD (SVCD)** which can hold up to 35-60 minutes of video on a 650/700 MB CD and can be played in many of the new standalone DVD players

Note that SVCD format supports higher quality video than your regular VCD but as you can see from the above descriptions is less compatible and holds less video. When creating a new multimedia project with Roxio's DVD Builder application, you can choose to create in either the VCD or SVCD format instead of the standard DVD format.

Ripping through those pesky audio formats

Audio file formats vary almost as much as CD and DVD formats. These formats, however, only contain information about the shape and duration of the audio's waveform. In addition, the format will specify the *sample rate* (the resolution of the audio that determines the sound quality), *bit-depth* (the number of bits, 0 and 1, used to describe the volume of the sample at any given point in the audio stream), and may include the type of compression used (assuming that the audio is compressed at all).

When an audio file uses an audio format without compression, it is naturally a larger file that requires more computer memory to play than files using different compression schemes. As a general rule, a second of uncompressed audio of the quality of your typical store-bought album on CD, which uses a sample rate of 44.1 kHz (kilohertz), a bit-depth of 16-bit, and is stereo, takes about 172 Kb (kilobytes) to store on your computer (that's about 10 MB per minute and 604 MB per hour).

On computers running Windows, uncompressed audio is almost always stored in the so-called WAV audio format (pronounced wave). This format is also known as PCM (Pulse Code Modulation) and carries a .WAV file extension. WAV files store are standard CD quality (44.1 kHz, 16-bit, stereo), meaning that they are big files that hog up your disk space.

In terms of compressed audio, you'll run into a number of different schemes — each of which is technically known as a *codec* (short for compress/decompress) — for compressing and later decompressing the audio stream.

The most popular audio codecs for computers running some flavor of Microsoft Windows are the ever-present MP3 (MPEG 3) and WMA (Windows Media Audio). The WMA format was developed by Microsoft for its Windows Media Player. This codec does not compress audio files as much as the much more popular, MP3 but it does tend to have slightly better sound quality. MP3 is, however, the most popular codec for storing and streaming music (thus the plethora of so-called MP3 players — see "I want my MP3" later in this chapter for details).

 MPEG actually stands for Motion Picture Experts Group, the name of a highly prestigious committee that sets standards for the encoding of digital video and sound. MPEG 3 actually uses the so-called MPEG 1, a video codec for compressing video in digital cameras and camcorders and in the creation of VCDs (Video CDs supported by DVD Builder) with what's called the Audio Layer 3 codec, thus the name MPEG 3 or, as it's more commonly known, MP3.

Codecs for more than just audio

Although this section deals solely with audio compression, codecs are by no means restricted to audio compression. Digital photos and video both use their own codecs in order to keep down the size of their visual media. The most popular codec for digital photos is JPEG (Joint Photographic Experts Group), which can vary in terms of its size/quality ratio. For digital video, the most popular codecs are MPEG 1, used primarily for video from digital cameras and camcorders, and MPEG 2, used primarily for commercially produced movies on DVD and in TiVo-type hard disk video recorders.

In addition to MP3 and WMA compression, in the Roxio Easy Media Creator components, you may also run across the OGG codec. OGG refers to Ogg Vorbis, an open, patent-free codec for audio encoding and streaming that is gaining some popularity. Ogg is not, as far as I can tell, an acronym like WMA or MP3 (perhaps it refers to Ogg, the former gamekeeper at Hogwarts in book four of *Harry Potter* before Hagrid takes over the post?). Where the name Vorbis comes from is anyone's guess.

If you're a user of Apple's iTunes, you run into another compression scheme known popularly as AAC (Advanced Audio Coding). This scheme uses MPEG 4 compression codec, and Audio files saved in AAC are often smaller than MP3 files with better sound quality (unfortunately, Roxio's Easy Media Creator 7 sound applications do not support this audio file format).

Don't you hate those "lossy" codecs?

There's one more consideration when it comes to compression schemes. When considering a codec to select for your audio, you need to reflect on whether or not the codec is lossy or lossless. A lossy codec is one that actually loses content that is considered to be duplicated or not essential in listening to the audio. A lossless codec is just the opposite: in compressing audio, it does not remove any of the bits from the original audio file that it cannot restore when the audio stream is decompressed for playback.

As you might guess, lossy codecs make for smaller compressed audio files but with slightly lesser sound quality. Lossless codecs, on the other hand, make for larger compressed files but usually with great fidelity to the original. This is the reason that MP3 audio files are generally a little smaller than the same WMA audio files and that WMA audio files are generally considered of slightly higher quality than MP3 files because MP3 is the lossy codec of the two and WMA the lossless one.

When applying lossy codecs such as MP3, JPEG (for digital images), and MPEG1 (for digital camera and camcorder video) to your media files, the Easy Media Creator applications and tools normally allow you to adjust the amount of compression to apply by selecting the relative quality for the compressed file. Select the best quality when larger file sizes aren't an issue and lesser quality when the relative size of the file is most important.

Ripping and burning those audio files

Before leaving behind the fascinating subject of audio file formats, you should be aware of a couple more procedures, namely *ripping* and *burning* audio files (terms, I admit, that suggest a degree of violence that is totally absent in their actual processes). Ripping refers to the process of taking audio tracks from one source in one audio format and saving them to another in a second audio format. The most common example of ripping is when you take tracks from a commercially produced CD and save them in another compressed digital format on your hard disk such as MP3 or WMA with the Creator Classic application.

Burning refers to the process of then taking the audio files that you've ripped to a new audio format such as MP3 and WMA on your computer's hard disk and then transferring them to a blank CD disc for playback on other devices (like a CD or MP3 player). Note that although you hear the term ripping applied mostly to audio files, it can also be applied to video files saved on DVD discs as well (although this requires special software besides Roxio Easy Media Creator, as most DVDs are highly copy-protected).

The term burning is, however, applied equally to the creation of both CD and DVD discs so that you find Burn buttons in both the Creator Classic and DVD Builder applications.

Make Mine Digital!

It's true that nowadays digital is king (and as the immortal Mel Brooks is so fond of telling us, "It's good to be king!"). Nowhere is this rush to digital seen more clearly than in the purchase of consumer electronics which today are almost entirely digital in nature, as in digital cameras, camcorders, DVD players, and digital audio players. It seems like the only electronics gear that is still analog is tape recorders and even you have the choice of going digital with DAT (Digital Audio Tape) recorders.

So what's this all about, this *analog* versus *digital* business? Well, let me start by giving you the textbook definition of each, followed by the classic example that hopefully makes their rather dry explanations all clear.

By definition, analog devices are apparatuses in which the data is represented by continuously variable physical quantities (you say what?). Digital devices, however, are machines in which the data is represented by discrete units, namely the binary number system which consists of just two measly numbers, 0 and 1.

Okay, now that that's clear as mud, take a look at the classic example of an apparatus that exists in both analog and digital forms, namely your wristwatch. If your watch happens to have a dial that shows the sequence of the twelve hours and represents the current time on this time with the placement of its hands (at least an hour and minute hand and perhaps even a hand to keep track of the passing seconds), then you're wearing an analog device. And this device represents its data (that is, the passing hours, minutes, and seconds on the twelve-hour dial) "by continuously variable physical quantities" (that's the moving watch hands to you and me).

If, however, you're wearing a wristwatch that has no hour dial and uses no hands but actually tells you the current time in Arabic numerals, as in 6:15:33 or 22:05:09, you are the proud owner of a digital device, one that represents its data (the same passing hours, minutes, and seconds) in discrete binary units (which clock manufacturer has skillfully disguised as a readout showing the current time).

Now nice as the wristwatch example is, it doesn't help too much in terms of the kinds of devices you'll be using with your Easy Media Creator software. For examples closer to the work you'll be doing with it, I prefer the examples of the long-playing record versus the audio CD and the videocassette versus video on DVD. Records are prime examples of analog audio media just as videocassettes are great examples of analog video media. And you guessed it; audio CDs and video DVDs are excellent examples of their digital audio and video counterparts.

One way to keep analog mechanisms straight from digital ones is to remember that the word "analog" is related to the term "analogous," denoting something that is similar to something else so that most analog devices capture their data by acting like the sense organs with which we collect data. So, analog cameras have lenses that capture light in similar ways that the lens in the human eye and analog audio recorders have microphones that vibrate like the tympanic membrane in the ear. Even the classic analog clock with its dial and moving hands in some ways mimics a sundial in the way that the sun's shadow moves across its disk.

Why digital rules

And now I can tell you the main reasons that digital has been crowned king. The first reason is that devices that play back such analog media as LPs and videocassettes can only access their data (sound and music, in this case) sequentially. The ramification of this fact becomes abundantly clear in the case of a videocassette when you go to try to find and replay a favorite scene in a movie on tape. Instead of being able to jump right to the scene as you can do with the controller for your DVD player (assuming that the movie is also available on DVD, which nowadays is almost always true), you have to fast forward or reverse until you recognize the place in the movie you want to replay. The discrete rather than continuous nature of digital audio and video media is what makes this kind of *random access* of the data possible.

The second reason that digital is riding so high and mighty comes from the fact that copies of any type of digital media (including sound, photos, and video) are every bit (pun intended) as good as the original, since both the original and copy contain the exact same sequence of 0 and 1s. This is definitely not true of analog media. The quality of each copy of an analog master is slightly degraded and copies made from copies are even worse (just as a photocopy made from a photocopy of an original is fainter and lacks much of the original detail).

So too, the quality of most media that store analog data (with film being the most notorious) naturally degrades with time (you have only to thumb through an album filled with your baby pictures to know what I'm talking about). By and large, this is not true of most digital media (hard disks and DVD discs stored properly should last you a really long time) and, of course, in the cases where it is, you can always create a new master from any copy that is still intact (thus the singular importance of making backups and the beauty of the fact that a copy made from a copy of an original is equal in quality to that copy and, indeed, the original itself).

Converting analog media to digital

The best way to protect your precious analog data (usually stored in photos, home movies, audio tape recordings, videocassettes, and LPs) is to convert the analog data from digital data. In fact, this may well be your primary motivation for learning how to use the applications and tools in the Roxio Easy Media Creator suite and may turn out to be your primary use for the software.

Like me, you may have shoeboxes of family pictures in the attic, a closet full of Super 8 home movies, drawers full of videocassettes, and a basement full of the most incredible collection of records, both LPs and 45s (now virtually abandoned and utterly unplayed). Fortunately, you can take steps to preserve this very precious data and all the wonderful memories it contains by making digital copies of their media. The device you use to convert analog data to digital depends upon the type of analog media you're converting. The next two sections look at two of the most common and most reasonably priced analog-to-digital conversion devices: the digital scanner that you can use to digitize photos and, in some cases, slides and the analog-to-DV (digital video) converters that enable you to convert video saved as home movies and videocassettes.

"Scotty, scan me up . . ."

A digital scanner is one of the most useful and cost-effective analog-to-digital conversion devices you can own. Scanners come in several flavors: film scanners designed specifically for scanning photos from film (including negatives) and 35mm slides and film, handheld scanners that you pass over the object or page you want digitized, sheetfed scanners where you feed the photo or page to scanned, and flatbed scanners designed for scanning any object that you can fit on its flatbed (especially printed text and images and photos developed from film).

For about a $100 or less, you can get a really decent flatbed scanner with which you can digitize all your family photos, news clippings, and favorite cards and letters and preserve them in digital form before they become too faded and stained to enjoy. If you want to be able to scan photo negatives, slides, and filmstrips as well, you'll have to pay more but you can still find a flatbed scanner that can scan these without having to resort to purchasing a special film scanner (which doesn't enable you to scan items like cards, letters, and pages of a book).

Note that almost any scanner that you buy today can connect to your computer through an USB (Universal Serial Bus) 2.0 cable (the type of cable connector typically used to connect a mouse to newer computers. Higher end (and more costly) scanners can also connect to your computer through the so-called FireWire (officially known by its much more boring designation, IEEE-1394) cable. Although a FireWire connection between your scanner and computer is not necessary, keep in mind that FireWire connectivity is completely necessary when it comes to transferring digital video from a digital camera or camcorder to your computer (in such cases, USB 2.0 just isn't fast enough).

Analog-to-DV converters

Analog-to-DV converters are standalone devices that enable you to connect analog devices such as an 8mm video camera or VHS format VCR to them via Composite video or S-video and RCA audio cables. The converter then converts the analog signal from the movie or tape to digital and sends the resulting 0 and 1 bits to your computer's hard disk via a FireWire cable. And once you've got the video data converted to digital and saved on your hard disk, you can then use Easy Media Creator applications such as VideoWave and DVD Builder to arrange and enhance the content (see Chapters 11 and 12 for details).

The nice thing about analog-to-DV converters like the Pyro A/V Link is that the conversion is not limited to analog to digital. After you arrange and enhance your digital video data with the Easy Media Creator software, you can then use the converter to convert it back to analog and transfer it out to a connected analog device such as a VCR. That way, you can save your final digital video project on VHS tape and then share the resulting videocassette with those in your family who haven't yet crossed over the digital divide.

Sorting Out Your Digital Recording Gear

While it's great to be able to convert your analog data to digital for use in your Easy Media Creator projects, it's even better (and a heck of a lot easier) to capture the data in digital form in the first place. To be able to capture digital media for use in your Easy Media Creator projects, at the very minimum you'll want to have access to a digital still camera (sometimes abbreviated to digicam) and a digital video camera (commonly called a camcorder, a truncation of camera-recorder).

When selecting a digital camera or camcorder, not only is the quality of the camera lens critical in determining the quality of your photos as with their analog counterparts but another unique factor comes into play, the resolution of a sensor called a CCD (Charge Coupled Device), whose pixels actually register the photographed image on the camera's disk. It is the resolution of the camera's CCD that most affects the sharpness of the photographed image.

Both digital still and movie cameras are rated by the highest CCD resolution they support (measured in megapixels that are a factor of the product of the number of horizontal and vertical pixels used on the CCD sensor). With still cameras, you can select a resolution beneath the camera's highest megapixel rating, enabling you to store a greater number of lesser resolution photos on the camera's storage disk. With camcorders, you can't modify the CCD resolution so that your movies are always recorded at the camera's highest setting.

In addition to the megapixel rating of the camera's CCD sensor, when selecting a digital still camera, you'll want to pay attention to the following factors:

- Whether or not the camera has a zoom lens (usually a mechanical zoom lens is superior to the so-called digital zoom that doesn't actually move the lens forward and back)

- How much built-in memory the camera has and whether this memory is expandable through some kind of flash memory disk or memory stick (the amount of memory determines how many photos you can take before you have to transfer them onto your computer's hard disk)

- Whether or not the camera has an LCD screen which enables you to preview the photo right after you take it

- The kind of computer interface the camera has (most support USB 2.0 connectivity, although the higher-end cameras also support FireWire connectivity

When selecting a digital camcorder, you apply many of the same criteria as when choosing a digital still camera (megapixel rating, zoom lens, LCD screen, and USB versus FireWire connectivity). Of course, the big difference between a digital still camera and camcorder is how they record their images.

Many camcorders still record their video on film, although a few of the smallest ones use flash memory cards and a few of the very newest ones can record their video directly on MiniDVD discs. Most camcorders, however, continue to record their video on Mini DV cassettes (which support the DV media format with CD quality sound). Mini DV cassettes are normally available in 30-, 60-, and 90-minute sizes.

Be aware that MiniDVD discs (3-inch diameter or about half the size of a standard DVD disc) do not play in all DVD players. Before you invest in a camcorder that uses MiniDVD discs, be sure that your DVD Player plays media this size. Otherwise, you'll end up always having to dump the video that you take with the camera onto your hard disk and then use one of the Easy Media Creator applications to burn it onto a standard-size DVD in order to play it in your machine.

When It's "Playback" Time

Getting your digital recording gear is truly only half the story, for what good is a digital camcorder if you have no way to play the movies you make with it outside of its tiny LCD screen or on your computer screen? The other half of the story has got to be what you are going to use to play all those great audio and video projects you create with the Roxio Easy Media Creator 7.

The next two sections give you an overview of the capabilities of today's crop of DVD and MP3 players. Both of these devices are surely among the hottest digital electronics on the market and ones that you want to consider investing in given the capabilities of your Roxio Easy Media Creator software.

Delving into the world of DVD players

DVD players have eclipsed videocassette players much faster than most people anticipated. This is probably not only due to their much superior video and sound quality but also to the dramatic decrease in their pricing: you can now get a decent player for anywhere between $100 and $200.

When choosing a DVD player, you have to consider what media formats (DVD and otherwise) that the player supports (see "Feeling at Home in the Digital Media Menagerie" earlier in this chapter for details). Some DVD players not only support a number of DVD media formats but audio DVD, CD, and MP3 as well. This feature enables you to play the audio DVD, CDs, and MP3 discs as well as the DVD video discs that you assemble and burn with your Easy Media Creator software.

If you still have a lot of videocassettes that you like to play (and you haven't yet bought into the idea of converting them all into digital DVD discs), you might want to consider purchasing a DVD/VCR player that can play both DVD video discs and your VHS cassettes.

If you're into recording your favorite television programs as well as being able to play your DVDs, you might consider investing in a DVD recorder (often abbreviated DVR). These beauties enable you to record your favorite programs onto DVD-R or DVD-RAM discs (remember that a DVD-RAM disc holds a whopping 9.4 GB of data and can be rewritten over 100,000 times). Some models are so fancy that they enable you to watch programs that have been recorded on a DVD-R or DVD-RAM disc while the recorder is in the process of recording another TV program on the same disc!

If you have a DVD recorder and you're like me and want to be able to record TV programs while you're away from home or watching another program, the TiVo service is the only to go. TiVo enables you to program your DVD recorder to save your favorite programs on a daily or weekly basis, any time of the day. In addition, TiVo offers a new Home Media Option that lets you program the recording of a TV program remotely through a computer, record a program on a DVR in one room of your house and then play it on another DVR in a different room, as well as use your MP3 playlists to play MP3s on MP3 discs and organize a slideshow for viewing digital photos saved on data CDs or DVDs.

1 want my MP3!

Today's DVD players enable you to play the audio CDs and MP3 discs that you burn with the Roxio Easy Media Creator software with no problem. But what about the times when you're on the move (which is probably more often than not) and you want to take your tunes with you? For that you're going to need a portable digital audio player more commonly referred to as an MP3 player.

MP3 players, like those in Apple's amazing iPod series, are now available in an array of music capacities and price points. In general, they run the gamut from $69 all the way to just over $500 (ouch!). The primary determinant of the price of an MP3 is, by and large, the amount of built-in memory the device has (which translates directly into how many MP3 music tracks it can store and how many minutes/hours of audio listening you have available). For example, at the low end, the $69 Rio has only 64MB of memory which gives you about two hours of music. At the high end, the $470 Apple iPod has 40 GB of memory which enables it to hold up to a whopping 10,000 tracks for more than 20 hours of back-to-back playback.

Because of the tight integration between the Roxio Easy Media Creator 7 suite and the Napster online music service (Roxio purchased and resurrected Napster), you might want to consider the Samsung Napster 20.0 MB YP-910GS MP3 player (shown in Figure 2-1). With 20 MB of memory, this player holds about 5,000 tracks of music for about 10 hours of playback. This player also has a built-in FM tuner (that lets you record songs from the radio) and transmitter (that enables you to play your MP3 tracks through your car's radio), along with a voice recorder. But the best part of this mighty little MP3 player is that it's tightly integrated with the Napster 2.0 music service, enabling you to download your playlists and MP3 tracks directly to the YP-910GS when it's connected to your computer via its USB 2.0 port (see Chapter 6 for details on using this device with Napster).

Technically speaking, the Apple iPod is not really just an MP3 player. It is, in fact, an MP4 player in that it's capable of not only playing MP3 audio but digital audio stored in the more advanced MPEG-4 audio codec with the so-called AAC (Advanced Audio Coding) compression. This type of compression not only makes for smaller files but ones that some people say are equal to their digital masters in sound quality. The only thing that you need to be aware of is that when you purchase an iPod, you're tied pretty heavily to the iTunes music store (which is great in its own right), while the Roxio Easy Media Creator software that you'll be using to rip and burn your MP3 tracks is tied heavily to the Napster music store.

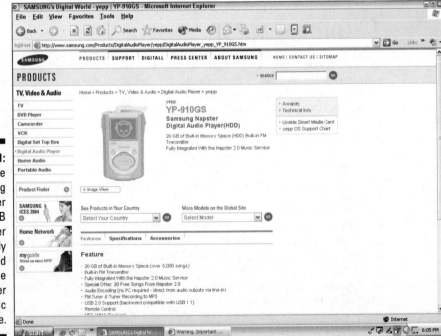

Figure 2-1: The Samsung Napster 20.0 MB MP3 player is tightly integrated with the Napster online music store.

The Care and Handling of CD and DVD Discs

Earlier in this chapter when I was extolling the virtues of digital and telling you why it's king, I went so far as to claim that if stored properly digital data should theoretically "last forever." Well, when it comes to the most popular forms of digital storage, CD and DVD discs, that statement is definitely an exaggeration bordering on a blatant untruth.

Although disc manufacturers claim a life expectancy of up to 100 years for their CD and DVD discs, you understand that this claim is not based on any real experience (as CD and DVD disc media haven't been around even half that long). Some skeptics even worry that instead of a century of good use, even CD and DVD discs stored under the most optimum conditions may not have a life expectancy much beyond 5 to 10 years (a bit on the short side of forever, I'd say).

With this lowball estimate comes a strong reminder to make multiple backup copies of your CD and DVD discs, especially those that contain data vital to your business. (And, of course, because Roxio's Disc Copier application is making this kind of disc backup so ridiculously easy that you now have no excuse for not doing it.) Of course, regardless of how long the actual life expectancy is for the CDs and DVDs that you create with the Easy Media Creator, improper handling of these discs can drastically reduce it to nothing at all (they're only made of pretty thin plastic after all).

When it comes to the proper care and handling of your CD and DVD discs, keep these important guidelines in mind:

- ✔ Always handle your discs by the outer edge or the center hole — avoid touching the shiny surface of the disc where the laser reads the data at all costs

- ✔ Keep dirt and dust and all other foreign material by storing your discs in their jewel cases

- ✔ Always store your discs upright (like books on a shelf) in their cases

- ✔ Store your discs in a cool, dry, dark environment (they don't take kindly to extremes of temperature and humidity)

- ✔ Remove any dirt, fingerprints, smudges, and liquids from the shiny bottom surface of your discs with a clean cotton cloth — always wipe in a straight line from the center toward the outer edge and never with a circular motion going around the disc

✔ Always use a non-solvent-based felt-tip permanent marker when marking the label side of your discs (and, of course, never, ever write on the shiny side which the laser reads)

✔ Remove stubborn dirt or gunk from the shiny, bottom surface of your discs with CD/DVD-cleaning fluid or isopropyl alcohol if no commercial cleaner is available

Most of you have the good sense to keep your hands off the shiny underside of a CD or DVD disc, knowing full that if you mess up this surface, your disc is toast. Unfortunately, many of you don't realize that you can destroy your precious disc just as fast by messing with the topside of the disc where you put the label. The truth is that this upper dye layer of a CD or DVD disc is actually the most sensitive part of the disc so that if you inadvertently scratch or damage this layer, your data is cooked as good as if you'd taken a butcher knife to the shiny underside! For this reason, it is not recommended that you ever apply an adhesive label to your CD or DVD discs, as the adhesive disc labels degrade rather quickly and if the label starts to peel off, it could take part of the dye layer with it.

Despite the potential danger, I still cover using the Easy Media Creator's great Label Creator tool for making professional-looking CD and DVD disc labels in Chapter 8. Just be aware that you're better off labeling a disc that contains important data that you want to last as long as possible with a non-solvent felt-tip marking pen rather than applying a printed adhesive label.

Part II
Creating Data Discs

The 5th Wave   By Rich Tennant

PLEASE

NO CD BURNER

In this part . . .

One of the primary tasks that you'll be doing in Easy Media Creator is backing up the vast amounts of data and media files that you accumulate on your computer system. Chapter 3 of this part presents all the information you need to use Creator Classic to create and burn these backup discs. Chapter 4 gives you the lowdown on using Easy Media Creator's very handy Media Manager tool to organize and manage these data files on your computer. Taken together, Creator Classic and Media Manager make it possible to finally get a handle on all that data you're sitting on and protect it from mishap.

Chapter 3

Backing Up and Copying Data Files

*T*hanks to the advent of CD and DVD discs and their great capacity for holding data (about 700MB for CD and an impressive 4.7GB for your average DVD), gone are any excuses for making disc backups of all your important data. The Roxio Easy Media Creator offers you two different applications for backing up the data you rely on all over your computer system. You can use the quick-and-easy Drag-to-Disc utility to make data backup discs on the fly or you can turn to Creator Classic when you want to create a data disc project that you can save and reuse to make copies of important folders and files. You can also use Creator Classic to create backup disc projects that make scheduled backup copies of such files on a regular basis.

This chapter gives you all the information you need to use either application for backing up your data. It also gives you some recommendations for which type of CD or DVD disc you should use in different kinds of backup situations (refer to Chapter 2 if you need a refresher in the differences between CD-R, CD-RW, DVD-R, DVD-RW, and so on).

Drag-and-Drop Magic

Drag-to-Disc is the program to use when you need to make a onetime backup of certain files and folders on your computer system. For example, suppose you've used the Easy Media Creator Capture tool to capture a whole bunch of video clips for later use in a DVD project with DVD Builder and want to back them up on disc so that you can free up the hard disk space. As you're not going to be backing up the video files on a regular basis, Drag-to-Disc is the perfect way to make the backup disc before deleting the video clips from your hard disk.

As good as its name, to make a data disc with Drag-to-Disc all you have to do is follow these easy steps:

1. **Insert a blank CD or DVD disc in your computer's CD or DVD drive.**

   Remember that you can't put a DVD disc into a CD drive but that you can put a CD disc into a DVD drive (see Chapter 2 for the reason).

2. **Double-click the My Documents, My Computer, or My Network Places icons to open them on your Windows desktop; then locate and select the folders or files in them that you want copied onto the disc.**

   Remember that you can select multiple folders and files by holding the Control key as you click their icons.

3. **Drag the selected folders and files over to the Drag-to-Disc program window and release the mouse button.**

That's all there is to it! If your CD or DVD disc needs formatting, the Drag-to-Disc program alerts to this fact (and takes care of necessary formatting). If your disc already has data on it (meaning you forgot to label it — shame on you), Drag-to-Disc alerts you to this fact and gives you an opportunity to replace it with a blank disc. If the disc is one of the rewritable types (see Chapter 2), you can choose to add the selected folders and files (assuming that they will all fit within the remaining free space) to the disc.

When the Drag-to-Disc application finishes copying the selected folders and files to the target CD or DVD disc, the program automatically opens a window for the disc showing you its new contents. If there's additional space, you can then add folders and files to the disc by dragging their icons either to this open window or the Drag-to-Disc desktop icon.

When you finish, be sure to eject the CD or DVD from its drive by clicking the Eject button on the Drag-to-Disc desktop icon or by pressing Alt+J (for eJect) after making the Drag-to-Disc desktop icon active rather than pressing the eject button on your CD or DVD drive. That way, the Drag-to-Disc application has the chance to prepare the disc for use in other computer drives. It also saves you from having to reach around and physically press the drive's eject button.

Launching Drag-to-Disc on startup

Most of the time, you'll want keep the Drag-to-Disc program icon (shown in Figure 3-1) on your desktop so that it's ready and available to do its backup magic anytime you're ready to feed it some files. With the installation of the Roxio Easy Media Creator 7 suite, the setting to routinely launch the Drag-to-Disc application whenever Windows starts up is automatically selected. This means that you should be able to find the Drag-to-Disc desktop shown in Figure 3-1 somewhere on your desktop.

Figure 3-1:
If you have Drag-to-Disc automatically launch on Windows startup, this desktop icon always appears somewhere on the Windows desktop.

If for some unknown reason you don't have this desktop icon on your Windows desktop after installing the Roxio Easy Media Creator 7 software, you can manually start Drag-to-Disc by following these four simple steps:

1. **Click the Start button on the Windows taskbar.**

2. **Position the mouse pointer on the All Programs item on the Start menu to highlight it and open the All Programs submenu.**

3. **Position the mouse pointer on the Roxio item on the All Programs menu to highlight it and open the Roxio submenu.**

4. **Click the Drag-to-Disc item on the Roxio submenu.**

 If the Easy Media Creator Home window is already open, you can forgo these steps involving the Start menu altogether and start the Drag-to-Disc application by clicking the Drag-to-Disc link near the bottom of the Applications area. So too, you can manually start Drag-to-Disc by clicking its icon (shown in the left margin of this paragraph) on the Systems Tray on the right side of the Windows taskbar.

By clicking the Drag-to-Disc icon in the Systems Tray on the Windows taskbar when the Drag-to-Disc application is already running, you can display the desktop icon on top of whatever window is currently obscuring your view of it. Use this technique to redisplay the Drag-to-Disc desktop icon when it's hidden beneath a window holding the folders and files that you selected for copying to the CD or DVD disc. That way, you can drag the selected folders and files to the redisplayed Drag-to-Disc desktop icon without having to first resize or close their window.

After manually starting the Drag-to-Disc application, you can ensure that it automatically launches on each Windows startup by following these steps:

1. **If the Drag-to-Disc desktop icon is not currently displayed, on the Windows taskbar either click the Show Desktop icon in the Quick Launch toolbar to minimize all open windows or click the Drag-to-Disc icon in the Systems Tray to bring the Drag-to-Disc desktop icon to the top.**

2. **Right-click the Drag-to-Disc program icon on the Windows desktop.**

   The Drag-to-Disc shortcut menu opens.

3. **Click the Settings item on the Drag-to-Disc shortcut menu or press Alt+S.**

   The Drag-to-Disc Settings dialog box, shown in Figure 3-2, opens.

4. **Click the Show Drag-to-Disc on Startup check box to put a checkmark in its check box.**

   If you want to have the desktop icon always appear in the lower-right corner of the Windows desktop, also put a checkmark in the Move to Lower Right Corner of Desktop check box.

5. **Click OK to close the Drag-to-Disc Settings dialog box and put your new settings into effect.**

You have to admit that compared to the other program icons on your Windows desktop, the Drag-to-Disc desktop icon (which is technically a program window and not an icon at all) is pretty large. You can, however, reduce this window to a more manageable size. To do this, click the Drag-to-Disc System tray icon to display the Drag-to-Disc desktop icon and then press Alt+I (as in Icon View). Note that you can also reduce the icon by clicking the Restore Down button — the one with the image of two windows, one in front of the other — on the title bar of the Drag-to-Disc icon, but pressing Alt+I is so much quicker and easier.

After you reduce the size of the Drag-to-Disc desktop icon, you can still use it to copy selected folders and files to a CD or DVD disc. Simply drag your selected folders and files and then drop them onto this smaller version. If you decide that it's too much effort to drag stuff onto this smaller desktop icon, you can enlarge it before doing your drag-and-drop operation by pressing Alt+I a second time.

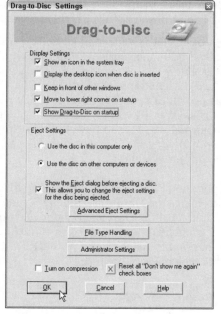

Figure 3-2:
Use the
Drag-to-Disc
Settings
dialog box
to change
the Display
and Eject
settings for
the Drag-
to-Disc
application.

Customizing other Drag-to-Disc settings

You may have noticed in Figure 3-2 that the Drag-to-Disc Settings dialog box controls more than just when and where the Drag-to-Disc desktop icon is displayed on your Windows desktop. In addition, this dialog box contains a bunch of Eject, File Type and Administrator settings that you can modify along with a check box that turns on disc compression and a button that resets all your "Don't Show Me Again" alert dialog boxes that sometimes pop up when using the Drag-to-Disc application.

In this dialog box, you can choose among these Eject settings:

- **Use the Disc in this Computer Only:** Choose this option button only when you're sure that the backup CD or DVD disc will be used in only in this computer's drive or a computer that uses the very same version of the Drag-to-Disc application

- **Use the Disc on Other Computers or Devices:** Keep this option button selected whenever there's a chance that you'll use the backup CD or DVD in a computer using a different type of operating system (such as UNIX or LINUX) or one where Drag-to-Disc isn't installed

- **Show the Eject Dialog before Ejecting a Disc:** Keep this check box selected to have the program display the Eject Dialog box whenever you physically attempt to eject the backup CD or DVD disc that enables you to choose between This Disc Will Be Used on This Computer Only

option button and the default This Disc Will Be Used on Other Computers
or Devices option button before physically ejecting the disc

✔ **Advanced Eject Settings:** Opens an Advanced Eject Settings dialog box
where you can individually modify the settings for non-rewritable and
rewritable discs that determine which version of UDF (Universal Disk
Format) is used (a standard designed to make optical media as compatible in various systems as possible) and whether or not ISO/Joliet setting
is used (enabling Macintosh systems to recognize the long filenames
from a Windows' disc — normally you won't have to fiddle around with
these settings as the they're already set to make your discs as readable
as possible by diverse computer systems)

In addition to the Display Settings and Eject Settings, the Drag-to-Disc Settings
dialog box also enables you to change the File Type Handling Settings and the
Administrator Settings. By default, all of the File Type Handling Settings prompt
you only with the options for a particular file type (such as audio files saved as
MP3, WAV, WMA, or OGG files or graphic images saved as BMP, JPG, or TIF files,
and the like) when you add that type of file to the disc.

Changing the File Type Handling Settings

If you want to predetermine how Drag-to-Disc handles a particular type of file
when you add that type of file to the disc, click the File Type Handling button
in the Drag-to-Disc Settings dialog box. Drag-to-Disc then opens the Default
File Type Handling dialog box (shown in Figure 3-3). Then, click the drop-
down button for the particular type of file (Audio Files, MP3 Files, Photos or
Images, and so on) and click the appropriate option on its drop-down menu.

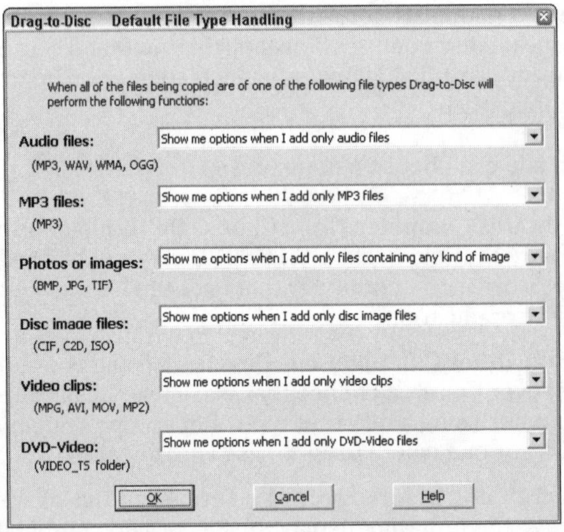

Figure 3-3:
Use the
Default
File Type
Handling
dialog box
to predeter-
mine what
Drag-to-Disc
does when
you add a
particular
type of file
to a disc.

For example, if you click the drop-down button to the right of Audio Files, you can choose between the following two handling options:

✔ Send the Files to Creator Classic to Make an Audio CD

✔ Send the Files to Drag-to-Disc to Make a Data CD

The handling options for the other file types listed in the Default File Type Handling dialog box are similar except that they target the Easy Media Creator application designed to deal with that particular type of file in addition to sending the files to Drag-to-Disc to make a data disc (so that the Video Clips option enables you to send the files to DVD Builder to make a video disc).

Changing the Administrator Settings (if you dare)

When you click the Administrator Settings button in the Drag-to-Disc Settings dialog box, an Administrator Settings dialog box appears with the following four check box options:

✔ **Verify RW Media on Full Format** (checked by default) to have Drag-to-Disc double check rewritable media (CD-RW, CD+RW, DVD-RW, and DVD+RW) for errors when fully formatting the disc

✔ **Verify Recording Using Read After Write** to have Drag-to-Disc verify the data it burns to disc by comparing it to the original data on your hard disc (selecting this option slows down the recording process but ensures greater data fidelity)

✔ **Enable EasyWrite (MRW) Support** (checked by default) to be able to perform a quick format of a rewritable disc on an EasyWrite recorder (also known as Mt.Rainier, this refers to types of CD and DVD recorders that use a standard developed by Philips for recording CD-RW and DVD+RW discs)

✔ **Use UDF 2.0 Instead of 1.5 (For DVD Only)** to burn the disc using an older, less compatible version of UDF (Universal Disc Format) — select this option only when you are using Drag-to-Disc to burn a DVD-R for playback in a consumer DVD recorder

For heaven's sake, don't go messing with these settings unless you know what you're doing or you're told to make changes to them by someone who does (or who you can blame if your data discs no longer work in the company's computers). Changing these settings may not only degrade the performance of these discs to a crawl but make them incompatible with different computer systems used in your organization!

Turning on disc compression

The last option on the Drag-to-Disc Settings dialog box (besides the Reset All "Don't Show Me Again" Check Boxes button that enables you to reactivate the display of all those lovely alert dialog boxes) is the Turn On Compression check box. When you click this check box option to put a checkmark in it, Drag-to-Disc automatically compresses all of the files that you drop on its desktop icon as it burns them to disc. This is great in that it reduces the size of each of the files you add, enabling you to add more files to a given disc.

Using compression does, however, mean that Windows computers which aren't running the latest copy of Drag-to-Disc won't be able to decompress and read the files unless the computer has a copy of the UDF (Universal Disc Format) reader installed on it. It also means that computers not running the Windows operating system (such as Macs and computers running under UNIX or LINUX) won't be able to decompress and read the files. Keep these limitations in mind when making discs for coworkers or clients who may not be so fortunate as to have the Roxio Easy Media Creator 7 suite or the UDF reader installed on their Windows systems or don't run Windows at all.

Also keep in mind that you can use the compression option when making a disc with an EasyWrite recorder.

Manually formatting a blank disc

Although Drag-to-Disc will automatically prompt you to format any blank disc as soon as you attempt to add folders or files to it, you can also manually format the disc before you start dragging-and-dropping your files. To do this, insert the blank CD or DVD disc in the appropriate computer drive; then follow these steps:

1. **If the Drag-to-Disc desktop icon is not already displayed on your computer, click the Drag-to-Disc icon on the taskbar's System Tray to display it.**

2. **Right-click the Drag-to-Disc desktop icon and then click Format Disc on its shortcut menu or press Alt+F.**

   The Drag-to-Disc Format Options dialog box shown in Figure 3-4 appears.

3. **Click the Volume Label text box and enter a descriptive volume label for your new disc.**

   Volume labels appear at the bottom of the Drag-to-Disc desktop icon after the drive letter. When entering a volume label, keep in mind that they can be no longer than 11 characters total and can't contain spaces or any of the following characters:

\(backslash)

/ (forward slash)

: (colon)

; (semicolon)

* (asterisk)

? (question mark)

" (double quotes)

< (less than)

> (greater than)

| (vertical bar)

+ (plus sign)

= (equal sign)

. (period)

, (comma)

[(open square brace)

] (close square brace)

4. **Click the Enable Compression on This Disc check box if you want to compress all the files you add to the formatted disc.**

   Keep in mind the limitations on using compression (listed under the Remember icon in the preceding section) before you select this option.

5. **If you're formatting a rewritable disc and you want to do a full rather than a quick format, click the Full Format the Entire Disc Before Using It option button.**

   Selecting this option button automatically deselects the default Quick Format Allows You to Begin Using the Disc Quickly option button.

6. **Click the OK button to begin formatting your blank disc.**

Instead of deleting the contents on a previously recorded disc that is rewritable (such as CD-RW, DVD-RW, DVD+RW, and DVD-RAM), you can completely get rid of all its files by manually formatting it using these same steps for manually formatting a blank disc. Just be sure that you don't want any of the files on the rewritable disc before you manually reformat it, as there's no way to retrieve files after a disc has been reformatted.

Figure 3-4:
The Disc
Format
options
dialog box
appears
whenever
you
manually
format a
blank disc.

You can use the Drag-to-Disc program's Rename Disc command to change the volume label for your CD or DVD disc. Make the program's desktop icon active; then right-click it and click the Rename Disc command on its shortcut menu or press Alt+R. Then replace the existing volume label with a new name (following the guidelines pointed out following Step 3 in the preceding steps) in the Name for Disc text box in the Drag-to-Disc Rename Disc dialog box before you click OK.

Note that renaming a disc's volume label in this manner does not change the disc name that appears on the title bar of any window you open on the disc with the Windows Explorer; the original volume label which gives rise to the disc name continues to be associated with this disc according to Windows. The new volume label does appear, however, in the Label text box if you open a Properties dialog box for the disc.

Also, the new volume name that you give the disc does not appear at the bottom of the Drag-to-Disc desktop icon until the next time you insert the disc in the drive. This is because ejecting and re-inserting the disc in the drive is the only way to force the Drag-to-Disc application to read the new volume label and display it in the desktop icon (in other words, there's no refresh button as in your Web browser).

Editing a data disc

After you copy files to a CD or DVD disc using Drag-to-Disc, you can use those files just as you would any files saved on your computer's hard disk or disks to which you have access on a network. The biggest question in editing a backup CD or DVD created with Drag-to-Disc is whether the disc is of the rewritable or nonrewritable type.

Although you can theoretically edit the contents of either type of disc, keep in mind that only rewritable discs actually update the disc contents to reflect your changes. Therefore, practically speaking, the editing of a rewritable can include reformatting the disc so that you can entirely replace its contents rather piecemeal editing of its folders and files.

Displaying the properties of a data disc

Before you start editing the contents of a data disc, especially before adding new files to it, you'll probably want to get the basic statistics on the disc, including whether the disc is rewritable or nonrewritable or how much disc space is used and how much is free. The easiest way to get this information is to follow these steps:

1. **Put the backup CD or DVD disc in the appropriate computer drive.**

2. **If the Drag-to-Disc desktop icon is not already displayed on your computer, click the Drag-to-Disc icon on the taskbar's System Tray to display it.**

3. **Right-click the Drag-to-Disc desktop icon and then click Disc Properties on its shortcut menu or press Alt+O (for PrOperties).**

Drag-to-Disc opens a Disc Properties dialog box similar to the one shown in Figure 3-5. Note in this figure that in addition to getting basic stats on the disc (including its type, total capacity, and used and free space), you can also change its volume name in it Label text box.

Figure 3-5:
Use the
Disc
Properties
dialog box
to ascertain
the type
of disc
(rewritable
or non-
rewritable)
and the
amount of
free space.

Displaying the contents of a data disc

The easiest way to perform routine editing operations on a data disc (such as adding, updating, or deleting files) is to open a window showing its contents and then manipulate the file icons in this window. To display the contents of CD or DVD disc, make the Drag-to-Disc desktop icon active and then right-click it and click View Disc Contents on its shortcut menu or press Alt+V (for View).

Drag-to-Disc then responds by opening a separate disc window showing all the folders and files that you've copied on it. Because this is a standard Windows Explorer window, you can manipulate its contents much as you would a window showing the contents of your computer's hard disk or any disk to which you have access on your network.

You can click the Details button at the bottom of the left panel of a window showing a data disc's contents to display the total capacity and free space on that disc instead of having to resort to using the Drag-to-Disc program's Disc Properties option to get this information.

Copying files from a data disc

After the folders and files on the data disc are displayed in its own window, you can then perform standard file operations on them such as cutting and copying their files to your computer's hard disk or disks that are available to you on your network.

To copy folders or particular files from the CD or DVD data disc to another disk on your computer system disk, open a window for its disk on your hard disk and then simply select and drag the icons for the folders or files you want to copy over to that window. To copy selected files into a particular folder on the computer disk, drop their files on the particular folder into which they're to be copied.

To cut files from the CD or DVD data disc that you can then copy onto one of your computer's disks, open a window with the data disc's files and then select their folder and file icons before you press Ctrl+X (you can also do this by selecting Edit⇨Cut on the disc window's menu bar). After cutting the files from the data disc, you can insert them one of your computer's disks by making its window active and then selecting Edit⇨Paste on its menu or by pressing Ctrl+V.

If you cut folders or files from nonrewritable CD or DVD discs (see Chapter 2 for a list), their names are removed from the disc, but the space they take up on the disc is not recovered. When, however, you cut folders or files from a rewritable CD or DVD disc, the space they took up is recovered and you can reuse by copying new files in their place. After all is said and done, this ability to reuse the space from file you've cut or deleted from the disc is the essential difference between a rewritable and nonrewritable CD and DVD disc.

Deleting files from a data disc

The story on deleting disc files or replacing them with newer, updated versions is pretty much the same as when cutting files from the disc. To delete files from a CD or DVD data disc, open its window, select the files' icons, and press the Delete key or choose Edit➪Delete on the disc window's menu bar.

When you delete files from a rewritable disc, their filenames are not only removed from the disc, but the file space they occupied is recovered on the disc. When, however, you delete them from a nonrewritable disc, their filenames are removed from the disc (rendering them impossible to access) but their file space is not recovered for later reuse.

Files that you delete from a data CD or DVD are not placed in your computer's Recycle Bin. Therefore, when you press the Delete key or choose Delete on the window's Edit menu, the files are gone for good. This means that you need to be really careful to not select files that you really don't want to delete, especially if you don't have copies of the files saved elsewhere.

You can use the Drag-to-Disc program's Erase Disc option (Alt+E) to delete all the files on a data disc. However, keep in mind that erasing all the files does not actually remove their data from the disc. Instead, this option removes only the list of folder and filenames on it. This means that it is possible for someone to reconstruct the list and have access to some or all of the disc's contents. If the disc contains extremely sensitive data, you're much safer physically destroying the disc so that it can never be read again (you can do this most easily by peeling off the disc's label, rendering it completely unreadable).

If your goal is to reuse the disc for backing up files, you're better off reformatting the disc (see "Manually formatting a blank disc" earlier in this chapter for details) and before copying new files, provided that you're using a rewritable disc.

Replacing files on a data disc

You can replace files on a backup CD or DVD disc by dragging file icons with the same filenames and dropping them onto the Drag-to-Disc desktop icon or the CD or DVD disc's open window. When you do this, Microsoft Windows opens a Confirm File Replace dialog box that gives you the opportunity not to go ahead with overwriting a particular file with one of the same name by clicking the No instead of the Yes button. If do click the Yes button, Windows replaces the identically named disc file with the one you've dragged onto the Drag-to-Disc desktop icon or into the CD or DVD disc window.

When you replace a file on a rewritable disc, the original file is deleted and only the new replacement file takes its place. When dealing with a nonrewritable disc, however, only the name of the original file is removed from the disc so that both the data in the original and replacement file remains on the disc, taking up twice the space.

Repairing discs with ScanDisc

ScanDisc is a great little utility that's part of the Drag-to-Disc application. It enables you often to repair CD or DVD data discs whose files have become corrupted and somehow rendered unreadable. To start the ScanDisc utility to scan a CD or DVD data disc for errors and then, possibly try to fix them, make the Drag-to-Disc desktop icon active and then right-click the icon and click Launch ScanDisc on its shortcut menu.

When you select the Launch ScanDisc option at the bottom of the Drag-to-Disc shortcut menu, the ScanDisc dialog box appears. Click the Scan button to have the program check your CD or DVD data disc for errors. The ScanDisc dialog box then changes to display its progress in checking the disc. When the utility finishes checking the entire contents of the data disc, a new dialog box showing files that have been pegged as damaged or lost (lost files are those that don't have filenames associated with them) may appear. Of course, if you're so lucky as to have a disc with no problems, no further dialog box appears and you can click the Finish button to close the ScanDisc program and go on your merry way.

If you do receive an indication of problems in the form of a File Recovery dialog box listing the damaged or lost files that are considered recoverable, you should take steps to copy these files to another destination on your hard disk before taking the final step of having ScanDisc try to repair the disc. That way, you'll have the data files intact even if ScanDisc can't repair the damaged disc.

To copy the recoverable or lost files (which are given sequential numerical filenames when they're copied that you can then later change), click the Yes button in the dialog box and then select the drive and folder that will serve as the place to which the damaged or lost files are copied in the Destination Drive drop-down list box.

When selecting the destination drive, you can select any local drive on your computer except for the one that contains the CD or DVD disc that you're scanning for errors. Also note that you're computer is part of a network; you can't copy the recoverable or lost files to any drive or folder on the network unless that drive or folder has previously been mapped as such, meaning that it's been assigned its own drive letter between A and Z (to do this, open the My Documents Window and then choose Tools⇨Map Network Drive and follow the prompts in Map Network Drive dialog box).

After designating the destination drive, you then designate the folder on that drive into which you want the recoverable files copied (do this by selecting the folder in the Destination Folder list or by clicking the New Folder button and creating a new folder). After indicating the drive and folder location, click the Copy button in the File Recovery dialog box to begin copying the files. When the copies are made, click the Done button.

After enabling you to copy and recover damaged and lost files to another location on your computer system, the ScanDisc utility then prompts you to attempt to repair the damaged disc to make it once again usable. Click the Yes button when the program asks you if you want to repair the disc; then click the Done button when the ScanDisc program finishes this operation (including checking the integrity of the files).

ScanDisc is not able to repair all damaged discs. You may find that even after attempting to repair a data disc, the disc is still unreadable in your computer's drive. You may also find that after repairing a disc, both Drag-to-Disc and Windows can no longer access the files on it. For this reason, be sure that your data disc is essentially a disc which backs up data that you also have elsewhere and from which you can generate a new backup CD or DVD.

Turning to Creator Classic for Your Backups

Creator Classic is the application you want to turn to when you need to make CD or DVD data discs on a regular basis from particular sets of data files or when you want to make a CD or DVD disc that mixes both audio tracks and data files. To start Creator Classic from the Easy Media Creator Home window, click the Copy Files to Disc link in the Data column or the Creator Classic link in the Applications area. If the Easy Media Creator Home window is already open, you can launch Creator Classic by clicking the Start button on the Windows taskbar, highlighting All Programs on the Start submenu, Roxio on the All Programs submenu, and clicking Creator Classic on the Roxio submenu.

Whichever way you choose to launch this application, after you do, the Creator Classic window shown in Figure 3-6 appears on your screen. As you can see in this figure, the Creator Classic window is divided into three areas: the Tasks pane on the left side where you indicate the type of project to create, the Select Source pane on the upper right where you locate the files you want to backup, and the Data Disc Project pane on the lower right which shows you all the files you add to the project.

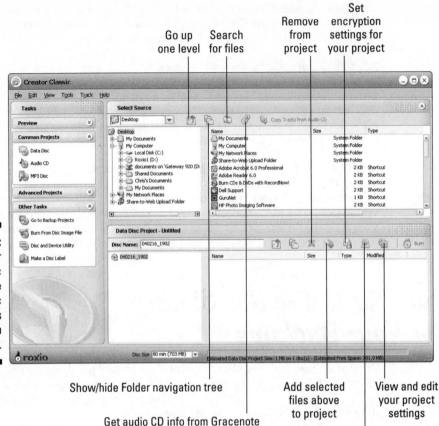

Go up one level
Search for files
Remove from project
Set encryption settings for your project

Show/hide Folder navigation tree
Get audio CD info from Gracenote CDDB online music database
Add selected files above to project
Import data from an appendable disc
View and edit your project settings

Figure 3-6:
Use Creator Classic to create data disc projects that you can reuse.

Opening a new disc project

When you first launch Creator Classic, the program is set to start a new data disc project, that is, a disc that contains only data files. If this is the kind of project that you need to make, all you need to do is start locating the files in the Select Source pane and then add them to Data Project pane.

Data disc projects are not the only ones supported by Creator Classic. In addition to the default Data Disc project, you can create the following audio projects as well:

✔ **Audio CDs** that contain only audio tracks for playback in any CD player (see Chapter 8 for details)

✔ **MP3 Discs** that contain only audio tracks saved in the MP3 codec for playback in CD and DVD players capable of playing MP3s (see Chapter 8 for details)

✔ **Enhanced CDs** that contain two sessions, the first consisting of audio tracks and the second consisting of data files for playback of the music in any CD player and the music and data in standard CD-ROM disc drives

✔ **Mixed-Mode CDs** that consists of a single session that contains both a track of computer data followed by one or more audio tracks for playback only in CD-ROM drives and recorders

Note that the big difference among the different types of projects in this list is whether or not they play audio tracks only or can deal with playing both audio tracks and some form of data file (such as a video clips). Because Audio CD and MP3 Disc projects consist of only audio tracks, you find information on creating these types in Chapter 8 in Part III on Creating Audio and Photo CDs.

Don't get confused by all this talk about Audio, Enhanced, and Mixed-Mode CDs into thinking that your Data Disc projects can only consist of standard data file types like those that contain text, financial data, graphic images, and the like. If your intention is to back up the music and video clips on a CD or DVD disc (as opposed to playing them in sequence on a standalone CD or DVD player), you can add any of these file types as data files to your data disc project (provided that the file type is not specifically excluded in the data disc project settings — see "Changing the Data Disc Project Settings" later in this chapter for details). Just keep in mind that the audio or video files saved to the resulting CD or DVD disc that you burn from the Data Disc project can only be accessed by computer programs such as the Windows Media Player when the disc is placed in your CD-ROM drive.

The Enhanced and Mixed-Mode CD projects create the two types of so-called hybrid CD discs. Enhanced CDs are more versatile because you can play their music in a standard Audio CD player and their data files in your computer's CD-ROM drive. They are often used to mix music tracks that can be played in audio CD players with an accompanying music video (that you can create in DVD Builder — see Chapter 11) that can be played only in your computer's CD-ROM drive. Mixed-Mode CDs, although limited to CD-ROM drives, are great for putting together educational and entertainment CDs whose subject matter naturally combines both data files and audio tracks.

Because both Enhanced and Mixed-Mode CD projects involve adding audio and data files (although in different ways), you find information on starting them and adding the data files to them in the following sections and information on adding their audio tracks in Chapter 8.

To open either an Enhanced or Mixed-Mode CD project, click the Expand button (the one with the two arrowheads pointing downward one over the other) to right of Advanced Projects in the Tasks pane on the left side of the Creator Classic window. The expanded Advanced Projects area contains the following three links:

- ✔ **Enhanced CD** to open a new Enhanced CD project in the Project pane

- ✔ **Mixed-Mode CD** to open a new Mixed-Mode CD project in the Project pane

- ✔ **Bootable Disc** to create bootable CD or DVD disc, that is, one that contains enough Windows system information to enable you to start your computer from the disc rather than your computer's hard disk (see "Making a bootable data disc" later in this chapter)

When you click the Enhanced CD link, the Project pane changes from Data Disc Project – Untitled to Enhanced CD Project – Untitled and an Audio Project icon appears above Data Project icon (reflecting the serial number default disc name that appears in the Disc Name text box) in the work area below.

When you click the Mixed-Mode CD link instead, the Project pane changes from Data Disc Project – Untitled to Mixed-Mode CD Project – Untitled and the Data Project icon (with the serial number disc name) appears above an Audio Project icon in the work area below.

To add data files to a new Enhanced or Mixed-Mode CD project, you just have to be sure that the Data Project icon is selected (indicated by highlighting) — if the icon is not currently selected, you need to click it to select and highlight it. Then you're set to start adding the data files as described in "Adding data files to a new project" later in this chapter.

Changing the Data Disc Project Settings

When you start a new Data Disc project, Creator Classic applies certain default settings that you may want to review and possibly change before you start adding files to the project. To review and change the Data Disc Project Settings, click the View and Edit Your Project Settings button to the immediate left of the Burn button (one of the few labeled buttons) at the top of the Project pane. The Project Properties dialog box shown in Figure 3-7 then appears with its three tabs: General, Advanced, and Exclude File Types.

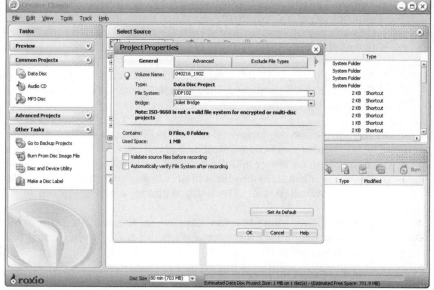

Figure 3-7:
Review and
change the
settings for
your new
Data Disc
project in
the Project
Properties
dialog box.

In addition to displaying information about the type of disc and the number of files and used space currently in the project, the General tab contains the following options that you can modify:

- ✔ **Volume Name** to change the volume label or name of the disc

- ✔ **File System** to choose between three file systems: ISO9660 (for discs to be used on diverse platforms including DOS, UNIX, Macs, OS/2, and Windows), Joliet (to support the use of filenames up to 64 characters long — ISO filenames are restricted to the DOS 8.3 naming system), and UDF 102 (for optical discs such as DVDs, especially when burning files larger than 1GB)

- ✔ **Bridge** to choose between ISO9660 Bridge (to support the UDF and Joliet file system), Joliet Bridge (to support the Joliet, UDF, and ISO file system), and No Bridge (to support no file system other than the one currently selected)

- ✔ **Validate Source Files Before Recording** when you want Creator Classic to verify that none of the source files have been moved, deleted, renamed, or otherwise modified since you added them (if Creator Classic does find such a file, it prompts you to remove the file from the Disc Project)

- ✔ **Automatically Verify File System After Recording** to have Creator Classic compare the files burned to the CD with the original source files on your computer system

You can't use the ISO9660 file system for any project that you intend to encrypt (see "Encrypting the data disc" later in this chapter) for any project that spans more than one disc (see "Burning a multi-disc data project" later in this chapter).

Note that if you want the modifications you make to these settings on the General tab to be new Data Disc default settings, click Set as Default button at the bottom of the this tab.

The settings on the Advanced tab of the Project Properties dialog box enable you to record various vital statistics about the disc's content such as the name of the disc's publisher and the name of the text file that contains the copyright information and to determine which date to use as the disc's publishing date. Click the Advanced tab to review and change any of these settings:

- ✔ **Publisher Name** to enter the name of the publisher (up to 64 characters long when using the Joliet file system and 128 when using the ISO9660 file system)

- ✔ **Prepared By** to enter the name of the person or company who prepared the disc (up to 64 characters long when using the Joliet file system and 128 when using the ISO9660 file system)

- ✔ **Copyright** to enter or browse for the name of the text file that contains the disc's copyright information (Creator Classic adds this text file to the root directory of the disc when you burn it)

- ✔ **Abstract** to enter or browse for the name of the text file that contains the a description or list of the disc's contents (Creator Classic adds this text file to the root directory of the disc when you burn it)

- ✔ **Bibliography** to enter or browse for the name of the text file that contains the bibliographic information about the disc's content (Creator Classic adds this text file to the root directory of the disc when you burn it)

- ✔ **Use Original File Date** option button to time stamp the disc with the date that the disc project is started (this is the date shown in the combo box to the immediate right of the date options)

- ✔ **Use Date When Disc is Written** option button to time stamp the disc with the date when you burn the disc

- ✔ **Use This Date** option button to time stamp the disc with the date you select (when you click this button, the date combo box to the right becomes active and you can type in a new date or click the drop-down button and select one on the pop-up calendar that appears)

The Exclude File Types tab on the Project Properties dialog box enables you to indicate what types of data files should not be added to the disc project. Any file types that you indicate on this settings tab are automatically not copied to the Project pane even when you've inadvertently selected them for adding in the Select Source pane. When you click the Exclude tab, the Project

Properties dialog box displays a list of all the individual file types you can keep out in the Add Files area. To exclude a particular type of file, simply click its check box to add a checkmark to it.

Below the Add Files area on the Exclude tab you find the following two check boxes and button:

- ✔ **Exclude All Hidden Files** to automatically exclude all hidden files in any group that you select in the Select Source pane

- ✔ **Exclude All System Files** to automatically exclude all system files in any group that you select in the Select Source pane

- ✔ **Select/Clear All** button that you can click to select all the file types in the Add Files area or, alternately, deselect them if they are currently all selected

When you finish changing all the settings on the Project Properties dialog box, click OK to close this dialog box and put your modifications into effect.

Titling the disc project

The first thing you may want to do after starting a new disc project is replace the temporary title that Creator Classic automatically assigns your project (that serial-number type volume label that appears in the Disc Name text box at the top of the Project pane) with a volume label of your own. To do this, drag through the serial-number type name in the Disc Name text box to select it and then type in your replacement volume label. When naming the disc project, you need to follow the naming guidelines outlined in the steps on manually formatting a disc for use with Drag-to-Disc (see "Manually formatting a blank disc" earlier in this chapter).

After you type in the new volume label name in the Disc Name, this new name automatically appears to the right of the Data Project icon in the work area of the Project pane below.

Adding data files to a disc project

When adding files to your disc project, you have a choice between two similar methods:

- ✔ Using the drag-and-drop method to drag selected files from the Source pane and drop them on the Data Project portion in the Project pane

- ✔ Select the files in the Source pane and then click the Add Selected Files Above to Project button and have Creator Classic add them to the Project pane for you

I happen to prefer the second method in adding the initial chunk of data files to a new project that are usually located in a common folder. I then find that later on I tend to rely on the first method to add an individual file or groups of files from diverse folders to the project.

When you use the drag-and-drop method to add files to a disc project, you don't have to be concerned about where you drop the files in the Project pane. Creator Classic automatically adjusts the list of data files to display all them all in strict alphabetical order of their filenames.

As you add data files to the Project pane, Creator Classic not only displays a list of their filenames but also indicates the current estimated size of the project and the free space remaining (both in terms of MB or GB free and in form of the slider that appears about these stats as shown in Figure 3-8). You can use these statistics to roughly gauge how many more files you can still add to the project.

Locating files you want to add to your project

If you're not exactly sure where the data files that you need to add to your project are located on your computer system, you can use the Windows XP Search Results feature to find them. To open the Windows Search Results window, click the Search for Files button at the top of the Select Source pane. When the Search Results window opens, you can use its search features to locate just the files that meet your search criteria.

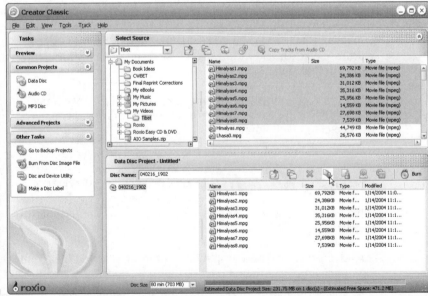

Figure 3-8: As you add data files to a project, their filenames appear in the Project pane along with the estimated project size.

You can also use the navigation tree in the Select Source pane to explore the contents of drives and folders on your computer system when trying to locate the files you want to add to a project. To expand a drive or folder in the tree so that its contents appear in its display area to the immediate right, click its icon's Expand button (the one with the plus sign).

To explore the contents of any folders that you add to the data portion of your project, click its folder icon in the Project pane's navigation tree. Creator Classic then displays its contents in the display to its right.

When exploring the contents of any subfolder in either the Select Source pane's or the Project pane's navigation tree, remember that you can always go back up one level to display the contents of the folder which contains it by simply by clicking the Go Up One Level button in the appropriate pane (it is the first button on each pane's toolbar).

Removing files from your project

If you find that you've added files to your data disc project in error, you can easily remove them from the project. Select their filenames in the Project pane and then click the Remove from Project button at the top of the pane. Creator Classic then displays a Warning alert dialog box asking you if you're sure that you want to remove the selected file(s) from the project. To go ahead and remove the files, click the Yes button. If you're not sure that you want to remove the files, click the No button instead.

Keep in mind as well that deleting files from a data disc project only removes them from the Project pane. It does not remove them from your hard disk, so you have no worries should you delete a file from a data project in error. You can always re-add it to the Project pane from its folder on the hard disk in the Source pane.

Encrypting the data disc

If your data disc project contains sensitive data such as personnel records or corporate financial data, you can encrypt and password-protect the CD or DVD so that only those who have the password can decrypt the data and gain access to its files. Just be careful when using this encryption and password-protection feature as you must know the password exactly as you entered it in order to be able to decrypt the disc files (don't lose that password or the data is as good as gone!). Also be aware that the only way to decrypt an encrypted disc so that you can open the data files and have access to their data is by using the Roxio Retrieve utility to retrieve the files to your computer's hard disk (see "Recovering Data with Roxio Retrieve" later in this chapter).

Technically speaking, you can encrypt the files on a data disc without password protecting the disc. In such a case, anyone to whom you distribute the disc must still use Roxio Retrieve to be able to read the files, although they could do so without having to worry about a password. In my view, if the files on the data disc are sensitive enough to encrypt their data, the disc should surely be password-protected as well.

To encrypt the files for the data disc project you're building in Creator Classic, you follow these steps:

1. **Click the Set Encryption Settings for Your Project button on Project pane's toolbar.**

   Creator Classic then opens the Encryption dialog box similar to the one shown in Figure 3-9.

2. **Click the Enable File Encryption (128 bit) check box.**

   This turns on the file encryption that requires the use of the Roxio Retrieve utility to decrypt.

3. **To password-protect the disc, click the Password text box, and then enter a password of at least six characters.**

   In order to complete the password-protection of the disc, you must now re-enter the password in the Re-enter Password text box exactly as you originally entered it in the Password text box.

4. **Press Tab or click the Re-enter Password text box and then re-type the password exactly as you originally entered it in the Password text box.**

   If you wish, you can hide the display of the filenames on the data disc as well as prevent their use by any unauthorized parties by performing Step 5. If you don't perform Step 5, anyone can get a list of the filenames on the disc using the Windows explorer (or some program like it) but they still can't open any of the files without being able to correctly reproduce the password and then using Roxio Retrieve to copy the encrypted files to their computer's hard disk.

5. **(Optional) Click the Hide File Names on Disc check box to block the display of the filenames in any Windows directory listing.**

6. **Click the OK button to close the Encryption dialog box and put your encryption settings into effect.**

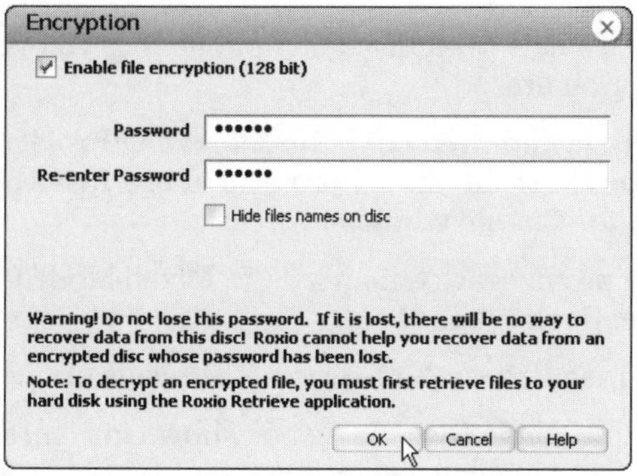

Figure 3-9:
Use the
settings
in the
Encryption
dialog box
to protect a
data disc
containing
sensitive
data from
prying eyes.

Encryption	✕

☑ **Enable file encryption (128 bit)**

Password ••••••

Re-enter Password ••••••

☐ Hide files names on disc

Warning! Do not lose this password. If it is lost, there will be no way to recover data from this disc! Roxio cannot help you recover data from an encrypted disc whose password has been lost.

Note: To decrypt an encrypted file, you must first retrieve files to your hard disk using the Roxio Retrieve application.

[OK] [Cancel] [Help]

Making a bootable data disc

Creator Classic makes it possible to create a bootable CD-ROM disc. A bootable disc in essence emulates a 1.44 floppy disk drive (the so-called A: floppy drive that is so often missing from today's computers, especially in laptops which are normally configured with only a CD or DVD disc drive) and that contains the Windows system files necessary to boot your computer. Such a disc enables you to boot your computer from your computer's CD or DVD drive in the event that you experience some kind of glitch with your computer's hard disk that prevents it from using its own Windows system files.

Before you can use Creator Classic to create a bootable disc, you have to ascertain that your computer system's BIOS settings support this feature. While most computers based on the Pentium-class computer chip support this feature, you may still have to check your computer documentation to learn how to access your system's BIOS settings and whether or not you have actually enabled a bootable CD-ROM option.

If your CD or DVD drive is connected to your computer via a SCSI host adapter, it may have its own BIOS. You still need to check the drive's documentation to verify that the SCSI adapter supports the bootable CD-ROM feature and, if so, how to activate it for your drive.

Assuming that your system supports the bootable CD-ROM feature and that you have activated it for your computer, you can then create a bootable CD-ROM using these steps:

1. **Place a blank CD-ROM into your computer's CD or DVD drive.**

   Make sure that this is a new CD-R disc and not one that you've burned before and then later on erased.

2. **Launch Creator Classic and then click the Advanced Projects Expand button to display the three advanced projects in the Tasks pane on the left side of the Creator Classic window.**

   The three advanced projects are Enhanced CD, Mixed-Mode CD, and the one you want to use, Bootable Disc.

3. **Click the Bootable Disc link in the Advanced Projects area.**

   The Choose Type of Bootable Disc dialog box shown in Figure 3-10 opens where you select between generating the disc from an existing floppy disk or from a boot image file that's installed on your computer's hard disk when you install the Roxio Easy Media Creator 7.

4. **If you have a bootable 1.44 MB floppy disk that you want used in making the bootable CD-ROM, click the Generate Image from Floppy option button. Otherwise, leave the Use Existing Image File option button selected and then click the Browse button and locate the boot image file on your hard disk.**

   If you click the Generate Image from Floppy option, you must insert the disk in your computer's floppy drive before you click OK in the Choose Type of Bootable Disc dialog box.

   If you leave the Use Existing Image File option selected but don't want to use the boot image file supplied by Roxio, click the Browse button to its immediate right and then locate and select the image file you want to use.

5. **Click the OK button at the bottom of the Choose Type of Bootable Disc dialog box to close it and have Creator Classic format your CD-ROM disc and copy the bootable system files to it.**

If you use the Generate Image from Floppy option, an alert dialog box appears prompting you to insert the disk in your computer's A: drive. Click OK to have Creator Classic continue with preparing the disc and copying the necessary files.

After preparing and copying the system files to your CD-ROM disc, Bootable Disc Project – Untitled appears at the top of the Project pane and you can then use Creator Classic to add any additional files that you want burned onto the disc (for example, you might want to add hard disk utilities, application installers, or other backup utilities to the disc in addition to the boot image files).

If you want to access information on your computer from your bootable disc (beyond just starting up the system), be sure to add these files to your Bootable Disc Project. These include the following:

- ✔ mscdex.exe
- ✔ cdrom.sys
- ✔ Device drivers for your computer's CD and/or DVD drives

After burning the files you add to your Bootable Disc Project (see "Saving the disc project and burning the disc" that immediately follows for details, you need to test out your bootable CD-ROM. To do this, restart your computer while the CD-ROM is still in your CD or DVD drive (by clicking the Start button on the Windows taskbar, the Turn Off Computer item on the Start menu and the Restart button in the Turn Off Computer dialog box). If your computer starts from the CD-ROM rather than from your computer's hard disk, your bootable CD-ROM has all the information it needs to start your system in case of any hard disk problems. Of course, this means that you have now to remove the CD-ROM from your CD or DVD drive to resume normal startup from the hard disk.

Figure 3-10:
Use the
settings in
the Choose
Type of
Bootable
Disc dialog
box to
create a
bootable
CD-ROM
that
emulates a
1.44MB
floppy disk.

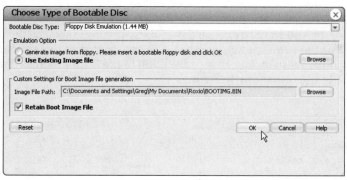

Saving the disc project and burning the disc

After you add all the files you want to your disc project, you can save it so that you can use it at a later time to burn additional CD or DVD discs without having to go through all that creation rigmarole all over again. To save the project you're working on:

1. **Choose File➪Save Project on the Creator Classic menu bar or press Ctrl+S.**

   The standard Windows Save As dialog box appears where you can select the drive and folder in which to save the project and the filename under which to save the project.

2. **Indicate the drive and folder where you want to save the project with the Save In combo box.**

3. **Replace Untitled in the File Name text box with the filename you want to use (just don't delete the .rcl filename extension).**

4. **Click the Save button to close the Save As dialog box and save your project settings on your hard disk.**

Note when you save the project, Creator Classic doesn't actually save the files in the project on your hard disk. This means that if you want to use the project again a later time to burn a disc, the files in the project must be in the same folders and disk locations as they were at the time you saved the project.

To burn the CD or DVD by copying the files in your project, all you have to do is click the Burn button on the right side of the Creator Classic toolbar. When you click this button, the Roxio Creator Classic - Burn Progress dialog box appears, giving you Project Summary and Device Summary statistics. To burn the disc using these stats, click the Burn button.

If, however, you want to change any of these settings (such as the destination device or the write speed), click the >>Details button at the bottom left of the dialog box to display an expanded version of the Burn Progress dialog box similar to the one shown in Figure 3-11.

Figure 3-11:
The expanded version of the Burn Progress dialog box enables you to select all the settings that determine how your disc is recorded.

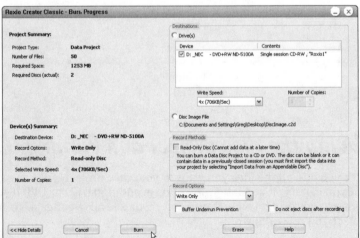

As you can see in Figure 3-11, this expanded version of the Roxio Creator Classic - Burn Progress dialog box enables you to select a new destination drive (if you have one), select a new write speed (if your CD or DVD media support this), and increase the number of disc copies to be made. In addition, you can select, deselect, or modify any of the following options:

- ✔ **Disc Image File** option button to save a complete copy of the disc project on your hard disk which can then be burned to a CD or DVD disc a later time using Creator Classic (keep in mind that the data files added to the project are not saved as part of this disc file image and so must be in the same folder and disk locations on your hard drive as they were when you created the project)

- ✔ **Read Only Disc (Cannot Add Data at a Later Time)** check box, which when selected prevents you from adding any more data files to this disc even when there's sufficient free space and you're using rewritable media

- ✔ **Record Options** drop-down to choose between Write Only to begin recording without doing any testing, Test Only to perform the recording test to determine whether or not files in the project can be successfully written to the disc, and Test and Write to perform the recording test and then, if the disc passes automatically continue and burn the files to the disc

- ✔ **Buffer Underrun Prevention** check box to enable or disable buffer prevention for your CD or DVD drive that creates a buffer in the memory to ensure that the data is recorded to the disc without any interruptions (this option is disabled for older drives that don't support this feature)

- ✔ **Do Not Eject Discs After Recording** check box to ensure or prevent Creator Classic from automatically ejecting each CD or DVD disc after it finishes recording all its data files

- ✔ **Erase** button to erase all the data on a rewritable CD or DVD disc (see Chapter 2 for details) before Creator Classic begins recording the files in your project on it

After adjusting all the necessary options in the Burn Progress dialog box, click the Burn button to begin recording your files. The information in the Burn Progress dialog box is then updated to a Disc 1 of x (where x is the total number of discs required to copy all the files in your disc project). This dialog box also shows you the progress of the data recording both in terms of the tracks and overall disc progress. This updated Burn Progress dialog box contains a Start Label Creator button that you can click to launch the Label Creator application for creating a custom label for your CD or DVD disc(s) after the recording is completed (see Chapter 9 for details).

If you don't want to make a label for your disc after the files are burned onto it, simply click the Close button to close the Roxio Creator Classic - Burn Progress dialog box and return to the Creator Classic window.

If you've added more files to your disc project than can be burned on a single CD or DVD disc, Creator Classic indicates the number of discs required along with the total size of the project at the bottom of the Project pane. When you burn the project, Creator Classic prompts to insert a new disc in the destination drive after it finishes copying as many files as fit on the current disc. This continues until all the files are copied. Because Creator Classic can split data in a single file across more than one disc, you need to use the Roxio Retrieve utility in order to access files burned on such a multi-disc project (see "Recovering Data with Roxio Retrieve" later in this chapter for details). Just be sure to label the discs in a multi-disc project sequentially (1, 2, 3, and so on) so that you identify each disc when using this tool to recover their files.

Adding files to an existing CD or DVD disc

Provided that a rewritable CD or DVD disc you've burned still has space free for additional files and was not recorded with the Read-Only Disc option (see "Saving the disc project and burning the disc" earlier in this chapter for details), you can append files to the disc by taking the following steps:

1. **Launch Creator Classic by clicking the Creator Classic link in the Applications area of the Easy Media Creator Home window.**

   If the Easy Media Creator Home window is not open, click the Start button on the Windows taskbar, highlight All Programs on the Start menu, followed by Roxio on the All Programs submenu, and then click Roxio Easy Media Creator Home on the Roxio submenu.

2. **Put CD-ROM disc to which you want append additional files in your computer's CD or DVD drive.**

   Remember that in order to add files to this CD-ROM disc, it must have sufficient free space and it must not have been originally burned as a Read-only disc.

3. **Click the Import Data from an Appendable CD button on the Project pane's toolbar (the one the second from left of the Burn button).**

   Creator Classic responds by starting a new Data Disc project to which it adds all the folders and files on the existing CD.

4. **Continue to add the other folders and files on your hard disk that you want recorded on the disc as you normally would (refer to "Adding data files to a disc project" earlier in this chapter for details).**

   If you think you might ever reuse this new project, name the project by replacing the numeric name in the Disc Name text box and then choose File⇨Save Project (Ctrl+S) on the Creator Classic menu bar.

5. **Click the Burn button at the right of the Project pane's toolbar; then select the appropriate burn options in the Roxio Creator Classic – Burn Progress dialog box (see "Saving the disc project and burning the disc" earlier in this chapter) and click its Burn button.**

Note that you don't have to burn the new data disc project to the same disc. If you want to burn it to a new CD or DVD disc, replace the one from which you imported most of the data with a blank disc before you click the Burn button on the Project pane's toolbar.

Creating a Backup project

Creator Classic supports the creating of a special Data Disc project called a Backup project. A Backup project differs from a regular Data Disc project in that you get to specify not only what files are copied to disc but how often. Backup projects are perfect for backing up files such as personnel or financial data files that require routine and regular backups as you add to and edit their contents during the course of business.

When creating a Backup project, you not only determine which files are backed up, how they are backed up, and whether or not they are encrypted, but also how often you should be prompted by Creator Classic to use the Backup project to burn the backup discs.

To start a new Backup project, you follow these steps:

1. **Click the Go to Backup Projects link at the top of the Other Tasks list in the Tasks pane on the left of the Creator Classic window.**

   The Creator Classic window is updated to show all the Backup projects you've created in the pane on the right and listing the individual Backup Tasks at the top of the Tasks pane on the left.

2. **Click the Create New Project link at the top of the Backup Tasks list in the Tasks pane. (See Figure 3-12.)**

   The Backup Options dialog box with the What, When, and How tabs shown in Figure 3-13 appears. Note that the What tab options are automatically displayed.

3. **Type in a name for the new Backup project in the Project Name text box.**

   Note that you can't later change the project name that you enter here.

4. **Indicate what folders to include in the Backup project by expanding their drives and folders so that they are displayed in the navigation tree and then click the check boxes in front of the their folder names to put checkmark in the boxes.**

After indicating what files to back up, you may then change the other options at the bottom of the Backup Options dialog box including which files types are excluded with the Exclude File Types button, whether or not source files are verified before they're copied to disc with the Validate Source Files before Backing Up check box, and whether or not the data backup files is verified after copying with the Automatically Verify File System after Backing Up (see "Changing the Data Disc Project Settings" earlier in this chapter for details).

5. **Click the When tab to display the When tab options indicating when and how often to be reminded to make the backup disc(s).**

   Here, you begin by specifying whether to use daily, weekly, or monthly reminders. By default, the new Backup project selects weekly reminders.

6. **Click the Set Reminder check box. If you want to be reminded daily or monthly, click the drop-down button and select Daily or Monthly on the Set Reminder pop-up menu.**

   The interval settings that appear in the area beneath the Set Reminder options depend upon which period you select. When you choose Daily, you can choose between the Every Day and Every Weekday options. When you choose Weekly, you can choose the day of the week you receive the reminder and whether you receive it every week, every two weeks, or every third week. When you choose Monthly, you can choose the day of the month you receive the reminder and whether you receive it every month, every two months, every three months, and so on.

7. **Make any necessary changes to the settings for reminder interval you selected.**

   Now all that's left to do on the When tab is to select the time of day to be reminded.

8. **Select the time of the day you want to be reminded in the Set Reminder At text box by clicking each part of the time and then adjusting it with the buttons.**

   The How tab contains all the options for encrypting, password-protecting, and hiding the files on the backup disc (refer back to "Encrypting the data disc" earlier in this chapter for help on changing individual settings).

9. **(Optional) Click the How tab and set any encryption and password settings that you want applied when making the backup disc.**

   Remember that if you encrypt the disc with a password, you must be able to produce the password exactly as you assigned it or you have no access to the disc and can just kiss the data goodbye.

10. **Click OK button to save your Backup project and return to the Creator Classic window.**

Delete the selected   View and edit the selected
Backup project   Backup project's settings

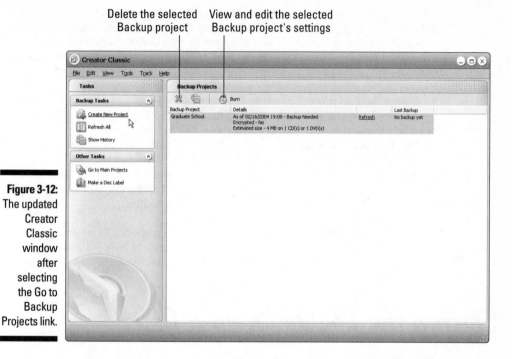

Figure 3-12:
The updated
Creator
Classic
window
after
selecting
the Go to
Backup
Projects link.

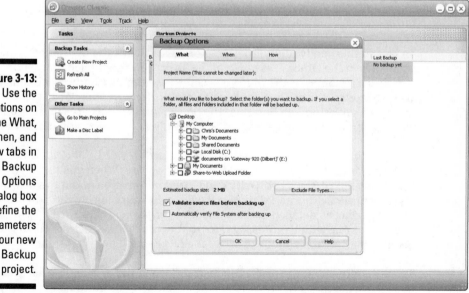

Figure 3-13:
Use the
options on
the What,
When, and
How tabs in
the Backup
Options
dialog box
to define the
parameters
for your new
Backup
project.

When you return to the Creator Classic, the Backup Projects pane now lists your new Backup project. This list includes the project name, details on whether or not the backup is needed (it is always needed when you first create the project), what kind of encryption, if any, is called for, as well as the estimated size of the project and the number of CD or DVD discs it requires.

To burn a Backup project listed in the Backup Projects pane, make sure that it's selected and then click the Burn button at the top of this pane. If you need to review or make changes to a particular Backup project, select the project in this pane and then click the View and Edit the Selected Backup Project's Settings button on the Backup Projects toolbar (the button to the immediate left of the Burn button). If you want to delete a particular Backup project instead, click the Delete the Selected Backup Project (the one with the red X at the beginning of the Backup Projects toolbar).

To return to the regular Creator Classic window after initially defining and burning a Backup project, click the Go to Main Projects link in the Other Tasks area of the Tasks pane.

Getting the Lowdown on a Disc

You can use the Disc and Device Utility to get all kinds of information about the discs that you burn with Creator Classic or Drag-to-Disc. You can also use this utility to erase and reformat discs so that you can reuse their media for burning other data disc projects.

To launch this handy utility from Creator Classic, click the Disc and Device Utility link in the Other Tasks area of the Tasks pane on the left. If Creator Classic isn't running at the time you want to use the Disc and Device Utility, you can launch it from the Easy Media Creator Home window by clicking the Extras & Utilities pop-up button at the bottom of the Tools area in the Home window and then clicking Disc and Device Utility at the very top of this menu.

Any way that you choose to launch it, a Disc and Device Utility dialog box very similar to the one shown in Figure 3-14 appears. When you first open this dialog box, it shows you only condensed information about the disc in your CD or DVD drive and the drive itself. To get more information on the disc, including as detailed Session and Disc properties, click the Expand button (the one with the plus sign) in front of the disc's description. To get detailed information about the drive, click its Expand button instead.

To erase or reformat the disc, click media's icon in the Disc and Device Utility dialog box and then click the Erase/Format button (this button may be grayed out and unavailable until you click the disc's icon). The Disc Erase/Format Confirmation alert dialog box then appears giving you the opportunity to choose between the Quick Erase/Format (selected by default) and the Full Erase/Format option button.

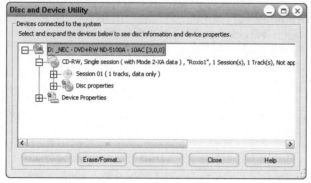

Disc and Device Utility

Figure 3-14:
Use the
Disc and
Device
Utility to get
information
about a
CD or DVD
you've
burned.

If you want to ensure that all the data on the disc is erased before the disc is formatted, click the Full Erase/Format option button before you click the Start button. If you're not worried about a full erase and want to be able to use the disc quickly, leave the default Quick Erase/Format option button selected when you click the Start button.

Recovering Data with Roxio Retrieve

You can use the Roxio Retrieve tool to recover files from the data disc projects you burn onto multiple discs or to recover files on discs that you have encrypted (see "Encrypting the data disc" earlier in this chapter).

Unlike the data disc projects burned onto a single CD or DVD where all the files are on that disc (and which you can readily access in any standard window opened with the Windows File Explorer), the data in some of files in a multi-disc project can actually be split across more than one physical disc. Because of this, you must use the Roxio Retrieve tool in order to copy such files to your computer's hard disk or some other network disk to which you have access.

Don't try to use the Windows Explorer to access files that are split across discs in a multi-disc project. Doing so can render the files on the discs in the set unusable. Therefore, always use the Roxio Retrieve tool to restore any of the files from a multi-disc project to your computer's hard disk.

To recover files from a multi-disc project with Roxio Retrieve, follow these steps:

1. **Put whatever disc of the multi-disc set into your computer's CD or DVD drive you think contains the files you want to restore.**

   Whenever you put in a disc from a multi-disc set, Roxio Retrieve shows you all the folders and files on the disc set along with the number of the disc on which they're stored.

2. **Launch the Roxio Retrieve tool by clicking the Extras and Utilities drop-down button at the bottom of the Tools area of the Easy Media Creator Home window and then clicking the Roxio Retrieve item on the pop-up menu.**

A Roxio Retrieve window similar to the one shown in Figure 3-15 then opens. This window shows the name of the disc with its navigation tree in the pane on the left and the names of all the folders and files at the current level along with its source disc number in the pane on the right. If the disc is encrypted, you will be prompted to enter the disc's password. If the disc is part of a backup disc project (see "Creating a Backup project" earlier in this chapter for details), the Roxio Retrieve window shows the backup history in the Backup History list. You can then choose the backup history you want to use (usually the most recent one, unless you're looking for an earlier version of a file before certain editing changes were made).

3. **Scroll up and down the navigation tree in the left pane and through the folder and file list in the right pane until you locate the files you want to copy to your hard disk.**

To open a folder and displays its contents, click its icon in the navigation tree to the left. To return to the previous level in the tree and display its folders and files, click the Up One Level button on Roxio Retrieve window's toolbar. Note that Roxio Retrieve indicates all files whose data is split across discs by listing the two disc numbers in the Source Disc column in the pane on the right (in Figure 3-15, you know that the file named LHASA22.MPG is split across two discs because its Source Disc information is listed as 1-2, telling you part of the information is on the disc 1 currently being scanned and part is on disc 2).

4. **Click the check box before the names of all the folders or files that you want copied to your hard disk so each of its boxes contains a checkmark.**

To copy all the files on the disc, click the check box in front of the disc's name in the pane on the left. Once you finish marking all the folders and files to copy, you're ready to start the copy procedure and indicate where the folders and files are to be copied.

5. **Click the Click to Copy Selected Files and Folders button on the Roxio Retrieve window's toolbar (the one the farthest to the right).**

The Choose Destination dialog box shown in Figure 3-16 appears. By default, Roxio Retrieve selects the Alternate Destination option button to save the selected files in the directory whose path is shown below. You can accept this default directory, change it with the Browse button, or have the files copied to their original directories by selecting the Original Location(s) option button.

6. **Indicate where you want the selected folders and files copied in the Choose Destination dialog box and then click its Retrieve button.**

As soon as you click the Retrieve button, Roxio Retrieve starts copying the selected folders and files to your designated location on your computer system. When copying a file that's not on the disc currently in your CD or DVD drive or one that's split across discs, Roxio Retrieve automatically ejects the current disc and prompts you to replace it with the number of the disc that contains the files or part of the file in question.

When Roxio Retrieve finishes copying all of the files, the utility displays a Roxio Retrieve alert dialog box indicating that the Retrieve process has been successfully completed.

7. **Click the OK button the Roxio Retrieve alert dialog box indicating the completion of the copying operation to close it and then click the Close button in the upper-right corner of the Roxio Retrieve window to close this utility.**

Note that you can resort the files displayed in the right pane of the Roxio Retrieve window by clicking on their column heading. For example, to sort the files by their Source Disc number in descending order (from highest to lowest), click the Source Disc column heading once. To then resort the files by Source Disc number in ascending order (lowest to highest), click the Source Disc column heading a second time.

Show folders ⌐ Click to copy
and select
Up one level ⌐ folders

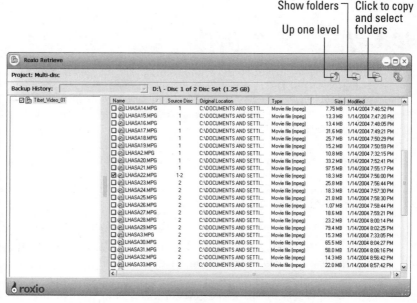

Figure 3-15:
Use the
Roxio
Retrieve tool
to recover
files from
multi-disc
projects by
copying
them
onto your
computer's
hard disk.

Figure 3-16:
Use the
options in
the Choose
Destination
dialog box
to tell Roxio
Retrieve
where to
copy the
selected
files.

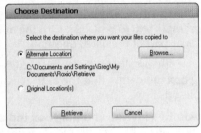

You can also use the Search for Files and Folders on the Disc Set button to locate particular files on the disc set. Simply enter the complete name of the file (including its filename extension) you want to find in the Named text box and click the Search Now button in the Search for Files and Folders dialog box that appears. Roxio Retrieve then expands the Search for Files and Folders dialog box to show you the number of the disc that contains your file.

Disc Copies in a Jiffy

The Roxio Disc Copier enables you to make duplicates of any noncopy-protected CD or DVD even if your computer system has only a single CD or DVD drive. This nifty application is especially useful when you need to make additional copies of CD or DVD discs that you burned either with Drag-to-Disc or Creator Classic.

To make a disc copy with Disc Copier, you follow these easy steps:

1. **Put the CD or DVD disc which you want copied in your computer's CD or DVD drive.**

   Now you're ready to launch the Roxio Disc Copier application.

2. **Click the Roxio Disc Copier link at the top of the Applications area in the Easy Media Creator Home window.**

   The Roxio Disc Copier alert dialog box warns you that unless you own the copyright or have the explicit permission of the copyright holder to copy the disc, you may be violating the Copyright law and be subject to legal penalties (such as fines and even perhaps damages). As soon as you click the OK button to close this alert dialog box, the Roxio Disc Copier window divided into a Source pane on the left and a Destination pane on the right appears.

3. **Click the Advanced button to expand the Roxio Disc Copier window to show information on the disc you want to copy and source and destination drive.**

   An expanded version of Roxio Disc Copier window similar to the one shown in Figure 3-17 then appears. This version shows the type or recorder and write speed and enables you to change these settings as well as to increase the number of copies to make.

4. **(Optional) If your computer has more than a disc drive (such as a CD-ROM and a DVD recorder), select the drive with the disc you want to copy on the Drive drop-down list in the Source pane and the drive that contains the blank disc to which the files are to be copied on the Recorder drop-down list in the Destination pane.**

5. **Click Copy button to begin the disc copy operation.**

   The Roxio Disc Copier – Burn Progress dialog box then appears, keeping you apprised of the copy operation by displaying Finished and Disc Progress sliders showing you the percentage completed and the elapsed time.

   If your computer has only one CD or DVD drive which acts both as the source and destination, after copying all the disc files to a temporary location on your hard disk, the Roxio Disc Copier automatically ejects the disc you're copying and displays an Insert Media dialog box that prompts you to replace the ejected disc with a blank disc of the same media type. After you click Continue Recording button to close this dialog box, a Select Write Speed dialog box may appear, enabling you to select a new write speed for the disc copy (to use the same write speed, simply click the Continue Recording button in this dialog box). When the Finished and Disc Progress indicators in Roxio Disc Copier – Burn Progress dialog box reach 100%, you can then either start the Label Creator to design and print a label for the newly copied disc (see Chapter 8) or close the Roxio Disc Copier application.

6. **To create a label for the disc copy, click the Start Label Creator button. To close the Roxio Disc Copier – Burn Progress dialog box, eject the disc, and return to the Roxio Disc Copier window, click the Close button instead.**

   If you don't choose to make a label for your new disc copy, you can then close the Roxio Disc Copier application by clicking its Close button in the upper-right corner of the window.

You can also use the Roxio Disc Copier application to burn copies of discs made either from a disc image file or a DVD-Video folder. A disc image file is one that contains DVD-video, audio, or video-CD content (a valid disc image file is marked with an icon showing two cascading discs, one on top of the other). A DVD-Video folder is one that contains only DVD-Video content that is not copy-protected (a DVD-Video folder is marked with a disc on top of the standard folder icon).

Figure 3-17:
Use the
Roxio Disc
Copier
application
to make
duplicates
of any
noncopy-
protected
CD or DVD
disc.

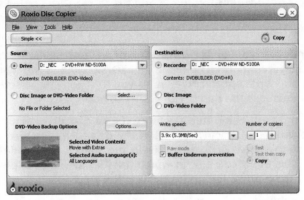

To use the Roxio Disc Copier to burn a disc image file onto a blank disc, click Disc Image or the DVD-Video Folder option button in the Source pane of the Roxio Disc Copier window and then click the Select button to the immediate right. Then, select the disc image file or the DVD-Video folder in the navigation tree in the left pane of the Select File or Folder dialog box or click the Search button to locate the disc image file or DVD-Video folder you want to copy.

When you select a DVD-Video folder, the right pane of the Select File or Folder dialog box displays all of its contents, including all the individual movies and any extras. It does this by showing the first frame of each movie along with a description of it in the right pane (to preview the content of any movie or extra, click its Play button). By default, the Roxio Disc Copier copies all of the video content in a DVD-Video folder. If you want to copy only a single movie in the folder, click the Copy Single Movie option button and then click the movie's key frame or description to select it.

After selecting the disc image files or DVD-Video folders in the Select File or Folder dialog box, click the OK button to close this dialog box and return to the Roxio Disc Copier window. From there, you can begin making the disc copy by clicking the Save As button (which replaces the Copy button when you select disc image files) or Burn (which replaces the Copy button when you select DVD-Video folders).

Chapter 4

Organizing Media Files with the Media Manager

*M*edia Manager is the place to go when you need to organize or find the various types of media files used in the creation of the various projects you build with the Easy Media Creator. These media files include photos, video clips, audio files, music tracks as well as the actual Easy Media Creator project files themselves.

This chapter gives you the lowdown on using Media Manager to keep tabs on the many types of files even when they're saved on widely divergent locations on computer system. As you find out, you can use Media Manager both to organize and quickly find and review all the different media files stored on various drives and on media (including CD and DVD discs) throughout your computer system.

This chapter also covers using Media Manager to make it possible to quickly locate particular types of media files by enabling you to assign keywords to them that you can then use in the searches you conduct for media files of a particular kind (you can even create media file collections based on your search results). Last but not least, you get vital information on using Media Manager to make backup copies of all your media files by burning them to CD or DVD discs (which then enables you to free up much needed hard disk).

Making the Most of Media Manager

If the Easy Media Creator Home window is open, you can launch Media Manager simply by clicking the Media Manager link at the top of the Tools column. If this window is not open, you can launch Media Manager from the Windows operating system by following these steps:

1. **Click the Start button on the Windows taskbar.**

   This opens the Start menu where you select the All Programs option.

2. **Position the mouse pointer on All Programs in the Start menu.**

   This opens the All Programs submenu where you select Roxio.

3. **Position the mouse pointer on Roxio in the All Programs submenu.**

   This opens the Roxio submenu where you select Media Manager.

4. **Click Media Manager in the Roxio submenu.**

Either way you go about it, when you launch Media Manager a window very similar to the one shown in Figure 4-1 opens. This window is initially divided into a Folders navigation pane on the left and the folder's Contents pane displaying all the subfolders in the My Documents folders on the right. Note that in the Media Manager, you can switch between the default Folders navigation pane and the Collections navigation pane that let you navigate all the collections you create and display the files and folders they contain in the Contents pane.

To switch to the Collections navigation pane, you click the Browse Collections button on the toolbar on the left below the menu bar (see "Browsing your collections" later in this chapter). Then you can return to the default Folders navigation pane by clicking Browsing Folders button (see "Browsing your folders" that follows for details).

Browsing your folders

The Folders navigation pane in the Media Manager window enables you to explore the folders and files on your computer's hard disk, removable media in your computer's CD and DVD drives, as well as the other drives on your network to which you have access. To display the contents of a particular drive or folder on your system, click the Expand button (the one with the Plus sign) in front the Desktop, My Computer, My Documents, or My Network Places system folder icons to display the drives and folders they contain. Then, to display the contents of a drive or folder contained within one of these system folders, click its drive or folder. Media Manager responds by displaying all the folders and files on that drive or in that folder in the Contents pane on the right. You can continue in this manner, expanding folders within folders to peruse their files and reacquaint yourself with the folders on your drives and their hierarchical relationship.

Figure 4-2 shows you the Media Manager after I expanded the My Documents system folder on my hard disk and then expanded the My Pictures folder before clicking the Mission Murals folder. Media Manager responds by displaying thumbnails of all the digital photos in this folder in the Contents pane. Note that after you use the Folders navigation tree to descend several levels deep within a particular drive or system folder, you can then ascend the tree, jumping back one level at a time by clicking the Up One Level button until you reach the very top of the tree (the Desktop in this case).

After you select a folder you want to explore in the Folders navigation pane, you can then use the following buttons on the pane's toolbar to manipulate the folder as follows:

- ✔ **Create a New Folder** to create a new subfolder within the current folder that you can name

- ✔ **Rename Selected Folder** to select the name of the currently selected folder so that you can replace it with a new folder name

- ✔ **Delete Selected Folder** to delete the current folder and everything within it (be careful with this button)

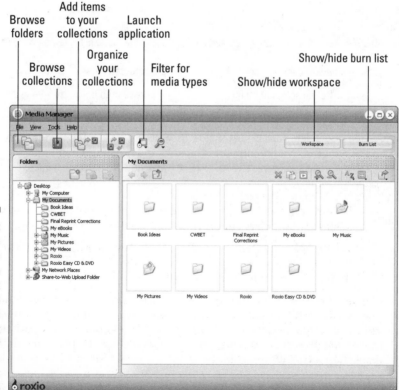

Figure 4-1:
Use the Media Manager to keep track of and organize all the different types of media files you use.

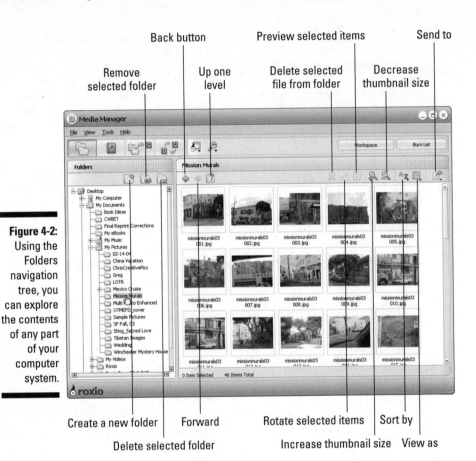

Back button   Preview selected items   Send to

Remove
selected folder   Up one
level   Delete selected
file from folder   Decrease
thumbnail size

Figure 4-2:
Using the
Folders
navigation
tree, you
can explore
the contents
of any part
of your
computer
system.

Create a new folder   Forward   Rotate selected items   Sort by

Delete selected folder   Increase thumbnail size   View as

When you select media files inside the currently selected folder in the Contents pane, you can then manipulate the selected files (and sometimes all the other files in the pane) using the following buttons that appear on the Contents pane's toolbar:

- **Delete Selected Items from Folder** to remove the selected files (and any selected subfolders) upon your confirmation

- **Rotate Selected Item(s)** to rotate the selected graphic files (this button isn't available when audio or video media files are selected) in 90-degree increments in a clockwise direction

- **Preview Selected Item(s)** to preview graphic or video media files (this button isn't available when audio files are selected) in separate windows that give you the file size and resolution — graphic file previews let you zoom in and out on the image, whereas video file previews let you play the video clip

✔ **Increase Thumbnail Size** to increase the size of all the thumbnail images used to identify media files and folders within the current folder (resulting in fewer being displayed in the Contents pane)

✔ **Decrease Thumbnail Size** to decrease the size of all the thumbnail images used to identify media files and folders within the current folder (resulting in more being displayed in the Contents pane)

✔ **Sort By** to modify the order of the files and folders within the current folder by such attributes as Date Modified, Date Created, Size, and Type in either ascending or descending sort order (Media Manager sorts them by Name in ascending order by default)

✔ **View By** to change from viewing thumbnails of the media files and folders to either Details which lists filename, size, date created and modified, and attributes along with a small thumbnail image of the file or List that just displays the filename to the right of the small thumbnail images

✔ **Send Selected Items To** to send the selected media files in the current folder to your printer for printing, your e-mail program for sending to others as attachments, as well as to any number of Easy Media Creator utilities including QuickShow to create an impromptu video movie, photo slideshow or audio playlist (see sidebar that follows), the PhotoSuite editor for enhancement, Photo Stitch to create a single panoramic photo from the individual shots, and to VideoWave for inclusion in the storyboard for a video project

TIP

Impromptu movies, slideshows, and playlists thanks to QuickShow

You can use the QuickShow option on the Send Selected Items To drop-down list to make a selection of video clips into a quick-and-dirty movie, photo images into an off-the-cuff slideshow, or audio files into a spur-of-the-moment track playlist. Open a folder that contains a bunch of the same type of media files (video, graphic, or audio) and then select their files in the Contents pane in the order in which you want to them to play in the impromptu show. Then click the Send Selected Items To drop-down button followed by QuickShow on drop-down list. Media Manager then switches to full-screen mode and plays the media in the selected files. This show screen contains a simple playback controller in the upper-right corner containing Play, Pause, Previous, Next,

and Exit buttons that you can use to control the show. This controller uses an AutoHide feature so that it automatically disappears from the screen after a few seconds of play (to make the controller reappear, position the mouse pointer in the upper-right corner in the vicinity of the unhidden controller).

To change the QuickShow settings such as the amount of time each slide is displayed or whether to play an audio track as background music for the show, choose Tools⇨Options on the Media Manager menu bar and modify any necessary settings (such as the Slide Duration or Play Background Sound) on the QuickShow tab of the Options dialog box before you click OK.

Browsing your collections

When you click the Browse Collections button right above the Folders navigation pane on the left side of the Media Manager window, the Folders pane changes to the Collections pane (see Figure 4-3). This pane enables you to browse all the special media collections files on your computer system (see "Creating Media File Collections" later in this chapter for details on creating collections), search for items within your collections, display a calendar view of your collections that groups media files by creation date, and a tag view that lets you assign keywords, comments, and sounds to media files in collection to make them easier to search.

When you click Browse Collections button, the following buttons appear in the Collections pane on the toolbar immediately beneath the Collections title bar. You can use these buttons to change the view in the Collections pane so that you can perform the following operations on your media file collections:

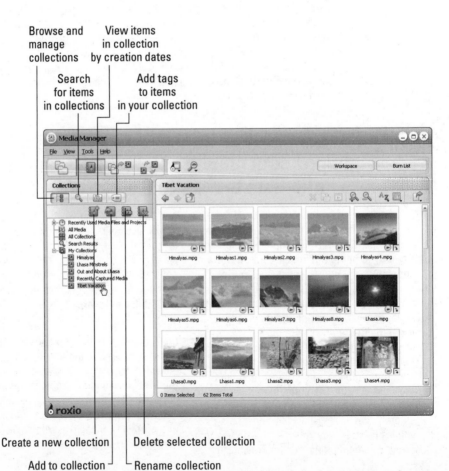

Figure 4-3:
Using the Collections pane's navigation tree, you can explore the contents of any media collections file on your system.

✓ **Browse and Manage Collections** to browse and select collections on your computer system. When you select the name of a particular collection in the Collections pane, the different types of media files are displayed in the Contents pane to the right.

✓ **Search for Items in Your Collections** to search for collections by name, keyword, or comments (see "Finding Wayward Media Files" later in this chapter)

✓ **View Items in Your Collections by Creation Date** to display the media files in your various collections by the month and year that they were created

✓ **Add Tags to Items in Your Collection** to assign keywords, sounds, and comments to a selected media file collection to make that collection easier to find when conducting a search for a particular type of media

Scanning your computer for media files

You can have Media Manager scan your computer system for all the media files that it contains, including supported audio, video, and graphic files as well as all Roxio project files. To have Media Manager scan your computer to locate all of its media files, you follow these steps:

1. **Choose Tools➪Scan for Media Files on the Media Manager menu bar.**

   Media Manager displays a Scan for Media Files dialog box that informs you that by scanning your computer for media files, Media Manager then enables you to more easily browse, search, and tag these files for quick retrieval.

2. **Click the Scan Settings button in the Scan for Media Files dialog box.**

   The Scan Settings dialog box (shown in Figure 4-4) appears where you can adjust which folders and disks on your computer system are scanned, what types of supported files are scanned, and how often Media Manager is to scan your computer.

3. **Click the check boxes in front of the disks and folders listed in the Scan In list box until they match the color and type of mark (x or standard checkmark) for the type of scanning you want in the legend to the right.**

   By default, most of the local disks and system folders (with the exception of the My Computer) are selected for scanning their folder and of their subfolders. In addition, all network disks and Web folders (indicated by the My Network Places and Share-to-Web Upload Folder check boxes) are not set up to be scanned at all. You can change any of these scan settings by continually clicking its checkmark until its color and mark (x or standard checkmark) match the desired kind of scanning listed in the Legend area of the Scan Settings dialog box.

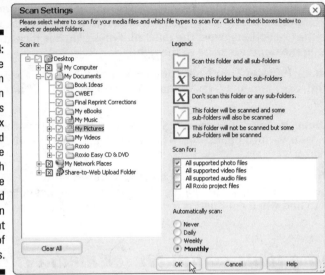

Figure 4-4:
Adjust the
options in
the Scan
Settings
dialog box
as needed
to determine
which
folders are
scanned
how often
for what
types of
files.

4. **Click the check boxes in front of the different types of media files listed in the Scan For list box to either clear its checkmark (so it's not scanned) or insert a checkmark in it (so that it is scanned).**

   By default, Media Manager scans all types of media files except for audio files on the designated disks and folders. To include audio files, click the check box in front of All Supported Audio Files. To remove any of the other three types (photo, video, or Roxio project files), click the check box in front of an option to remove its checkmark.

5. **Click the option button in the Automatically Scan list box to indicate how often to scan your computer (Never, Daily, Weekly, or the default, Monthly).**

   By default, Media Manager is automatically set to scan your computer (using the Scan In and Scan For setting you designate here) on a monthly basis to check for media file updates. To switch to a more frequent interval, click the Daily or Weekly option button. To prevent Media Manager from automatically scanning your computer, click the Never option button instead.

6. **Click the OK button to close the Scan Settings dialog box and return to the Scan for Media Files dialog box.**

   Now you're ready to have Media Manager begin scanning your computer for the specified types of media files.

7. **Click the Scan Now button in the Scan for Media Files dialog box to have Media Manager begin scanning your computer.**

As soon as you click the Scan Now button, the Scan for Media Files dialog box disappears and Media Manager begins scanning the disks, folders, and subfolders you specified for your designated media files. Media Manager keeps you apprised of its progress in the scanning process by showing you which folder it is currently scanning on the status bar at the bottom of the Scan for Media Files dialog box.

When Media Manager finishes scanning your computer for all the designated file types, it then adds an All Media icon to the Collections pane (displayed by clicking the Browse Collections button directly below the menu bar). When you click this icon in the Collections pane, thumbnails of all the designated media files (of the types included in the scan) are displayed in the Contents pane to the right.

Once you've got all your media files scanned and identified in the All Media folder, you can then easily add them to collections that you're building (see "Creating Media File Collections" later in this chapter), tag them for quicker retrieval (see "Tag, You're It!" later in this chapter), or bring them into the workspace (see "Working that Workspace" that immediately follows).

Working that Workspace

Media Manager has a special Workspace pane (similar to the one shown in Figure 4-5) that you can use to assemble media files from diverse folders and collections on your computer to that you can then perform a particular activity to all the files at the same time (such as saving them all in a new collection or printing or e-mailing them). For example, you can use the Workspace to collect a bunch of photos saved in different folders all across your hard disk and then display them sequentially in an onscreen slideshow by clicking the QuickShow item on the Send Selected Items To button's pop-up menu from the Workspace toolbar.

To open the Workspace pane, click the Workspace button on the right side of the Media Manager toolbar. The Workspace pane opens at the bottom of the Media Manager containing its own toolbar for processing the assembled media files.

To bring files into the Workspace for simultaneous processing, select their folders in the Folders navigation or Collections pane and then drag their icons from the Contents pane and drop them on the Workspace pane. When you finish using the Workspace pane, you can clear it of files by clicking the Clear All button on the pane's toolbar and then clicking the Yes button in the Confirm Clearing Workspace alert dialog box (note that these files are then removed *only* from the Workspace and not deleted from their respective folders on your computer's disks). To close the Workspace pane when you no longer are using it, click the Workspace button on the right side of the Media Manager toolbar a second time.

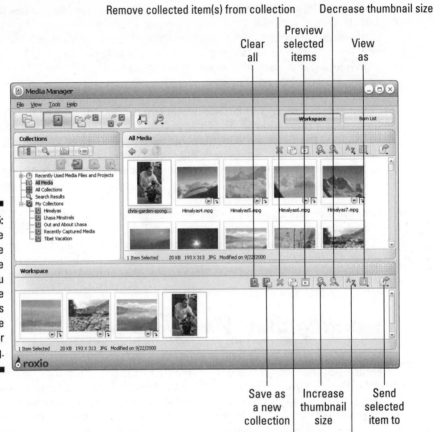

Remove collected item(s) from collection   Decrease thumbnail size

Clear all   Preview selected items   View as

Figure 4-5:
The Workspace pane enables you to assemble media files from diverse locations for processing.

Save as a new collection   Increase thumbnail size   Send selected item to

Rotate selected items   Sort by

Burning up that Burn List

In place of the Workspace pane, you can open a Burn List pane at the bottom of the Media Manager window that enables you to assemble all the media files that you want burned on a backup CD or DVD disc. To open the Burn List pane (similar to the one shown in Figure 4-6), click the Burn List button (to the immediate right of the Workspace button on the toolbar at the top of the Media Manager window).

After you open the Burn List pane, you can add folders, files, and collections to it by selecting their folders or collections in the Folders or Collections pane and then dragging their icons from the Contents pane and then dropping them into the Burn List pane. As you add files to this pane, the status information at the bottom of the Burn List pane keeps you informed of the amount of free space left on the type of disc you're using (see "Backing Up Media Files on Disc" later in this chapter for details on using the Burn List pane to make a backup of your media files).

REMEMBER

Keep in mind that the free-space gauge is dependent upon which type of disc you select with the Select Disc Type drop-down list button (the one to the immediate left of the gauge that uses a disc icon). To select a CD or DVD disc with a different capacity, click this drop-down button and then click the type you intend to use in the burn process (650 MB CD, 700 MB CD, 4.7 GB DVD, 185 MB MiniCD, or 210 MB MiniCD).

TIP

Close the Burn List pane when performing other tasks in Media Manager by clicking the Burn List button on the far right side of the Media Manager's toolbar when you haven't yet added enough files to fill a CD or DVD disc. Then, when you come upon some more media files that you want to burn to disc, you can open the Burn List pane (by clicking the Burn List button once more) so that you can drag-and-drop them into this pane.

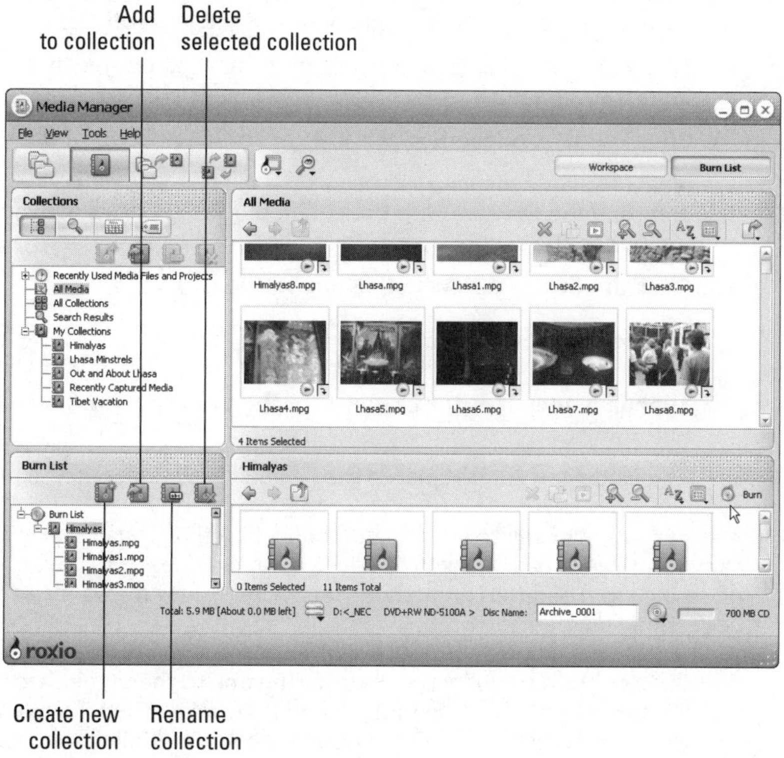
Add to collection
Delete selected collection
Media Manager
Workspace
Burn List
Collections
All Media
Burn List
Himalyas
roxio
Create new collection
Rename collection

Figure 4-6: The Burn List pane enables you to assemble the media files that you want to back up together on a CD or DVD disc that you burn.

Creating Media File Collections

Media file collections are a key element in the struggle to organize and keep on top of the many media files of different types that you use in the various projects you create with the Roxio Easy Media Creator suite. Collections enable you to associate different types of media that you might want to use together in a particular project (such as a DVD movie as described in Chapter 12). The great thing about Collections is that you don't have to physically move or copy all the media files you want to associate with one another into the same folder. A Collection can keep track of all the different files regardless of where they're actually located on your computer system (this includes files saved in folders on your hard disk, files saved in folders on a network drive to which you have access, and files saved in folders on backup CD and DVD discs (that you can actually create with Media Manager — see "Backing Up Media Files on Disc" later in this chapter for details).

To create a new media file Collection, follow these steps:

1. **Launch the Media Manager and then click the Browse Collections button on the right side of the Media Manager toolbar.**

   Media Manager displays the Collections navigation tree in the Collections pane.

2. **Click the My Collections icon to expand this portion of the tree.**

   Media Manager displays all the collections you've created in the Contents pane and the Create a New Collection button becomes active on the toolbar on the second row of the Collections pane.

3. **Click the Create a New Collection button.**

   Media Manager adds a Collection to the navigation tree named New Collection and gives you the opportunity to rename it (see Figure 4-7).

4. **Type in a new descriptive name for the Collection and then press the Enter key.**

   The name you enter replaces the default "New Collection" name.

As you can see in Figure 4-7, any new collection that you create is automatically empty and ready for you to add your media files to it. Media Manager offers a couple of different methods for adding a new media file to the Collection you create:

✔ Click the Add to Collection button (the one to the immediate right of the Create a New Collection button) and then select the folders and files to associate with the new Collection in the Add to Collections dialog box.

Add to collection ─┐   ┌─ Rename collection

Create
new
collection

Delete
selected
collection

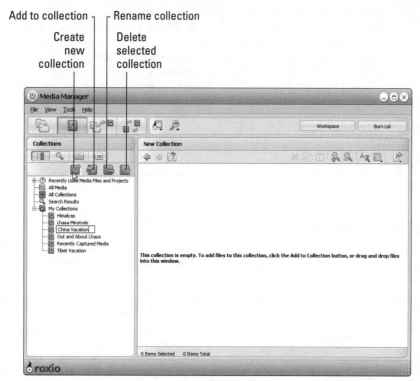

Figure 4-7:
Adding a
new China
Vacation
Collection
to the My
Collections
node on the
Collections
navigation
tree.

✔ Click the Add Items to Your Collections on the left side of the Media
Manager toolbar to split the window into four panes: the Folders
Navigation and Folders Contents panes above the Collections Navigation
and Collections Content panes below. Next select the media files in the
upper Folders Contents pane to add and then click the downward-
pointing arrow button to the left of the Add button to add them into the
Collections Contents pane below.

To select all the media files in the currently selected folder, click somewhere
in the Contents pane and then press Ctrl+A. Media Manager then selects all
the media files in the folder (including the ones you can't see in the Contents
pane).

Saving Workspace files as a Collection

Instead of going through the steps to create a new Collection outlined in the
previous section and then adding media files to it, you can create a new

Collection by adding all its media files to the Workspace pane and then creating the new collection out of its files. This second method for creating a new Collection is sometimes superior to the first in that it enables you to do other things to its media files such as preview all media files of a certain type with the QuickShow utility (see the "Impromptu movies, slideshows, and playlists thanks to QuickShow" sidebar earlier in this chapter) or print all the graphics files as well as associate all of them in a new Collection.

To create a new Collection from the contents of the Workspace pane, follow these steps:

1. **Click the Workspace button to open the Workspace pane at the bottom of the Media Manager window.**

   An empty Workspace pane opens at the bottom of the Media Manager window.

2. **Select the folder containing the media files you want to add in the Folders navigation pane and then select the media files in the Contents pane on the right.**

3. **Drag the selected files to the Workspace pane and then release the mouse button to drop them into this pane.**

   Repeat Steps 2 and 3 until you have added all the media files to the Workspace pane that you want in the new Collection.

4. **Click the Save as New Collection button on the Workspace pane's toolbar (the second button from the left).**

   The Save as New Collection dialog box opens.

5. **Click the Enter a Name for the New Collection text box and then type in the name for the new Collection and then click the Save button.**

   Media Manager closes the Save as New Collection dialog box and creates a new Collection with all the media currently in the Workspace pane.

6. **Click the Clear All button at the beginning of the Workspace pane's toolbar and then click the Yes button in the Confirm Clearing Workspace dialog box to clear the pane.**

   After clearing the media files from the Workspace pane, you are ready to close it.

7. **Click the Workspace button on the Media Manager's toolbar to close the Workspace pane.**

You can then check new Collection you created by clicking on the left side of the Browse Collections button on the Media Manager toolbar and then clicking the Expand button in front of the My Collections icon and finally clicking the name of the new Collection. All the media file that you added to the Workspace pane now appear in the Collection's Contents pane.

Filtering the files in a Collection

Media Manager makes it easy to filter out the types of media files that you don't want displayed in the Folders or Collections Contents pane. This is useful when you're dealing with the Contents pane for a folder or Collection that contains a bunch of different types of media files and you want "narrow down the field" so that it displays only a single type of media file (that you can then review).

To filter out all but a single type of media file, click the Filter for Media Types drop-down button on the Media Manager toolbar and then click the type of media file that you *do* want displayed in the Contents pane (Photos, Audio Files, Video Files, or Roxio Projects) in the pop-up menu. Media Manager temporarily removes the display of all files except for the type you selected in the Contents pane. To redisplay all of the media files in the Contents pane for the currently selected folder or Collection, click the Filter for Media Types drop-down button on the Media Manager toolbar and this time click All Media Files at the very top of the pop-up menu.

Tag, You're It!

Media Manager enables you to tag the media files you assemble into Collections (see "Creating Media File Collections" earlier in this chapter) so that later you can more easily identify their contents or search for them. The program supports three different types of tags:

- **Keywords** that enable you to find related groups of files when doing searches in Media Manager (see "Finding Wayward Media Files" that immediately follows)

- **Comments** that enable you to add text notes that describe the contents of a media file (such as adding the location where a photo was taken and the names of the people who are in it)

- **Sounds** that enable you to add audio notes that describe the contents of a media file (if your digital camera supports adding sound notes to your photos, these are automatically imported along with the image when you use the Capture tool to bring it into a Roxio project — see Chapter 10 for details)

To check a media file for tags, right-click its file icon and then click Properties on its shortcut menu. Then click the Tags tab in the Properties dialog box. This tab displays all the keywords, the text of any comments added to the file, as well as the name of any sound file associated with the media file.

Adding keywords to Collection files

To add keywords to the media files in a Collection in Media Manager, follow these steps:

1. **Click the Browse Collections button on the Media Manager toolbar.**

   The Collections pane appears.

2. **If necessary, expand My Collections in the navigation tree and then click the name of the Collection with files you want to tag.**

   Next, you need to switch from Browse Collections to Assign and Manage Keywords in the Collections pane.

3. **Click the Add Tags to Items in Your Collection button (the one to the farthest right on the Collections toolbar.**

   Media Manager opens the Assign and Manage Keywords portion of the Collections pane with its own toolbar of three buttons (see Figure 4-8).

4. **Select all the media files in the Collections Contents pane that you want to tag with the same keyword(s).**

   Now you're ready to select the keyword(s) to assign to the selected files.

5. **Click the check boxes in front of all applicable keywords listed near the bottom of the Collections navigation pane.**

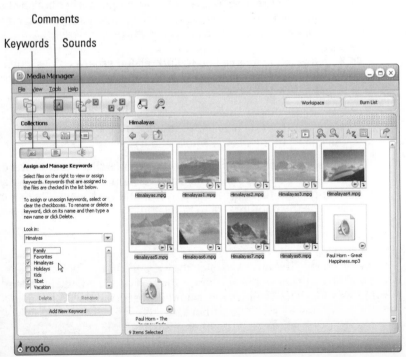

Figure 4-8:
Use the Assign and Manage Keywords portion of the Collections pane to add keywords, comments, or sounds to your media files.

If none of the currently listed keywords applies, you can create a new keyword(s) to apply.

6. **(Optional) Click the Add New Keyword button and then type in the keyword in the blank box and press Enter.**

   If you add a new keyword in Step 6, then you still need to take the next step to apply it to the selected files.

7. **(Optional) Click the check box in front of the new keyword you just added to apply it to the files selected in the Contents pane on the right.**

After you assign keyword(s) to different groups of media files in a Collection, you can then view which keywords apply to what files in the Collection in the Assign and Manage Keywords portion of the Collections pane by simply selecting the media file's icon in the Contents pane. As soon as you click the files' icon, checkmarks appear in all the keywords that you've applied to it (if all the check boxes are empty, this means that you haven't yet applied any keywords to the file).

To remove a keyword that you've applied to a file, all you have to do is to click the keyword's check box to remove its checkmark.

Adding comments to Collection files

In addition to or instead of keywords, you can add explanatory comments to a media file that help you identify its contents. To add a comment to a media file, make its Collection active in the Collections navigation pane and then select the media file in the Contents pane. Next, click the Add Tags to Items in Your Collection button on the Collections toolbar and then click the Comments button in the middle of the second toolbar below.

When you click the Comments button, View and Edit Comments portion of the Collections pane appears containing a Look In drop-down list box where you can select the Collections file whose contents you want displayed in the atten-dant Contents pane. Below this, you find a Comments list box which displays the text of your comments. To add a comment, click the comments list box and then type the text of your note. To edit the contents of a note that you've added, use the I-beam mouse pointer to select the text that needs editing and either delete it with the Delete key or replace the text by typing over it.

Adding sound tags to Collection files

In place of a written comment, you can add a sound tag to a particular media file that explains something about the file's contents or how the file should be edited or used in any of the other projects you create with Roxio Easy Media Creator 7. The process for assigning a sound tag is very similar to that for assigning a comment except that instead of clicking the Comments button in the lower toolbar in the Collections pane, you click the Sounds button (the one on the far right with the speaker icon).

When you click the Sounds button, the Associated Sounds portion of the Collections pane appears. This area contains its own Look-in drop-down list box and below that a Select Sound drop-down list box (where you can select audio files with sound notes that you've already recorded for other media files). To record a new sound note, click the Record a Sound button near the bottom of the Collections pane.

Media Manager then launches the Roxio's Capture tool, which you can use to record your sound note (see Chapter 10 for details on recording sound with Capture). After you finish recording your sound note in Capture, click its Done button with the Go Back to the Launching Application option button still selected to return to Media Manager where the newly recorded sound note is assigned to the selected media file (indicated by the presence of a speaker icon at the bottom of the selected file's thumbnail image).

To listen to the sound note that you've assigned to a media file, click the Play This Sound button that appears right above the Record a Sound button in the Collections pane. Media Manager then plays back the sound note you just recorded and the Play this Sound button turns into a Stop button (which you can click as soon as you've heard enough of the note).

To remove a sound note from a selected media file, click the Select Sound drop-down button and then click the None item at the top of this box's pop-up menu. To delete the file with the sound note you recorded, click its file icon in the Contents pane, press the Delete key, and then click the Yes button in the Confirm Removal of Selected Media File(s) alert dialog box.

Finding Wayward Media Files

Media Manager enables you to find just the media files you want to work with by searching all the media files or Collections on your computer system. When searching for media files, you can do the search on the name of the file or Collection as well as on keywords that you've assigned to the files and even the text of comments that you assigned to them (see "Tag, You're It!" earlier in this chapter for details on assigning keywords and comments to your media files).

Media Manager supports two kinds of media searches:

> ✔ **Simple search** in which you just enter search text and Media Manager then searches for it in all media filenames and Collection names, keywords, and comments in all the media files scanned on your

computer system (see "Scanning your computer for media files" earlier in this chapter)

✔ **Advanced search** in which you specify what text to search for in media filenames and Collection names and what type of media files and Collections to include in the search

To conduct a simple search, you follow these simple steps:

1. **Click the Browse Collections button on the Media Manager toolbar.**

   Media Manager opens the Collections pane.

2. **Click the Search for Items in Your Collections button on the Collections pane's toolbar (the one second from the left with the magnifying glass icon).**

   Media Manager opens the Simple Search portion of the Collections pane similar to the one shown in Figure 4-9.

3. **Type the text to search for in the names of your Collections or filenames they contain and in the keywords and comments you've assigned to these files in the Simple Search text box.**

   The search text that you enter can be just part of a Collection name (such as **vacation** to find both the Collection called Europe vacation and Last summer's vacation) or media filename.

4. **Click the Search button to initiate the search.**

Simple search   Advanced search

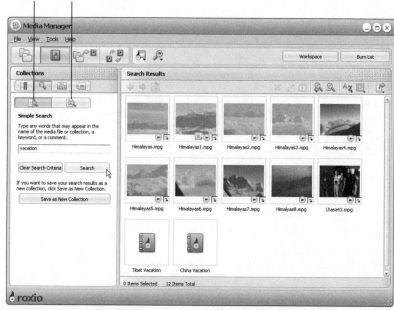

Figure 4-9:
Use Media Manager's simple search feature to locate collections and the media files they contain on your computer system.

Media Manager then displays all the icons for the collections and thumbnails for the media files that contain the search text either in their Collection name or filename or in their keywords or comments. These matching Collections and files appear in the Search Results pane on the right side of the Media Manager window (this pane replaces the usual Collections Contents pane when you click the Search for Items in Your Collection button).

Conducting an advanced search is very similar except that you get to specify the text to search for in collection names and media filenames and to what types of media files and what collection(s) to include in the search. You conduct an advanced search from the Simple Search portion of the Collections pane (by following the first two steps of the simple search procedure given at the beginning of this section). Then you follow these additional steps:

1. **Click the Advanced Search button to the immediate right of the Simple Search button on the Collections pane's toolbar.**

    The Collections pane changes from Simple Search to Advanced Search similar to the one shown in Figure 4-10.

2. **Enter the file or collection name to search for in the Search Text box.**

    You can then narrow the search by selecting which types of media files to include in the search.

3. **(Optional) Click the check boxes in front of the types of media files that you do *not* want included in the search under Search For to remove their checkmarks.**

    You can even further narrow the search by selecting what collection(s) to include in the search.

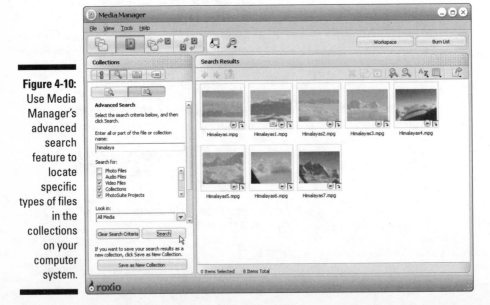

Figure 4-10: Use Media Manager's advanced search feature to locate specific types of files in the collections on your computer system.

4. (Optional) Click the Look In drop-down button and click the name of the collection to include in the search on the Look In drop-down list box.

To search all the collections on your computer, click All Collections in Look In drop-down list. To search all media files that Media Manager scanned on your computer system, click All Media instead.

5. Click the Search button to conduct the advanced search using all your search criteria.

As with the Simple Search, Media Manager displays all the collections and media files that match your search criteria in the Search Results pane on the right side of the Media Manager window.

If you want to make all the collections and media files displayed in the Search Results pane into its own collection file, click the Save as New Collection button near the bottom of the Simple Search and Advanced Search portion of the Collections pane and then give a new name for the collection in the Save as New Collection dialog box.

Backing Up Media Files on Disc

In addition to enabling you to preview and organize all the different kinds of media files you use with the Roxio Easy Media Creator suite, Media Manager also makes it easy to backup these media files by burning them to CD or DVD discs. To do this, you use the Media Manager's Burn List pane opened and closed by clicking the Burn List button on the far right side of the Media Manager's toolbar.

When the Burn List pane is displayed at the bottom of the Media Manager, you can then add all the collections and individual groups of media files that you want burned to disc. As you drag-and-drop these files into the Burn List pane, its status bar at the bottom of the pane keeps you informed of the amount of space that added files will take up on the type of media that you use (see Figure 4-11). This status bar also contains a Disc Name text box in which you can add your own volume name for your backup disc, a Disc Recorder pop-up button which enables you to select a new CD or DVD recording device, and a Disc Type pop-up which enables you to select the type of disc media — 650 MB CD, 700 MB CD (the default), 4.7 GB DVD, 185 MB MiniCD or 210 MB MiniCD — on its pop-up menu.

When you finish adding all the collections and individual media files to the Burn List pane that you want (or can fit) on your CD or DVD backup disc, click the Burn button to start burning the disc. The Media Manager - Burn Progress dialog box then appears, which you can expand to display further burn options or just start burning the disc by clicking its Burn button (the options in this dialog box work exactly like the ones in the Burn Progress dialog box described in Chapter 3). When you do this, the Media Manager - Burn Progress dialog box appears that keeps you informed of the burning process. When all the files in the Burn List pane have been burned to the disc, Media Manager automatically ejects the disc from its CD or DVD drive.

Keep in mind when adding media files to the Burn List pane that you can add folders that contain these files as well as collections. However, when you drag a folder icon from the Folders navigation pane into the Burn List pane, Media Manager automatically converts the folder into a new collection (with the same name) that appears both in the Burn List navigation pane and the Burn List Contents pane.

After burning a CD or DVD disc, you can then empty the Burn List pane by selecting all its collections and media files (do this by clicking the Burn List contents pane and then pressing Ctrl+A) and then clicking Remove Selected Item(s) from Burn List button on its toolbar). Before you empty the Burn List pane, you can save all its files in its own collection by Clicking the Create a New Collection button on the Burn List navigation pane's toolbar when the Burn List disc icon is selected at the top of the navigation tree.

Figure 4-11:
Use the
Media
Manager's
Burn List
pane to
assemble
the
collections
and media
files you
want to
back up by
burning to
CD or DVD
disc.

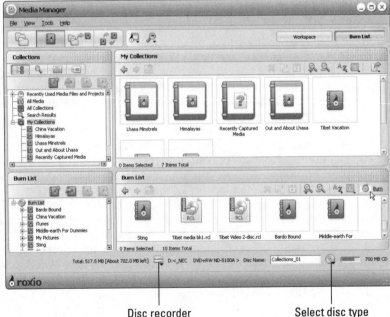

Disc recorder   Select disc type

Part III

Creating Audio CDs and Photo Projects

The 5th Wave
By Rich Tennant

"You know kids — you can't buy them just any media creation software."

In this part . . .

Undoubtedly, the digital audio and digital photos that Part III deals with represent some of the most fun media to work with (who doesn't love a good tune and the memories that photos of our favorite activities engender?). This part begins with Chapter 5, which covers all aspects of digital audio, from recording it (both live and from pre-recorded sources, including those beloved old LPs and audio cassettes) to editing and enhancing it. Chapter 6 is the place to go for information on acquiring, editing, and using your digital photos. Part III concludes with Chapter 7, which gives you the ins and outs of compiling and burning audio CDs and MP3 discs, and Chapter 8, which covers Easy Media Creator's Label Creator tool that makes it as easy as can be to design and print disc labels and case inserts for all your CDs and DVDs.

Chapter 5

Recording and Editing Audio with Sound Editor

As you find out in this chapter, Sound Editor is the place to go when you need to preview, edit, or enhance audio files (assuming that they're non-licensed files which are not copy-protected) that you want to use in various projects you create with Roxio Easy Media Creator 7. You can also use this tool to record audio from analog playback devices such as LP records and audio cassettes.

The Sound Editor also lets you save your recorded and edited audio files using a variety of different audio formats (MP3, WMA, OGG, or WAV) and compression settings. Because Sound Editor can open audio files saved in any of these formats and then save them back out in any of these formats, you can use the Sound Editor to convert audio tracks that you receive saved in one audio format into another more compressed or manageable format for use in your other Roxio projects. You can then use the edited files you create in Sound Editor as part of the tracks that you burn to standard audio CDs or MP3 discs with applications such as Roxio's Creator Classic (see Chapter 8 for details).

Getting Cozy with Sound Editor

Just like with the other Roxio Easy Media Creator tools, you can launch Sound Editor from the Easy Media Creator Home window or from the Windows XP operating system. To launch the tool from the Easy Media Creator Home window, click the Sound Editor link in its Tools column. To launch Sound Editor from the Windows taskbar, click the Start button, position the mouse pointer on All Programs on the Start menu, then on Roxio on the All Programs submenu, and finally click Sound Editor on the Roxio submenu.

An empty Sound Editor window then opens where you can record a new audio file or edit an existing audio file already saved to disk. To open an audio file for editing, click File➪Open on the Sound Editor's menu bar or press Ctrl+O. Then locate the audio file to edit in the Open dialog box using the Look In drop-down list box or one of the buttons in the left panel (My Recent Documents, Desktop, My Documents, My Computer, or My Network Places) and click the Open button.

When you open an audio file for editing, Sound Editor represents its sound visually as a waveform (as shown in Figure 5-1). This waveform shows the relative amplitude of the sound (that's volume to you and me) with its different spikes, peaks, valleys, and dips over time.

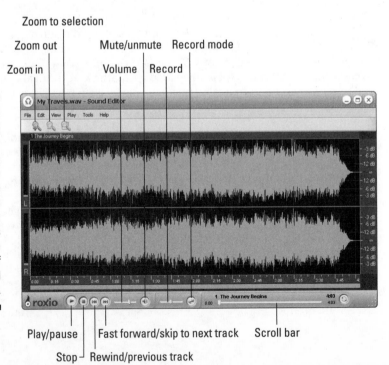

Figure 5-1:
The Sound Editor visually represents the audio file as a waveform that shows the relative amplitude of the sound over time.

If you try to open an audio file for editing in Sound Editor to which you don't have the rights and which is protected (as is the case with all audio tracks that you download or purchase from a music service such as Napster, the Sound Editor displays an alert dialog box letting you know that the file is protected and cannot be opened with Sound Editor.

As you can see in Figure 5-1, the Sound Editor shows the waveform for both the left and right channels (which are identical when editing a sound file that wasn't recorded in stereo). Both the left and right channels of the waveform are plotted against a decibel (abbreviated dB) scale on the right side of the Sound Editor window.

These left- and right-channel dB scales measure the voltage gain of the amplifier against the strength of its original signal (indicated by the red baseline that runs through the middle of each scale). When the audio file's waveform rises above this baseline, the scales measure how much stronger the audio signal is than the original carrier signal. When the waveform dips below this baseline, the scales measure how much weaker the audio signal is when compared to the original carrier signal.

At the far left side of the Sound Editor window, Peak meters appear for both the left and right channels. These meters indicate how close the recording level comes to the zero dB clipping point where the sound literally goes off the chart. Volumes in the safe zone are indicated in green and yellow bars and sounds that actually exceed this point where sounds are clipped are indicated in red bars.

Zoom, zoom, zoom . . .

You can use the zoom controls at the top of the Sound Editor window to zoom in and out on the waveform:

- ✓ **Zoom In** to zoom in on the waveform so that you can see more detail of the waveform over less time in the Sound Editor window

- ✓ **Zoom Out** to zoom out on the waveform so that you can see less detail but over more time in the Sound Editor window

- ✓ **Zoom to Selection** to zoom in just the portion of the audio waveform that you've selected in the Sound Editor window

As you click the Zoom In and Zoom Out buttons, the scale on the time track beneath the waveform changes to show the how much of the recording's waveform is currently displayed in the Sound Editor window (this timescale shows the number of minutes and seconds that have elapsed from the start of 0:00.0).

When you zoom all the way out on the audio file, the recording's entire wave-form is displayed in the Sound Editor window and the Zoom Out button becomes grayed out (indicating that it's temporarily unavailable). As you zoom in on the recording and not all of its waveform is displayed in the Sound Editor window, the scroll bar (the green bar that appears immediately beneath the timescale) no longer extends the entire width of the window. You can then drag this bar to the left and right to bring different parts of the recording's waveform into view in the Sound Editor window.

To zoom in on just a particular portion of the waveform, click the mouse pointer at the starting place in the waveform and then drag through the waveform until you've selected through the entire of portion of the waveform you want to examine up close. Then click the Zoom to Selection button (the zoom button on the far right underneath the Sound Editor menu bar) to display just the selected section of the waveform in the Sound Editor window. To return to the previous view of the waveform, click the Zoom Out button once. To deselect the waveform selection, click the mouse pointer anywhere in the waveform (a position cursor indicated by a thin, white dotted vertical line replaces the waveform selection at the place you click).

You can use the plus (+) and minus (-) keys on your keyboard to zoom in and out on a recording's waveform. In fact, by pressing the plus key you can actually zoom out on the waveform many times more than by clicking the Zoom Out button until only fractions of a second of the recording is displayed in the Sound Editor window and the left and right channels of the waveform appear as very spaced-out waves extending above and below the dB scale's baseline.

Playing with the playback and recording controls

You can use the playback controls at the bottom of the Sound Editor window to play the audio file that you're editing or enhancing. When you click the Play button to play back the file's recording, Sound Editor begins the playback from the Position indicator (the thin, yellow vertical line that moves across the waveform from left to right as you playback the audio). This Position indicator begins playback at the beginning of the audio file unless you double-click the mouse pointer at some other, later point in the waveform (doing this not only starts the playback at that position in the recording but also leaves a cursor indicated by a white, dotted vertical line at that position).

When you click the Play button to start the audio playback, this button changes to a Pause button, which you can then click to pause the playback. Note that if you click the Stop button, Sound Editor stops the playback and resets the Position indicator at the very beginning of the waveform. To the immediate right of the Stop button, you find a Rewind/Previous Track button that you can click to move the Position indicator to the beginning of the previous track (which is the same as the beginning of the recording if the recording has only one track in it). Likewise, you can click the Fast Forward/Next Track button located to its immediate right to jump to the beginning of the next track in the recording (or to the very end of audio file if it has only a single track).

Drag the Volume slider to control the volume (drag left to reduce the volume and right to increase it). If you need to temporarily mute the volume altogether, click the Mute/Unmute button to the immediate right of the Volume slider. The first time you click this button, Sound Editor mutes the playback. The second time you click this button, the program removes the muting, returning to the original playback volume.

Table 5-1 gives you a list of the most common keystroke shortcuts that you can use to control the playback of a recording in Sound Editor. You can use any of these keystrokes instead of having to click the controls at the bottom of the Sound Editor window.

Table 5-1	Sound Editor Playback Keystroke Shortcuts
Keystroke	*What It Does*
Ctrl+P	Play/Pause
Ctrl+T	Stop
Ctrl+R	Record mode
Ctrl+F	Next track
Ctrl+B	Previous track
Ctrl+Shift+F	Fast forward
Ctrl+Shift+B	Rewind
F8	Mute/Unmute
F9	Decrease Volume
F10	Increase Volume

Recording Audio

You can use Sound Editor to record audio from analog sources such as LP records and audio cassettes. To do this, you must first connect your analog audio equipment to your computer's sound input with the appropriate cables. Most of the time, this cable will be a y-shaped cable with one red and one white stereo-jack connector on one end that come together in a single earphone- or microphone-type connector on the other.

You then connect the red and white stereo-jack connectors to the left and right-channel line out connections on your analog audio equipment (tape deck, stereo receiver, and so on). On most personal computers that aren't equipped with a special analog-to-digital converter (see Chapter 2), you then connect the other connector to the microphone connection on your personal computer so that this acts as the sound input when recording your LPs or cassette tapes with Sound Editor.

Note that when trying use Sound Editor to record audio from a record player, you must take the line out of a stereo receiver or some other type of amplifier to which the record player is connected (if you were to cable the record player directly to your computer's sound input, the audio would be too weak for Sound Editor to record it).

After connecting your analog device to your computer's sound input, you take these steps in the Sound Editor program to record audio played through the device:

1. **Click Tools on the Sound Editor menu bar and then click Recording Device on the Tools menu and the actual name of your recording device on the Recording Device submenu.**

   If you can't get Sound Editor to work when selecting your actual recording device, try selecting Default Mapper Device on the Recording Device submenu to use the Windows' sound mixer.

2. **Click Tools on the Sounder Editor menu bar and then click Recording Source on the Tools menu and the name of your computer's recording source on the Recording Source submenu.**

   For example, if you're recording through a microphone connected to your computer's sound input, click Microphone on this submenu. If you're recording through a line connected to an analog device such as a cassette recorder, click the option on this submenu that mentions Line or Line In (the actual items on this submenu vary according to the sound card your system uses). Note that if you select Default Mapper Device on the Recording Device submenu, this same choice is automatically selected for you on the Recording Source submenu.

3. **Click the Record Mode button at the bottom of the Sound Editor window to the immediate right of the Record Level slider.**

   When you click this button, the Record Mode button's icon turns red and the Play/Pause button turns into a red Record/Pause button that you can use to start and temporarily pause the recording of your audio.

4. **(Optional) Drag the Record Level slider to the right (maybe midway) to set a test volume for recording.**

Next, you want to test the recording level by playing the audio track you want Sound Editor to record.

5. **Start playing the track(s) you want to record on the analog device connected to your computer (record player, cassette player, and the like).**

   When playing the track(s) you want to record with Sound Editor, you should hear the audio through your computer's speakers and see the L (left channel) and R (right channel) peak meters light up with green, yellow, and, hopefully, on occasion red bars.

6. **Adjust the volume by dragging the Record Level slider as needed so that the L and R peak meters mostly display in the green, infrequently in the yellow, and seldom, if ever, in the red.**

   If the peak meters display persistently in the red, then clipping has occurred. You must click the meters to clear them and then reduce the volume by dragging the Record Level slider to the left and then retesting your recording levels by replaying the audio track(s) you want to record. Once the recording levels on both the L and R peak meters check out, you're ready to record the track.

7. **Cue up the LP record or cassette to the point at which you want to start recording in Sound Editor.**

   If you're recording tracks on an LP, place the needle near or at the end of the track previous the one you want to record and then when the record player reaches the silence in between the tracks, proceed to Step 8. If you're recording a track on cassette, cue up to the silence in between the two tracks and immediately after you follow Step 8, click the play button on the cassette player.

8. **Click the red Record/Pause button in the playback controls at the bottom of the Sound Editor window.**

   As Sound Editor begins to record your audio, it draws the waveform of the left and right channels in the Sound Editor window. If you need to pause the recording to switch the tape or turn over the LP, click Sound Editor's Record/Pause button. To begin recording again, click the Record/Pause again.

9. **Click the Sound Editor's Stop button when your analog source finishes playing all the audio you want to record.**

   Now you're ready to save the new digital version of the audio you just recorded under a new filename, using appropriate encoding and compression options.

10. **Choose File⇨Save on the Sound Editor menu bar to open the Save dialog box. Indicate where you want to save the file in the Save In location, the name you want to give the file in the File name text box, the type of audio file in the Save as Type drop-down list, and the type of encoding in the Encoder drop-down list box, and then click the Save button.**

As you see in Figure 5-2, by default Sound Editor saves your recorded audio in stereo using the uncompressed WAVE audio format with the PCM encoder (which eats up a lot of disk space fast). If you need to save space, select a different audio format such as MP3 or OGG that use compression and then modify their compression settings as appropriate (see "Choosing Audio Formats and Compression Settings" later in this chapter for more on this topic).

Removing silences from a recording

One of the first things you may want to do after saving your new recorded audio to disk is remove any leading or trailing silences that you may have recorded. You will get a leading silence if you have a delay between the time you cue up the analog audio, click the Sound Editor's Record button, and actually start playing the LP or cassette tape that you want to record. You will get a trailing silence if you have a delay between the time the LP or tape finishes playing and the time you click the Sound Editor's Stop button to stop the recording.

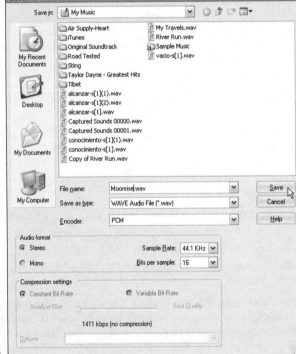

Figure 5-2:
In the Save dialog box, you select the type of audio file, encoder, and compression to use in saving your newly recorded audio.

To get rid of a recording's leading silence, you choose Edit⇔Select Leading Silence on the Sound Editor's menu bar. Sound Editor then automatically locates and selects the silence at the very beginning of the recording (see Figure 5-3) and you can delete this silence simply by pressing the Delete key. You can also do this by right-clicking the selection and then clicking Edit⇔ Delete on the shortcut menu.

Figure 5-3:
To delete a leading or trailing silence, select it and then right-click the selection and click Edit⇔Delete on the shortcut menu.

To get rid of trailing silence, you choose Edit⇔Select Trailing Silence on the Sound Editor's menu bar and then either press the Delete key or right-click the selection and then click Edit⇔Delete on the selection's shortcut menu.

If you delete a leading or trailing silence only to suddenly realize that you need to retain that silence in this recording (perhaps to act as a track break when combining this recording with another audio track in one of your Easy Media Creator projects), press Ctrl+Z to Undo your deletion of the silence and put it back in your file before you do any more editing. Then click the mouse pointer anywhere in the recording's waveform to remove the selection.

Inserting silences into a recording

Should you find that you need a leading or trailing silence in a recording that you don't already have, you can use the Edit⇔Insert Silence command on the Sound Editor menu bar to insert one. Simply click the mouse pointer at the place in the recording where you want the silence to be inserted before you choose Edit⇔Insert Silence.

Sound Editor then opens the Insert Silence dialog box shown in Figure 5-4 where you indicate the number of seconds of silence to insert (two seconds is the default and is usually quite sufficient) in the Seconds text box before you click the OK button.

Figure 5-4:
To insert a
silence into
a recording,
open the
Insert
Silence
dialog box
and indicate
the number
of seconds
of silence to
insert.

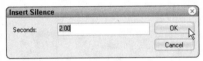

The Edit➪Insert Silence command can come in real handy after you've used the Edit➪Insert Audio File command to insert another track or recording into your current audio and need a gap between the two to mark and separate the individual tracks.

Adding track breaks to a recording

If the audio file that you've recorded with Sound Editor had more than one track, you can use Sound Editor's Tools➪Auto Locate Tracks command to have the program detect the silences in the recording and add track breaks at each of them. You can then click the Fast Forward/Next Track button on the Sound Editor's playback controls at the bottom of the window to advance through each of the tracks. You can also rename any of the tracks by right-clicking the temporary track name, Untitled Track, which appears after its sequential number at the top of left track's waveform and then clicking Rename Track on its shortcut menu. Replace Untitled Track by typing over it and then press Enter.

If Sound Editor's Auto Locate Tracks' command doesn't correctly identify all the track breaks in the recording because some of the tracks have no silences between them, you can manually insert track breaks at the appropriate places. To do this, follow these steps:

1. **Open the audio in Sound Editor by choosing File➪Open on the menu bar and then selecting the audio file into which to insert tracks.**

Next you locate the place in the recording where you need to insert the first track break. You can do this either by listening to the recording or, if you know the place in the timeline where one track ends and the other begins, scrolling to that place in the recording.

 2. **Locate the position where the track break is to be inserted and then click this place with the mouse pointer to insert the cursor there.**

Now you're ready to insert the track break at the cursor's position.

 3. **Choose Tools⇨Insert Track Break on the Sound Editor menu bar.**

Sound Editor inserts a new break at the cursor's position in the waveform. This new track break is given the next sequential track number and the temporary name, Untitled Track.

 4. **Right-click Untitled Track that appears above the left-track waveform, click Rename on its shortcut menu, and then type in your name for the track break and press Enter.**

When Sound Editor inserts a new track break at the cursor's position, it does not automatically add a silence between it and the previous track. If you want to do this, you must take an additional step.

 5. **(Optional) Choose Edit⇨Insert Silence on the Sound Editor menu bar and then type in the number of seconds in the Seconds text box of the Insert Silence dialog box before you click OK.**

Be sure to remember to save your audio file after inserting the track breaks with the File⇨Save command (Ctrl+S). Note, however, that each time you save changes to the recording you're editing in Sound Editor, the program opens the Save dialog box, giving you the opportunity to change various settings as well as save your changes (most other Windows' programs only do this when you choose File⇨Save As). You must then click the Save button to close the Save dialog box and click the Yes button in the alert dialog box that appears, asking you to confirm the replacement of the original audio file even when you're only saving the track breaks you've added to the recording!

Selecting the Audio to Edit

After you've saved the recording you made with Sound Editor with all the superfluous silences removed and the track breaks identified, you may still need to edit all or just portions of the audio by adding any of Sound Editor's many audio effects (see the section "Enhancing Audio Files" that follows immediately for details). To apply an effect to the entire audio file, you need to select its entire waveform: you can do this either by choosing Edit⇨Select All on the Sound Editor's menu bar or simply by pressing Ctrl+A.

If your recording has multiple tracks and you want to apply a particular audio effect to only that track, you can quickly select it by choosing Edit⇨Select

Track on the Sound Editor menu bar and then clicking the number and name (if it has one) of the track whose audio is to be selected in the Select Track submenu. Sound Editor then selects the entire portion of the waveform that contains the audio for the designated track.

If you only want to apply an audio effect to a portion of a track, you need to manually select that part of the waveform before applying the particular enhancement. To do this, you click and drag the mouse pointer through the portion of the waveform to be modified. Of course, you can use Sound Editor's playback controls to locate the portion of the track to be enhanced by listening to it. Just be sure to note the starting and ending times on the timeline as you listen to it.

Keep in mind that you can zoom in on the portion of the waveform that you select by pressing the plus key (+). If you want to zoom in on the first half of the selected portion of the waveform so that it appears at the beginning of the Sound Editor window, choose View➪Zoom In to Left on the Sound Editor menu bar or hold down the Shift key located on the left side of the keyboard as you press the plus key (+). To zoom in on the last half of selected waveform, choose View➪Zoom In to Right on the Sound Editor menu bar or hold down the Shift key located on the right side of the keyboard as you press the plus key (+).

Enhancing Audio Files

Sound Editor supplies you with a multitude of different kinds of audio effects that you can apply to the recording you make with it. To apply an effect to the waveform that you've selected (using any of the selection techniques outlined in "Selecting the Audio to Edit" that immediately precedes this section), you choose Tools➪Apply Effect to Selection command on the Sound Editor menu bar. Sound Editor then opens a submenu listing all the following audio effects you can apply to your selection by clicking its menu item:

- **Invert** to flip the positive and negative offsets of the selected audio

- **Reverse** to play the selected audio backward (in hopes, I guess, of hearing its secret message!)

- **Fade In** to apply a fade-in effect so that beginning of the selection begins at zero volume increasing to full volume by the end of the selection (apply this effect only to the start of tracks in your audio file)

- **Fade Out** to apply a fade-out effect so that beginning of the selection is at full volume decreasing down to zero volume at the end of the selection (apply this effect only to the end of tracks in your audio file)

- **Normalize** to level out the peaks in the volume in the current audio selection (apply this effect when the audio file contains tracks recorded at different volume levels and you want the combined audio recording to play at a uniform volume)

✔ **Alienizer** to add metallic and alien synthesized effects to your audio by dragging the Alpha and Beta sliders to the left or right in the Alienizer dialog box — click the Play button in this dialog box to hear the result on the selected audio of your adjustments to the Alpha and Beta values before clicking OK to apply them

✔ **DeClick** to remove distinctive clicks or crackles in the selected audio by dragging the DeClick and/or DeCrackle sliders to the right — click the Play button in this dialog box to hear the result on the selected audio of your adjustments to the DeClick or DeCrackle percentages before clicking OK to apply them

✔ **DeTuner** to adjust the pitch of the selected audio without affecting the speed by clicking the Pitch or Demi-Tone option button and then adjusting its slider to the left or right in the DeTuner dialog box — click the Play button in this dialog box to hear the result on the selected audio of your adjustments to the Pitch and Demi-Tone values before clicking OK to apply them

✔ **Enhancer** to adjust three aspects of the selected audio by manipulating three sliders: Bass Boost to increase the amplitude of the low frequency (bass) sounds; Brighten to increase the amplitude of high frequency (treble) sounds; and Stereo Width to increase the perceived separation between the left and right channels of stereo audio

✔ **Equalizer** to display a 10-band equalizer (as shown in Figure 5-5) that enables you to boost or cut the amplitude (volume) for ten bands of sound frequencies by dragging their respective frequency sliders (note that this equalizer contains a Master slider that you can use to adjust overall volume for the selected audio) — click the Play button in this dialog box to hear the result on the selected audio of your amplitude adjustments to individual frequencies before clicking OK to apply them

Figure 5-5:
Use the Equalizer effect to adjust the amplitude within ten bands of sound frequencies for the selected audio.

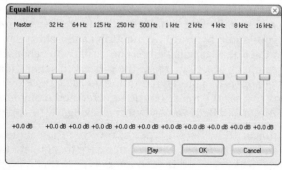

✔ **Maturizer** to adjust the quality of the selected audio (especially LPs recorded from older "vintage" equipment) by adjusting any or all of five different sliders: Noise (for tapes that have a lot of noise), Hum, Crackle, Click (for 33 rpm or 78 rpm LPs), and Bandlimit — click the Play button in the Maturizer dialog box to hear the result on the selected audio of your particular adjustments to these five areas before clicking OK to apply them

✔ **Parametric Equalizer** to display a 4-band equalizer (shown in Figure 5-6) that enables you to boost or cut the gain (amplitude) and bandwidth (Q) for four bands of sound frequencies by dragging their respective Band sliders (note that this equalizer contains a Master slider that you can use to adjust the overall gain for the selected audio) — click the Play button in this dialog box to hear the result on the selected of your gain and bandwidth adjustments to the different bands before clicking OK to apply them

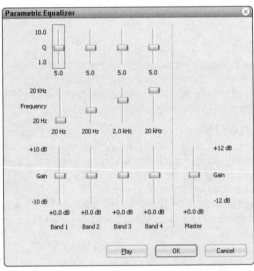

Figure 5-6:
Use the Parametric Equalizer effect to adjust the gain and/or bandwidth within four bands of sound frequencies for the selected audio.

✔ **Robotizer** to add metallic and robotic synthesized effects (similar to the Alienizer) to your audio by dragging the Alpha and Beta sliders to the left or right in the Robotizer dialog box (note that you can also click the Broaden Stereo check box to increase the perceived separation of the left and right channels of a stereo recording) — click the Play button in this dialog box to hear the result on the selected audio of your adjustments to the Alpha and Beta values before clicking OK to apply them

✔ **Room Simulator** to add different types of reverberation audio effects on the selected audio: Box, Room, Church, or Space to simulate these various environments as reverberation chambers (note that for any of the four options you choose, you can adjust the amount of reverberation and echo by adjusting the Reverb Time and Echo Level sliders) — click the Play button in this dialog box to hear the result on the selected audio of your Box, Room, Church, or Space Option button selection and any adjustments you make to the Reverb Time and/or Echo Level sliders before clicking OK to apply them

Keep in mind that Sound Editor's audio effects are cumulative, that is, they are layered on top of the other. This means that you need to test each effect as you apply it by listening to the result before applying another effect. That way, if you find that you goofed up and really don't like the audio effect you just applied, you can remove it by choosing Edit⇨Undo on the Sound Editor menu bar or pressing Ctrl+Z (remember that you can also reapply an effect that you remove with the Undo command by immediately choosing the Edit⇨Redo command or pressing Ctrl+Y).

Choosing Audio Format and Compression Settings

When you first save a recording that you make with Sound Editor, the program defaults to saving the resulting audio file in the WAVE audio format (using the .wav filename extension). This default audio format saves audio files that sound nearly identical to the original source recordings (as identical as is possible for digital audio made from an analog counterpart to sound). The only problem with WAVE audio files is that they're completely uncompressed, meaning that they can be really huge files (especially for recordings of any length).

When disk space is a question (and when isn't it), you often need to select a different audio format whose encoder supports the use of different sample rates, bit rates, and compression settings. That way, you can experiment with saving a version of the resulting audio file so that it is as compact as possible while retaining whatever sound quality that you feel is crucial given its ultimate use.

If you have the disk space available, always save the original recording using the uncompressed WAVE audio file format. Then you can experiment creating versions saved in other audio file formats, using different compression settings until you find the optimal combination for your particular needs while still retaining an uncompressed original sampled at the highest rate.

To save a more compact version of the audio you've recorded in Sound Editor, you need to modify the settings in the Save dialog box (these settings are available to you not only the first time you save a new recording but each time you save editing changes to it), starting with the audio file type. In addition to the default WAVE audio file, Sound Editor also gives you a choice among these other three audio file formats in the Save as Type drop-down list box in its Save dialog box:

- **MPEG Layer 3 Audio (*.mp3)** which gives you a choice between the Coding Technologies MP3 encoder (the default) and the Fraunhofer MP3 encoder (a version of MPEG developed and patented by Fraunhofer IIS, that is, Institut Integrierte Schaltungen)

- **OGG File (*.ogg)** using the OGG Vorbis 1 encoder

- **Windows Media Audio File (*.wma)** using the Windows Media-Audio encoder

When you select the MP3, OGG, or WMA as the audio file type instead of WAVE, you cannot only modify the Audio Format settings but the Compression Settings as well (see Figure 5-7) in the Save dialog box to create more compact versions of your Sound Editor recordings.

The Audio Format settings include the following options that you can modify depending upon which of the four available audio formats (WAVE, MP3, OGG, or WMA) you select:

- **Stereo** or **Mono** option buttons to choose between two-channel stereo sound and a single-channel monographic sound: choose Mono when dealing with a monographic recording to save valuable disk space

- **Sample Rate** drop-down list box to select the rate at which the audio source is sampled: you can choose a value in range between 8 KHz up to 48 KHz depending upon the audio file type selected, with the higher the rate the better the sound, and 44.1 KHz the default and standard for most audio CDs

- **Bits per Sample** drop-down list box to select between a sample size of 8 or 16 bits (the default) when you select WAVE as the audio file type (the higher the number of bits per sample, the higher the quality of the resulting audio)

When you choose MP3, OGG, or WMA as the audio file in the Save as Type drop-down list box, you can change the following Compression Settings as well:

- **Constant Bit Rate** or **Variable Bit Rate** option buttons to choose between a constant bit rate and a variable bit rate (which can sometimes give you better sound audio)

- **Smallest Size** to **Best Quality** compression rate slider to determine the bit rate/compression factor to be applied to the audio file: drag the slider to the left to increase the amount of compression, resulting in a smaller file size with less sound fidelity, and to the right to decrease the amount of compression, resulting in a larger file size with greater sound quality

- **Options** drop-down list box to select between Normal Stereo (the default), Joint Stereo (which can sometimes reduce the size of the audio file slightly without greatly compromising the stereo quality), and Dual Channel

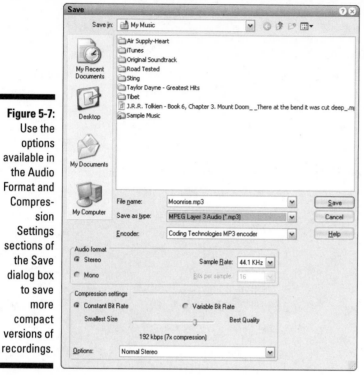

Figure 5-7:
Use the options available in the Audio Format and Compression Settings sections of the Save dialog box to save more compact versions of recordings.

When experimenting with these Audio Format and Compression Settings, keep in mind that you usually want to strike a balance between decent sound and huge file sizes. When dealing with a recording where two-channel stereo is not important or the original recording is not stereo, always start with your file-size savings by selecting the Mono option button in the Audio Format area of the Save dialog box.

When selecting compression settings for stereo recordings, start by saving the audio file with the Smallest Size to Best Quality compression rate slider at dead center so that your bit rate/compression factor matches the sound quality equally against the file-size savings. Then, if that resulting audio file is still too big for your needs, you can delete that compressed version and then open the original WAVE audio file and try saving another compressed version of the file, this time after dragging the compression rate slider left toward the Smallest Size end so that the file-savings factor outweighs the sound quality slightly.

Chapter 6

Managing Digital Photos

. . . .

In This Chapter

▶ All the things you can do with the PhotoSuite application

▶ Getting comfortable with the PhotoSuite window and interface

▶ Fixing your digital photos with PhotoSuite's editing features

▶ Creating custom projects from PhotoSuite's project templates

▶ Printing your photos

▶ Sharing your photos with friends and family by sending them by e-mail

. . . .

*W*orking with digital photos has become one of the more important functions of today's computer software. In the PhotoSuite application in the Roxio Easy Media Creator 7 suite, you have one of the most powerful tools for fixing and editing your digital photos. Coupled with the capacity of the suite's Media Manager tool for organizing your digital photos (see Chapter 4) and the ability of its VideoWave application to arrange photos into a slideshow (see Chapter 11), you have at hand all the software you need for maintaining and arranging all your digital photo collections from now on.

In this chapter, you find out how to use the PhotoSuite application to fix, edit, and enhance your digital photos. You also discover how easy it is to use PhotoSuite to print your photos either individually, in groups on a single page, or as a contact sheet. In addition, this chapter covers sharing your digital photos with your friends and family. As you see in this chapter, with PhotoSuite you not only can send your photos as e-mail attachments or in the body of your e-mail message, but you can also package a group of them into a slideshow that your recipients can then play in sequence (complete with background music, if you decide to add it).

Launching PhotoSuite Your Way

If you have the Easy Media Creator Home window open, clicking the PhotoSuite link in the Applications area is the easiest way to launch the program. It is, however, not the only way to launch PhotoSuite from the Easy

Media Creator Home. If your intention is to edit a bunch of photos with PhotoSuite's many editing features, you can launch the program and have it go directly to the Open dialog box in the My Pictures folder by clicking the Edit and Fix Photos link under the Photo column in the Tasks area at the top of the Easy Media Creator Home.

So too, if your intention is to e-mail photos to your friends or family with PhotoSuite, you can launch the PhotoSuite and have it automatically select the program's E-mail task pane by clicking the E-mail Photos link in this Photos column. Finally, if your intention is to create any of the several photo projects (such as a greeting card , collage, or calendar) using your digital photos, you can launch PhotoSuite and have it open the program's Create a Project task pane by clicking the Create a Greeting Card link at the very bottom of the Photo column in the Tasks area.

If, however, the Easy Media Creator Home window is not open, you can also launch PhotoSuite from the Windows taskbar by clicking the Start button, highlighting All Programs on the Start menu with the mouse pointer, followed by highlighting Roxio on the All Programs submenu, and then finally clicking PhotoSuite on the Roxio submenu.

Don't forget that if you've recently edited photos in PhotoSuite or used its project templates to create your own photo projects and you haven't yet finished working on them, you can both launch PhotoSuite and go directly to work editing the particular photos or photo project by double-clicking the photo or project in the Recent Projects area at the very bottom of the Roxio Easy Media Creator Home window. Click the Expand button on the far right side of the bar that says Recent Projects (the one with the two arrowheads pointing downward) if none of the thumbnails of your recently created projects appear at the bottom of the Easy Media Creator Home window.

Getting Familiar with PhotoSuite 7

When you launch PhotoSuite from the Start menu on the Windows taskbar or by clicking the PhotoSuite link in the Applications column of the Easy Media Creator Home, the PhotoSuite Home Page window shown in Figure 6-1 appears. PhotoSuite's Home Page window contains two panes, Edit & Create at the top left and Print & Share at the bottom left each of which contains several hyperlink options that you can click to perform various functions with PhotoSuite.

Note that you can display more information about any of the options on the right side of the PhotoSuite Home Page window by positioning the mouse pointer on its link. This descriptive information then appears beneath the general PhotoSuite 7 welcome information that always appears at the top right of the initial PhotoSuite window.

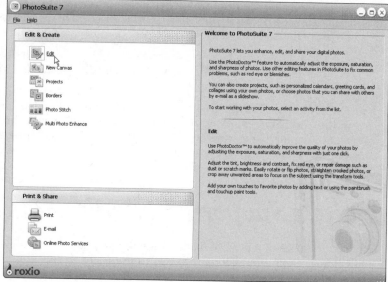

Figure 6-1:
The
PhotoSuite
Home Page
window
offers its
many
options in
two panes:
Edit &
Create and
Print &
Share.

The Edit & Create pane contains these links:

- **Edit** to display the Open dialog box where you can select the photo(s) to edit with PhotoSuite

- **New Canvas** to display the New Canvas task pane in the PhotoSuite window that enables you create a new photo collage made up of different photos that you arrange on the canvas

- **Projects** to display the Projects task pane on the left side of the PhotoSuite window that enables you to create a new photo project using any of the several project templates included in PhotoSuite 7 (Collage, Album, Calendars, Cards, Gift Tags, Magazines, Postcards, and Posters)

- **Borders** to display the Open dialog box where you can select the photo to which to add a frame of your choice

- **Photo Stitch** to display the Photo Stitch task pane in the PhotoSuite window where you can select the photos that you want to join together as a single, panoramic photo

- **Multi Photo Enhance** to display the Multi Photo Enhance task pane in the PhotoSuite window where you can select the photos you want to fix, edit, or enhance as a group at the same time

The Print & Share pane of the PhotoSuite window contains the following three links:

- **Print** to display the Print task pane in the PhotoSuite window where you can select the photo(s) you want to print and designate how they are to be printed

- **E-mail** to display the E-mail task pane in the PhotoSuite window where you can select the photo(s) you want to send and designate how they are to be sent

- **Online Photo Services** to display the Online Photo Services task pane in the PhotoSuite window where you select the photos that you either want to upload and store on a Web page on the Roxio Photo Center's site or have printed by the Photo Center

PhotoSuite's Supported File Formats

PhotoSuite makes it a snap to fix damaged digital photos, edit their contents, and enhance their overall look with the program's extensive editing features. PhotoSuite can open and edit photos saved in any of the following graphics file formats:

- **BMP** (Bitmap) with the .bmp, .rle, or .dib filename extension

- **JPEG** (Joint Photographic Experts Group) with the .jpg, .jpe. or .jpeg filename extension

- **PNG** (Portable Network Graphics) with the .png filename extension

- **TIFF** (Tagged Information File Format) with .tif or .tiff filename extension

BMP or Bitmap is the Microsoft Windows' standard graphics file format. Bitmap files come in 2, 16, 256, and 16.7 million (24-bit) color and most use no compression. The so-called RLE or Run-Length Encoded variation of the basic Bitmap does use some modest compression (RLE files use 16 or 256 colors and are primarily used in saving graphics used as the Windows desktop's wallpaper and background images).

The JPEG file format is one of the most popular graphics file formats for digital photos (many digital cameras save their photos as JPEG files). This graphics file format uses a "lossy" compression scheme that attempts to reduce the overall file size by reducing detail in certain areas which often results (especially in photos with lots of details) in a slight degradation of the overall picture quality. JPEG is an especially good format to use for photos that you intend to display on Web pages on the Internet.

The PNG file format was developed as an alternative to the GIF (Graphics Information Format), the ever-popular file format for displaying Web page graphics. PNG files come in 256-color, True Color, and 32-bit color varieties and use a lossless compression scheme to cut down on the overall size.

The TIFF file format was developed as a portable format for bitmap images. TIFF files come in monochrome, 16-color and grayscale, 256-color and grayscale, and 16.7 million-color (24-bit) varieties. This file format gives you the highest quality in terms of bitmap images but their files are notoriously large, especially for high-resolution images.

Although the PhotoSuite can both open for editing and save edited photos in the Bitmap, JPEG, PNG, or TIFF file format, the program's native graphics file format is something known as DMSP (using the .dmsp filename extension). This file format was developed for editing photos in PhotoSuite and developing photo projects using the program's templates (see "Playing with PhotoSuite Project Templates" later in this chapter for details). This file format supports the use of a layer scheme (somewhat akin to that used in Adobe Photoshop) that enables you to undo changes made to specific graphic objects (even when you've combined multiple photos and other objects together in a collage).

When editing photos originally saved in the other supported graphics file formats with PhotoSuite, after opening the photo, use the File⇨Save As command to save the file in the PhotoSuite's DMSP format — you do this by selecting PhotoSuite Format (*.dmsp) in the Files of Type drop-down list in the Save As dialog box before clicking the Save button. Then, after you finish making all your editing changes to the photo in PhotoSuite, you can save the final edited version in its original graphics file format (BMP, JPEG, PNG, or TIFF) for distribution to others.

The process of saving the original file as a DMSP file for the editing process and then saving it back out in its original file format when the editing's done is especially important when it comes to dealing with JPEG photos. That's because continually saving the editing changes made to a JPEG photo in PhotoSuite contributes to the overall degradation of its quality (especially when the photo has a lot of detail).

Photos saved in PhotoSuite's native DMSP file format can only be opened with PhotoSuite. For this reason, never send a DMSP photo to anyone you aren't completely certain has PhotoSuite installed on his or her computer. Also, photos saved in PhotoSuite's DMSP native file format can't be opened on the Internet (always save photos bound for the Web either in the JPEG or PNG file formats).

Fixing, Editing, and Enhancing Photos

To edit a photo in PhotoSuite, you can click the Edit and Fix Photos link in the Photo column of the Tasks area if the Easy Media Creator Home window is displayed, or if you're in PhotoSuite itself, click its Edit link that appears at the top of the PhotoSuite window. The Open dialog box shown in Figure 6-2 then opens where you can select the collection (see Chapter 4 for details) or folder that contains the photo you want to edit.

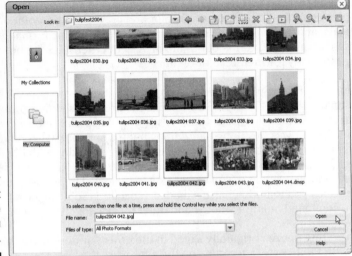

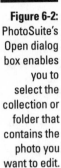

Figure 6-2:
PhotoSuite's
Open dialog
box enables
you to
select the
collection or
folder that
contains the
photo you
want to edit.

When you locate the photo you want to edit in the Open dialog box, click its thumbnail and then click the Open button. The selected photo then appears on the right side of the PhotoSuite window along with either the All Edit Features task pane (shown in Figure 6-3) or the Common Edit Features task pane. If the program displays the Common Edit Features task pane, you can click the Show All Features button to switch to the All Edit Features task pane which contains nine editing buttons. You use the features on the pop-up menus associated with the nine buttons in the All Edit Features task pane to fix, transform, and add special effects to the photo you're editing.

If you click the Show Common Features button right below the Cutouts & Masks button, PhotoSuite switches to the Common Edit Features task pane that only contains the PhotoDoctor, Crop, Rotate, Red Eye, and Add or Edit Text buttons (these five represent the most commonly used photo editing features and they are found on the pop-up menus associated with the Overall Quality, Transform, Facial Flaws, and Text buttons on the All Edit Features task pane).

Fix me up

Two buttons, Facial Flaws and Damaged Photos, on the All Edit Features task pane contain options designed to help you improve the quality of photos by fixing particular flaws such as the ever-present red eye (especially problematic in pet photos) and other types of flaws such as dust motes (speaks caused by dust on the photo) and scratches or tears (usually associated with older photos developed film that you scan into your computer).

Figure 6-3:
The photo you selected for editing appears in the PhotoSuite window along with the All Edit Features task pane.

The Facial Flaws button contains these three options for fixing problems with the subjects in your digital photos:

- **Red Eye** to remove red eye from the subjects in your photo
- **Wrinkles** to remove particular wrinkles from subjects in your photo
- **Blemishes** to remove particular blemishes from the subjects in your photo

The Damaged Photos button contains these three options for fixing problems with the photos themselves:

- **Dust** to remove the presence of specks (dust motes) throughout the photo
- **Scratches** to repair and remove particular scratches that appear in the photo
- **Clone** to repair a particular damaged area in the photo by using pixels from a similar, undamaged area to replace it

The Red Eye option on the Facial Flaws menu and the Dust option on the Damaged Photos pop-up menu have an AutoFix button that you can click to attempt to have PhotoSuite automatically find and take care of the problem.

If you use the AutoFix button in the Red Eye task pane and it doesn't eliminate all your red eye problems, you can use its three-step manual process for finding and eliminating those goblin eyes (see "Get the red out!" that follows). If you use the AutoFix button in the Dust task pane and it doesn't remove all your dust imperfections, you can try using the Clone option to remove individual dust motes as described in "Bring in the clones" later in this chapter.

Get the red out!

Red eye is a prominent problem in portraits (often caused when the subject's eyes reflect lights from a flash). To take care of red eye in the photo you have open in PhotoSuite, click the Facial Flaws button in the All Edit Features task pane and then click Red Eye on its pop-up to open up the Red Eye task pane. You can then click the AutoFix button at the top of this task pane to try and have PhotoSuite take care of the problem automatically.

If the AutoFix button doesn't take care of the problem, you can still take the red out of the eyes of particular subjects in the photo by following this manual procedure:

1. **Click the Zoom In button on the toolbar above the photo on the right side of the PhotoSuite window or choose File⇨Zoom In on the program's menu bar and then drag the vertical and horizontal scroll bars to bring the subject whose red eye you want to fix into view on the screen.**

   Repeat Step 1 until you've zoomed in the subject's eyes so that they're clearly visible on the screen and big enough to manipulate.

2. **Position the mouse pointer (which assumes a circular shape with a crosshair in the middle) over of one of the subject's red eyes.**

   The mouse pointer must be the same size as the eyes you're going to treat (see Figure 6-4) before you can go ahead and click the mouse button to replace red eye with blue coloring.

3. **Drag the brush size slider in the Red Eye task pane to the left (to decrease the diameter of the mouse pointer) or to the right (to increase the diameter of the mouse pointer) until the mouse pointer is the same size or just slightly smaller than the subject's eyes.**

   Now you're ready to replace the red eye by clicking the mouse button.

4. **Position the mouse pointer so that it covers one of the subject's eyes and then click the mouse button.**

   When you click the mouse button, PhotoSuite replaces the red in the eye with blue pixels.

5. **Repeat Steps 2 through 4 to remove the red from the subject's other eye.**

Figure 6-4:
Zoom in and
then use the
brush size
slider in the
Red Eye
task pane to
manually
remove red
eye from
subjects in
the photo.

After you finish manually removing red eye from the subjects in the photo you're editing, click the Done button at the bottom of the Red Eye task pane to return to the All Edit Features task pane. If you screw up and replace more than the just the red eye area with blue, click the Undo Last Stroke button until the unwanted color is removed. If you decide that you want to close the Red Eye task pane without retaining the changes you've made to red eye in the photo, click the Cancel button.

Bring on the clones

The Clone task pane, opened by clicking the Damaged Photos button and then clicking Clone at the bottom of its pop-up menu, contains the controls for sampling an area of the photo and then painting another area with the same pixels. This feature is great for repairing damaged or washed out areas of a photo by taking a part of the nearby background and using it to fill in the missing or damaged places.

To use the Clone task pane to repair an area of your photo, you follow these steps:

1. **(Optional) Click the Zoom In button and drag the horizontal and verti-cal scroll bars until both the damaged area and the area whose pixels you want to clone are prominently displayed in the PhotoSuite window.**

2. **Position the mouse pointer (which assumes a circular shape with a crosshair in the middle) over the one edge of the undamaged area whose pixels you want to paint with.**

   Next you may need to adjust the size, transparency, and edge fading settings with their respective sliders. Use the Size slider to adjust the size of the circular mouse pointer, keeping in mind that its diameter becomes the size of both the source brush you use to sample the pixels you want to clone and the destination brush you use to paint the damaged area with the cloned pixels. Use the Transparency slider to determine the intensity of cloned pixels: drag to the right for a lighter effect and to the left for a more opaque effect. Use the Edge Fading slider to increase or decrease the amount of fading around the edge of the destination brush (that is, the one you paint the damaged area of the photo with).

3. **(Optional) Manipulate the Size, Transparency, and Edge Fading sliders until you've got the settings you think you want to use in cloning.**

   Now you're ready to establish the starting point for the cloned pixels by clicking the mouse pointer. This establishes the starting point for the source brush that clones whatever pixels it passes over.

4. **Click the mouse pointer to establish the starting point for the source brush which clones the pixels it passes over.**

   All that's left to do now is paint with the mouse pointer over the damaged or washed out portion of the photo using the pixels in the area around the cloning start point.

5. **Drag the mouse pointer over the damaged or washed out area of the photo, replacing its pixels with those passed over by the source brush.**

When painting the damaged or washed out area, be aware not only of the strokes of your destination brush that's repairing the damaged area but also keep your eye on the strokes of your source brush picking up the pixels you're painting with. If the strokes of your source brush go outside of the area you want cloned in the damaged area, you start painting with part of the image that don't want copied to the damaged area. If this happens, click the Undo Last Stroke button near the bottom of the Clone task pane until the cloned pixels that don't belong are removed from the photo.

If you find that you keep painting with an unwanted part of the picture, try resetting the start point of the source brush at a place where there are more pixels you want to use. To do this, click the Reset Start Point button near the top of the Clone task pane and then click the mouse pointer at a new, safer starting point for the source brush before dragging the mouse pointer to paint with the destination brush.

When you've repaired all the damaged or washed out areas in the photo, click the Done button to return to All Edit Features task pane. If you want to forgo all the changes you've made with the Clone task pane, click the Cancel button instead.

Transform me

Between the options on the pop-up menus attached to its Overall Quality and Transform buttons, PhotoSuite includes all the features that you should ever need for improving the quality of your digital photos. The Overall Quality options include those for modifying such things as the photo's exposure, color saturation and tint, as well as its overall brightness and tint. The Transform options include those for doing such things as cropping, rotating, flipping, straightening, and resizing the photo image.

In matters of exposure and color

As all photographers know, you can't always take your shot in the most optimal lighting conditions. The worst lighting conditions, of course, are those outdoor settings where it's way too bright, as when shooting right into the sun rather than having the sun at your back and those indoor settings where it's way too gloomy as when taking a shot in a fairly dimly light room and the flash doesn't go off. As a result, like it or not, the quality of many of the pictures you shoot ends up being compromised by the presence of some really overexposed and/or underexposed areas.

Fortunately, digital photo editing often enables you to compensate for most extreme lighting conditions, making it possible to return a certain amount of balance and detail to your favorite photo. This is especially true in the case of grossly underexposed photos where the color and detail is washed out throughout. It also works pretty well with photos which are overexposed overall. Where it's not so successful is with digital photos that suffer from both extremely over- and underexposed areas. In these cases, you usually have to split the difference and settle for just a certain amount of improvement in toning down the washed out effect in overexposed areas and in bringing back a little of the color and detail to the underexposed ones.

To improve the quality of a digital photo, you turn to the help of the options on the Overall Quality button at the top of the All Edit Features task pane. The very first option on this button's pop-up menu is PhotoDoctor. The PhotoDoctor automates the process of trying to find the correct exposure, saturation, and sharpness settings for a photo that suffers either from some underexposure or overexposure deficiencies.

To let the PhotoDoctor diagnose and attempt to cure your photo's ills, you click PhotoDoctor on the Overall Quality's pop-up menu, the PhotoDoctor task pane opens containing only an Auto Fix button as shown in Figure 6-5. When you click this Auto Fix button, PhotoSuite attempts to diagnose problems in the photo's exposure, color saturation, and sharpness, and then proceeds to reset them. After transforming the photo, the PhotoDoctor task pane lists which settings have been modified, while showing you the result in pane on the right (see Figure 6-6).

Figure 6-5:
Click the
Auto Fix
button in
the Photo
Doctor task
pane to
have
PhotoSuite
rectify the
photo's
exposure,
saturation,
and
sharpness
settings.

Figure 6-6:
After you
click the
Auto Fix
button, the
Photo
Doctor task
pane tells
which
settings
have been
applied to
the photo.

If you don't like the results (and often, you won't), click the Cancel button at the bottom of the PhotoDoctor task pane to dump the modifications and return to the All Edit Features task pane. If you do like what you see and want to retain the modified photo, click the Done button instead and then save the changes to the file (Ctrl+S). Of course, if you take the added precaution of working on a copy of the original digital photo, you can always fall back to opening the original photo in PhotoSuite.

If the PhotoDoctor isn't able to cure what ails your photo, you can try using one or more of the individual controls, Exposure, Saturation, Sharpness, Tint, and Brightness & Contrast to fix the problems. Like the PhotoDoctor task pane, the Exposure, Saturation, and Sharpness task panes (opened by click-ing their respective options on the Overall Quality pop-up menu) all contain their own Auto Fix buttons that you can click in the hope that PhotoSuite will correctly diagnose and fix problems with the photo's exposure, color satura-tion, and sharpness settings.

I often find that I get better results by fiddling with the Exposure, Saturation, and Sharpness controls individually and in the order of their appearance on the Overall Quality pop-up menu rather than by using the PhotoDoctor. After making corrections in each of these areas, I very seldom, if ever, have to go on and fool with the Brightness & Contrast control as well.

The Exposure, Saturation, and Sharpness task panes also have their own slid-ers that you can use instead to manually achieve the amount of correction your photo needs:

✔ **Exposure** task pane contains Dark Areas, Midtones, and Bright Areas sliders that enable to adjust the exposure in just the darker or brighter areas of the photo or only in the mid ranges in between

✔ **Saturation** task pane contains a Saturation slider for adjusting the over-all saturation of color in the photo and a Midtones slider for adjusting color saturation in just the mid ranges of the photo

✔ **Sharpness** task pane contains an Amount slider for adjusting the amount of contrast in the photo's edge pixels, a Radius slider for adjusting the number of pixels radiating from the edge pixels that you want to sharpen, and a Threshold slider for adjusting how different pixels must be to be considered as the edge pixels for sharpening

The controls in the Tint task pane enable you to correct the overall hue and balance of color in a photo. It's useful when you're dealing with an old photo print that shows yellowing from age that carries over into the digital photo during scanning. To change the tint of a photo, in the Tint task pane, you click the area of the photo that should be white or gray with the mouse pointer (which appears in the guise of an eyedropper). PhotoSuite then automatically adjusts the tint of the photo.

In cases where you're not trying to get rid of yellowing by restoring the whites and grays but rather want to "tint" the photo in a particular color (often to add a mood to it), you use the Tint Color slider to select the color you want to tint the photo and then the Tint Balance slider to increase or decrease the amount of color tinting applied.

The Brightness & Contrast task pane, as its name implies, enables you to modify the amount of brightness and contrast in the photo by manipulating its Brightness and/or Contrast sliders. This task pane is one of the very few associated with the Overall Quality button that don't offer any control for automatically selecting the optimal brightness and contrast settings. Here, you have to manipulate the appropriate slider(s) to make any modifications.

The Exposure, Saturation, Sharpness, Tint, and Brightness & Contrast task panes all contain Show Preview check boxes that are all automatically checked so that you immediately see the effects of all the modifications you make with the various sliders. You can use this check box to compare the changes you've made to the original photo. Simply click the Show Preview check box to remove its checkmark and display the original photo and then click this check box again to reapply its checkmark to once again display the modifications you've just made.

In matters of size, shape, and orientation

The pop-up menu attached to the Transform button in the All Edit Features task pane contains a number of important options (Crop, Rotate, Flip, Straighten, and Resize) that enable you to manipulate the size, shape, and orientation of your photo. This menu also contains Position and Change Order options which are only available when you superimpose more than one photo on another (see "Superimposing one photo on another" later in this chapter for details).

Here we come a cropping

The Crop option on the Transform button's pop-up menu enables you to cut out whatever parts you consider extraneous in the photo so that it concentrates on whatever you consider to be the photo's primary subject or subjects. Cropping is one of the most used editing tools for photos. When you click the Crop option, crop marks (indicated by dashed lines with resizing handles shown as circles at each corner) surround the perimeter of the photo and the Crop task pane similar to the one shown in Figure 6-7 appears.

The Crop task pane enables you to select a crop shape (other than the default rectangular shape matching the proportions of your original photo) and then drag the crop marks so that only the part of the photo you want is within the dotted lines (referred to as "the area of interest"). Note that PhotoSuite also indicates which part of the photo will be cropped and which part is in the area of interest (and will be retained) when you finish the cropping procedure (by clicking the Done button) by making the display of the cropped area fairly transparent while continuing to display the area of interest as normal.

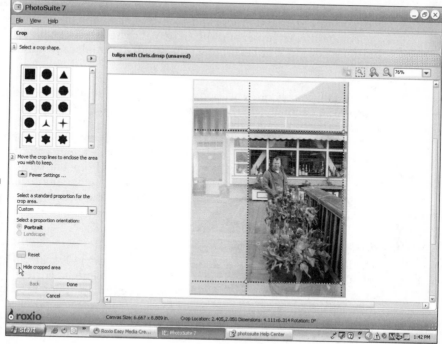

Figure 6-7:
Use the controls in the Crop task pane to cut out all extraneous portions of the photo.

This differentiation is important when using any non-rectangular crop shape as the program continues to display the crop marks that you manipulate as a rectangle that contains the crop shape you select. This means that when using a non-rectangular crop shape, you need to pay attention to which areas are transparent and which are in the area of interest (which no longer correspond to the crop marks) order to tell what is going to be cropped and what is going to be retained.

When defining the area of interest with the crop marks, keep these techniques in mind:

✔ Drag anywhere on the vertical or horizontal dashed crop lines to move them individually

✔ Drag the resize handles at a corner to resize both the vertical and horizontal lines extending from that corner while at the same time maintaining the current aspect ratio

✔ Press and hold down the Shift key when dragging a resize handle when you want to move the vertical and horizontal lines extending from it without maintaining the current aspect ratio

✔ Drag the entire area of interest within the photo by positioning the mouse pointer somewhere within this area and then dragging the open hand mouse pointer

To select a new proportion for the crop marks, click the new proportion setting from the Standard Proportion drop-down list. The proportion refers to the comparative relation of width to height (when the default Portrait option button is selected) or height to width (when the Landscape option button is selected).

To see how your photo will appear when the area indicated for cropping is cut out (without actually going ahead with the cropping), click the Hide Cropped Area check box to put a checkmark in it. PhotoSuite then temporarily removes all but the indicated area of interest until you click the Hide Cropped Area check box again to remove the checkmark. If you're happy with the results and want to go ahead with the cropping, click the Done button at the bottom of the Crop task pane. If you decide against cropping the photo, click the Cancel button instead to return to the All Edit Features task pane without modifying the photo.

Getting reoriented or resized

The Rotate, Flip, Straighten, and Resize options on the Transform button's pop-up menu enable you to quickly put the photo into its correct orientation or modify its overall size. Of all these four, the Rotate option is probably the most important, given that whenever you turn the camera up to get a tall, vertical shot, this photo appears as a picture in landscape mode (as though it were laying on its side) that needs to be rotated either ninety degrees counterclockwise (to the left) or clockwise (to the right).

When you open the Rotate task pane, this pane contains the following three buttons you can use to quickly correct the orientation of most photos:

- **90° Left** to rotate the photo ninety degrees counterclockwise

- **90° Right** to rotate the photo ninety degrees clockwise

- **180°** to rotate the photo so that it's completely turned upside down

If you want to rotate the photo to any other angle, you can use the combo box right below the 180° button by typing in a particular value (representing the number of degrees between 1 and 359 that the photo should be rotated in a clockwise direction). You can also select the number of degrees to rotate the photo by clicking the combo box's Plus (+) or Minus (–) button until the desired number of degrees is displayed in the combo box.

If you're more of the hands-on type, you might want to manually rotate the photo. You do this by positioning the mouse pointer on the rotation handle that appears from the dashed line hanging down from the top center. Then, when the mouse pointer changes its shape so that it matches that of the rotation handle's icon (the arrow curving around and up to the right), drag the rotation handle (and by extension the entire photo) in the direction you want the photo oriented and then release the mouse button when it's oriented exactly as you want it.

The Flip option enables you to reverse the orientation of your photo. The Flip task pane contains three buttons that you choose among when flipping your photo:

- **Horizontally** so that what appears on the right in the original photo now appears on the left
- **Vertically** so that appears at the top in the original photo now appears on the bottom (this is equivalent to rotating the photo 180 degrees)
- **Both Ways** so that the photo is flipped both horizontally and vertically

The Straighten option enables you to straighten your photo (something I always seem to need help with). To use this feature, you open the Straighten task pane and then follow these simple steps:

1. **Click the mouse pointer at one end of some object in the photo that should be perfectly horizontal or vertical.**

   You now need to draw a horizontal or vertical line that PhotoSuite can use as a guideline when straightening the photo (see Figure 6-8).

2. **Drag the mouse pointer along the object to draw the guide line to be used in straightening the photo horizontally or vertically.**

   Now you're ready to have PhotoSuite actually straighten the picture.

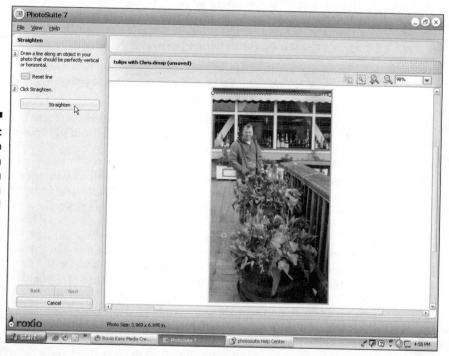

Figure 6-8:
To straighten a photo, you draw a horizontal or vertical guideline that the program can use when straightening it.

3. **Click the Straighten button in the Straighten task pane.**

   PhotoSuite straightens the photo along the line you've drawn.

4. **Click the Next button at the bottom of the Straighten task pane.**

   Because straightened photos often need to be cropped, PhotoSuite displays the Crop task pane (see "Here we come a cropping" earlier in this chapter for details).

5. **(Optional) If your newly straightened photo needs some cropping cleanup, crop the photo and then click the Done button at the bottom of the Crop task pane.**

The Resize option lets you resize your photo by dragging the picture's borders. To increase or decrease the overall photo size in the Resize task pane, you follow these steps:

1. **Click the More Settings button in Resize task pane.**

   PhotoSuite then displays the Width and Height text boxes along with the Units drop-down list box that you can use to keep an eye on how small or large you're actually making the picture (it's often hard to tell on the screen when the magnification setting is anything other 100%).

2. **Drag the sizing handles (the circles at each corner and in the center of each side) around the photo until it is the size you want.**

   If you're making the photo larger and you're having trouble dragging the sizing handles, decrease the picture's magnification by clicking the Zoom Out button or by selecting a new magnification setting in the Select Zoom Level drop-down list and then try Step 2 again.

   Before setting the new picture size, you should now check its dimensions (this can be important if you intend to print the photo and it's now larger than the paper size your printer can handle).

3. **Check the new dimensions in the Width and Height text boxes and if they're okay, click the Done button at the bottom of the Resize task pane to actually resize the photo.**

Of course, if you happen to know the exact dimensions you want to use in resizing the photo, you can enter them into the Width and Height text boxes. However, keep in mind that as long as the Maintain Proportions check box has a checkmark in it, entering a new value into either one of these text boxes automatically changes the value in the corresponding text box. (By the way, to have PhotoSuite actually change the size of the photo in the work area after you've typed in a new value into either the Width or Height text box, you must click the I-beam mouse pointer in the other text box.)

Don't remove the checkmark from the Maintain Proportions check box before you start resizing the photo either manually or by entering new values into the Width or Height text boxes unless you are sure you know what you're doing. By resizing a photo without regard to the aspect ratio between the width and the height (that's the proportions that are being maintained), you can end up with a photo that's really distorted.

Achieving that perfect photo effect

PhotoSuite is the best when it comes to easy-to-apply special effects. In addition to the ready-made special effects you have to choose from, you can also lighten a photo by increasing its transparency setting or give the photo a real old-fashioned look by using the Edge Fading control to dissolve its edges.

In addition to applying these filters, transparency, and edging effects, you can also add text to your photos, paint and draw on them, and even add cutouts that remove particular shapes from the photo (a really handy technique when combined with non-rectangular crop shapes where you want to cut off the white areas that fill in the original rectangle that are left behind after cropping the photo to the new shape).

Dazzling special effects for every mood

PhotoSuite includes a wide array of special effects that can really change the look of your photo. To have a gander at all the effects and experiment with what they do (or don't do for your photo), click the Effects button in the All Edit Features task pane and then click Special Effects at the top of its pop up menu.

PhotoSuite then opens the Special Effects task pane that contains an Effects list box that displays thumbnails of but a small portion of all the effects offered by the program. To narrow the list by displaying only a particular category of special effects, click the drop-down list button to the right of All Effects and then click the category (Adjust Color through Warp) in the drop-down list whose effects you want displayed in the Effects list box. You can also display thumbnails of all the special effects on a pop-up palette (as shown in Figure 6-9) by clicking the Palette pop-up button (the one with the arrowhead pointing to the right) immediately to the right of the Effects drop-down list button.

When you click one of the special effect thumbnails, PhotoSuite immediately applies that special effect to the preview of your photo shown in work area on the right side of the PhotoSuite window. If you don't like the effect, you can just go ahead and choose another (PhotoSuite's special effects are *not* cumulative so you don't have to cancel one effect before trying another).

Note that some of the special effects enable you to adjust their settings (this is especially true of the more radical effects in such categories as Blur, Distort, Pattern, and Texture). You can tell when the special effect you've selected allows you to modify its settings because the Adjust Settings button in the Special Effects becomes active (that is, it is no longer grayed out).

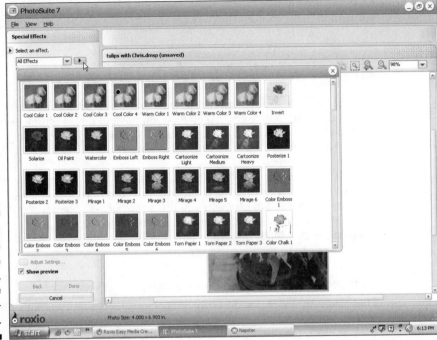

Figure 6-9:
To display a pop-up palette of special effects to apply to your photo, click the Palette pop-up button.

When you click the Adjust Settings button to modify the settings for the special effect you've selected, the Special Effects task pane displays whatever controls that that particular special effect offers for modifying its settings (usually in the form of sliders). After you've finished modifying the special effect's settings, click the Done button to return to the normal Special Effects task pane (you can also abandon your changes when returning to this task pane by clicking the Cancel button instead).

When you've got the special effect that you want to stay with, click the Done button at the bottom of the Special Effects task pane to return to the All Edit Features task pane. If you want to dump the special effect that you thought was so cool a moment ago, click the Cancel button instead.

Adding text to your photos

PhotoSuite makes it easy to annotate your pictures with text. You can use this feature to add titles to your photos. To do this, click the Text button and then click the Add or Edit Text item at the top of its pop-menu. PhotoSuite then displays the Add or Edit Text task pane like the one shown in Figure 6-10 where you can enter the title or whatever label you want to add and then select the text color, font, font size, font attributes, and alignment for it.

Figure 6-10:
You can add
titles to your
photos
using the
controls in
the Add or
Edit Text
task pane.

To annotate your photo with text in the Add or Edit Text task pane, follow these steps:

1. **Click the Add a New Text Object button.**

   After you click this button, PhotoSuite puts the cursor in the Edit Text list box and adds a new text box in the center of your photo.

2. **Type the text you want to appear in the photo in the Edit Text list box.**

   To add line breaks to the title or comments you're typing, press the Enter key.

   Now you're ready to adjust the text settings beginning with the text color. By default, PhotoSuite selects black as the text color which only works when placing the text on a very light background in the photo.

3. **(Optional) Click the Color drop-down button and then click the text color you want to use on the pop-up palette.**

   If you want to use a color that appears in the photo, click the eyedropper icon in the lower-right corner of the color palette and then click the color you want to use in photo. If you want to mix a sample color, click the More Colors button in the lower-left corner of the color palette and then create a new color by entering the appropriate Red, Green, and Blue values or by dragging the crosshairs in the Hues and Shades sample boxes before clicking OK.

By default, PhotoSuite picks Tahoma as the font in which to display the text. If you wish, you can select another font to use from a wide variety of fonts that PhotoSuite makes available.

4. **(Optional) Click the Font drop-down button and then click the name of the font you want to use in the drop-down list.**

   By default, PhotoSuite selects 7 points as the font size (pretty small by any reckoning). If you wish, you can select a larger font size to use.

5. **(Optional) Type a new point size in the Font Size combo box or use its Plus (+) or Minus (–) buttons to select a new point size.**

   In addition to adjusting the font and font size, you can also change the alignment of the text in its text box (which is centered both horizontally and vertically by default), add the bold, italics, or underlining attribute to the text, and even scrunch up or spread out the text in the text box by modifying the horizontal spacing percentages (percentages below 100% bring the text closer together and percentages above 100% spread it out).

6. **(Optional) Make any necessary adjustments to the text alignment, text attributes, or to the horizontal scaling.**

   PhotoSuite positions the new text box in the dead center of the photo. Almost all the time, you'll want to move the text box to a more appropriate location in the photograph.

7. **Position the mouse pointer inside the text box and when the pointer changes to an open hand, drag the text box to the desired position on the photo.**

   In addition to repositioning the text box in the photo, you may also want to re-orient the text by rotating the text box.

8. **(Optional) Position the mouse pointer on the rotation handle (the larger ball in the middle at the top of the box) and then when the mouse pointer turns into a circular arrow drag it until the text is oriented just as you want it to appear in the final photo.**

   When you have the text positioned and oriented the way you want it, you're ready to set it.

9. **Click the Done button to return to the All Edit Features task and then click outside the text box to remove the box's outline as well as its sizing and rotation handles.**

After returning the All Edit Features task pane, don't forget to save the changes you've made to the photo (and by extension, the text you added) with the File⇨Save or File⇨Save As commands on the PhotoSuite menu bar.

Touching up your photos with painting and drawing

You can use PhotoSuite's painting and drawing tools to touch up your photos or even add either freehand or predefined shapes to your photos. These tools include a paint brush tool that you can use to add brushstrokes to your photo, a flood fill tool that you can use to fill particular areas of the photo with color, and a touchup paint tool that enables you to add color to the photo by actually painting on it (when you use the paint brush and flood fill tool, you create and add new graphic art objects to the photo, which means that you can continue to edit it because the object is on its own layer).

In addition to adding painting and drawing to your photo, you can also add standard shapes such as circles, squares, triangles, and the like with the Predefined Shapes item on the Paint & Draw pop-up menu as well as create custom shapes of your own design with the Custom Shapes menu item. Note, however, that you will mostly want to reserve the adding of shapes to photo projects where they can combine with the photos you're adding rather than literally overshadow them (see "Playing with PhotoSuite Project Templates" later in this chapter for information on creating projects).

In the Paint Brush task pane (opened by selecting Paint Brush on the Paint & Draw button's pop-up menu), you need to select the brush shape and paint color. You can then use the three sliders to refine your brush settings:

✔ **Size** to increase or decrease the size of the paint brush (reflected in the size of the mouse pointer in the photo)

✔ **Transparency** to determine how solid or faint the brush strokes are

✔ **Edge Fading** to determine how much each stroke blends into the background

After you finish setting your brush settings, you can drag the mouse pointer to paint strokes on the photo. If you make a mistake and want to erase a particular stroke, click the Undo Last Change button to remove it.

Note that working with the touchup brush in the Touchup Brush task pane is similar except that in addition to selecting your brush shape, paint color, brush size, transparency, and edge fading settings, you need to select a particular style of the touchup brush that determines what kind of painting you do. These brush style selections include a wide variety of effects which the PhotoSuite attempts to illustrate through the use of butterfly thumbnails displayed above the name of each brush type in the Select a Touchup Brush list box (you can also display a pop-up palette of brush styles by clicking the pop-up button to the right of this list box).

Note that the function of most of the brush styles in this list is far from evident from their thumbnails. You should experiment with them to see just what effects they produce, as some are quite surprising. For example, the Lighten brush style actually lightens the colors of whatever object you paint with it rather than putting down the paint color you've selected. So too, the Transparency brush style actually removes all color acting like an eraser in other paint programs.

When you paint with the touchup brush using the settings you've chosen, PhotoSuite does not put down each stroke as a separate graphics object (indicated by the lack of selection handles along the brushstroke). This does not mean that you can't delete a brushstroke made with the touchup brush (you do this by clicking the Undo Last Change), but it does mean that you can't do any more editing to the brushstroke, such as move or rotate it after you've finish painting with this brush (something you can do when using the regular paint brush).

Getting ready to use the flood fill tool in the Flood Fill task pane (opened by clicking Flood Fill on the Paint& Brush button's pop-up menu) is very similar to getting ready to use the touchup brush tool in that you must select a fill style in the Select a Fill Style list box (using the exact same list of styles illustrated with the very same butterfly thumbnails as in Select a Touchup Brush list box), fill color, transparency, and edge fading.

Instead of setting the brush size as you do in the Touchup Brush task pane, in the Flood Fill task pane, you indicate how the pixels in the photo are selected for filling using the Tolerance slider. If you set a low tolerance with this slider, PhotoSuite fills the pixels area you click with the paint bucket mouse pointer that are the same color or very close in hue. If you set a high tolerance with this slider, PhotoSuite fills the pixels that are similar but not exactly same in the area you click.

After making your modifications to the flood fill settings, you can fill sections of the photo by clicking the paint bucket mouse pointer on the area you want filled. Which pixels are filled with the selected color using the designated fill style in the area you click depends upon the tolerance you use. If you want to fill more areas than the current tolerance allows, you can drag the paint bucket mouse pointer around the area to be filled. If PhotoSuite ends up filling more of the photo that you wanted, click the Undo Last Fill button in the Flood Fill task pane to remove it.

Now, cut that out!

The Create Cutout feature enables you to separate an area of special interest in a photo from its background by cutting that area out so that you can save it in it own graphics file. When defining the object or area in a photo to cut out, you can either enclose the area in a wide variety of predefined shapes or you can select the area by tracing it or having PhotoSuite automatically attempt to trace the area by its edges or its color.

To create a cutout using a predefined shape, you follow these steps:

1. **Open the Create Cutout task pane by clicking Create Cutout option on the Cutouts & Masks button's pop-up menu.**

   The initial step in this pane is labeled 1, How Would You Like the Selected Item to be Cutout. It contains two option buttons: By Using

Preset Shapes (selected by default) and By Freehand Tracing, Edge Tracing, or Picking Colors.

2. **Make sure that the By Using Preset Shapes option button is selected and then click Next button at the bottom of the Create Cutout pane.**

   The Create Cutout pane now contains the next two areas: 2 where you choose the shape(s) you want to use in defining the area of the photograph to cut out and 3 where you can adjust the cutout selection by inverting it.

3. **Click the shape that you want to use in defining the cutout in the list box and then click the Add Selected Shape button.**

   When you click the Add Selected Shape button, PhotoSuite inserts that shape in your photo surrounded by a rotation and sizing handles.

4. **Move, size, and rotate the shape as required so that it encloses the area to be included in the cutout.**

   When enclosing the cutout area with preset shapes, you can use more than one shape (Figure 6-11 shows an example of this where I combined a triangle and rectangle to enclose Transamerica Pyramid building in downtown San Francisco). When the Combine with Current Selection option button is selected (as it is by default), PhotoSuite adds each new shape to the cutout. When you click the Subtract From Current Selection option button, each new shape reduces the cutout area (depending on how you make them overlap the original cutout shape, you can end up with very interesting effects). PhotoSuite differentiates between the shape enclosing the cutout and that outside of the cutout by displaying the cutout area normally and all that beyond the cutout as transparent.

   If you're happy with the cutout selection and are ready to save it in a new file or make it into a new graphics object, proceed to Step 6. If, however, you want to cut out everything but what's in the shape(s) you've set in the photo, you need to take Step 5 first.

5. **(Optional) If you want to make the cutout everything in the photo but what's enclosed within the preset shapes, click the Invert Selection button.**

   Now you're ready to proceed to area 4 where you take the last steps in the process.

6. **Click the Next button at the bottom of the Create Cutout task pane.**

   The area marked 4 in the Create Cutout task pane contains three option buttons to choose from: Cut It Out to copy the cutout selection to a new graphics file, Create a New Object (the default) to copy the cutout as a new graphics object in the same photo (so that's superimposed on the original photo), or Cookie-cut It Out to turn the cutout into a new graphics object in the photo that is removed from the rest of the photo (and therefore leaves a hole in it when you move the graphic).

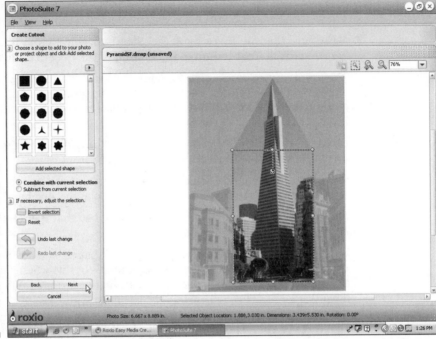

Figure 6-11:
You can
combine
preset
shapes
when using
shapes to
define the
area to
cutout.

7. **Select the type of cutout you want to create by selecting the Cut It Out, Create a New Object, or Cookie-cut It Out option button and then click the Next button.**

   Depending upon which option button is selected when you click the Next button, the final Create Cutout task pane either contains one or two additional steps. When the Cut It Out option button is selected, you can only modify the transparency and edge fading settings before saving the cutout either to a new file or to the Windows Clipboard. When you select either of the other two, you can also move, resize, or rotate the cutout in the current photo.

8. **Make any necessary adjustments to the cutout's transparency or edge fading settings by dragging the appropriate slider.**

   If you want, you can now save a copy of the cutout in a separate file or copy it to the Windows Clipboard so that you can quickly paste it into another photo you're editing or into another photo project you're creating.

9. **(Optional) Click the Save Cutout to a File button and then select the folder into which to save the file and enter its filename in the Save As dialog box before you click the Save button.**

   Note that PhotoSuite allows you to save your cutout only in the PNG graphics files format. If you need the file in another graphics file format, open the resulting PNG file and then use the program's File⇨Save As command to convert it to another format by selecting that format in the Files of Type drop-down list before clicking the Save button.

10. **(Optional) To copy the cutout to the Windows Clipboard for later pasting in other projects and programs, click the Copy Cutout to the Clipboard button.**

   If you used the Create a New Object or Cookie-cut It Out options, you can still move, resize, or rotate the selected cutout before leaving the Create Cutout task pane.

11. **(Optional) Reposition, resize, and/or rotate the cutout shape as needed in the photo.**

   Now you're ready to close the Create Cutout task pane and return to the All Edit Features task pane.

12. **Click the Done button at the bottom of the Create Cutout task pane.**

   If you retained a copy of the cutout in the original photo (as opposed to saving the cutout in a separate PNG file), you may want to save your changes in a new or the original graphics file.

13. **(Optional) To save the cutout in the original photo file, choose File⇨ Save on the PhotoSuite menu bar. To save the modified photo with cutout in a new file, choose File⇨Save As and modify the folder location and/or filename before you click the Save button in the Save As dialog box.**

Note that once you're back in the All Edit Features task pane, you can still manipulate the cutout in the photo and even delete it, if you decide it's no longer necessary (by pressing the Delete key or right-clicking the object and then clicking Delete on its shortcut menu).

Cutouts using predefined shapes are great for giving whimsical or meaningful shapes to the parts of photos that you intend to put into a collage project (see "Calling all collages" later in this chapter). For example, you can cut out heart-shaped figures in photos intended for valentines or wedding collages and cards or starburst-shaped ones for graduation albums.

The procedure for creating a cutout by freehand tracing, edge tracing, or picking colors is similar in every way except for the procedure of actually selecting the cutout area. After clicking the By Freehand Tracing, Edge Tracing, or Picking Colors option button in the initial Cutout task pane, you have a choice among the following methods:

   ✔ **Freehand Tracing:** choose this option button to manually designate the cutout area by clicking a starting point (which appears as a white circle) and then tracing all around the area until you meet back with and connect the selection by clicking on the starting point (as you trace, you can click to establish intermediary points that enable you to turn corners and change direction)

✔ **Edge Tracing:** choose this option button to manually designate the cutout area by clicking a starting point (which appears as a white circle) and then clicking all around the area until you close the selection by clicking on the start point and then clicking the Done Tracing button in the Create Cutout task pane

✔ **Picking Colors:** choose this option button to select the cutout area simply by clicking on its color in the photo with the magic wand mouse pointer (you can use the Tolerance slider to determine how much the hues can differ when making the selection)

After selecting the cutout area using any of these three methods, the rest of the steps outlined for creating cutouts from predefined shapes apply (that is, from Step 5 on in the step-by-step procedure that appears earlier in this section).

Mask that effect!

The Create Mask feature enables you to apply a special effect to just a particular area in your photo by masking out and thereby protecting all the other areas in the picture. The procedure for actually creating the mask (which, remember, defines the area that you can then apply special effects to) is identical to that for creating cutouts: you can either create a mask using any of the preset shapes or by freehand tracing, edge tracing, or picking colors (see "Now, cut that out!" earlier in this chapter for details).

Once you've defined the mask in the Create Mask task pane (opened by clicking Create Mask on the Create Cutouts & Masks button's pop-up menu), you are ready to use it when applying special effects in the Special Effects task pane (opened by clicking Special Effects on the Effects button's pop-up menu — see "Dazzling special effects for every mood" earlier in this chapter for details).

You can tell when the effect that you select is going to be applied only to the area in a mask because of the addition of the Disable/Enable Mask button to the toolbar in the photo's viewing area. This toggle button enables you to temporarily remove the mask so that the effect you select applies to the entire photo and not just the area within the mask you created (because it is a toggle button, you can re-enable the mask and limit a special effect to it by clicking the Disable/Enable Mask button a second time).

Figure 6-12 illustrates how this masking thing works. For this photo, I created a mask that included only the buildings on Columbus Street in San Francisco, featuring the blue sky. I then applied the Antique special effect to the photo. Because of the mask, only the buildings within the mask are given the sepia tone, leaving the sky its deep, azure blue (a fact that you surely can't appreciate seeing the photo only in black-and-white).

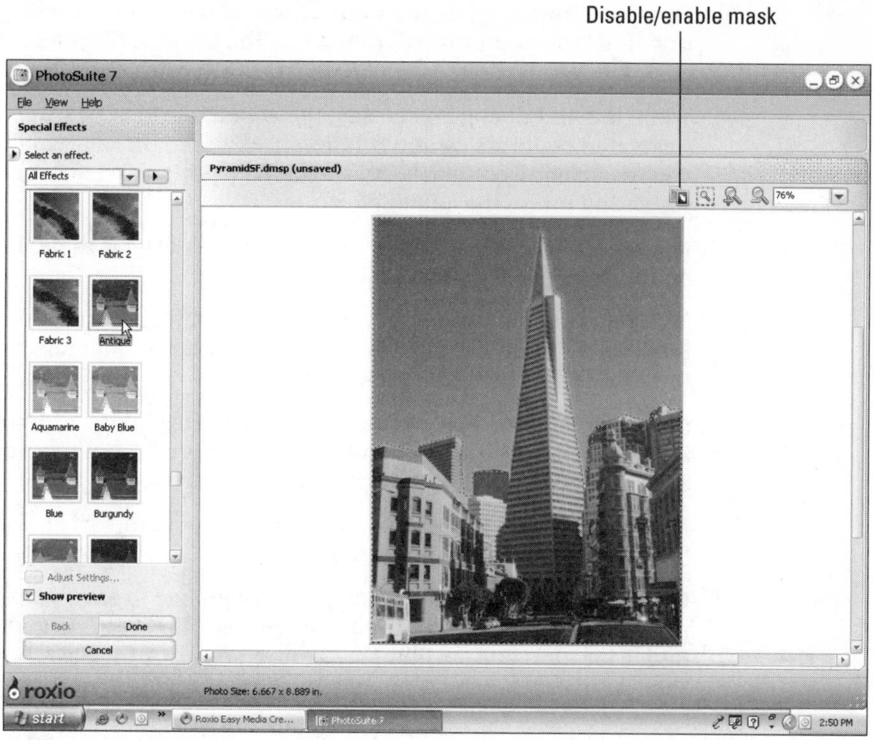

Disable/enable mask

Figure 6-12:
When you
apply a
special
effect to a
masked
photo, only
the areas
within the
mask are
modified.

Superimposing one photo on another

PhotoSuite's Add Photos button in the All Edit Features task pane makes it easy to combine photos by superimposing one on top of the other. This feature makes it easy to put together a photo montage that combines different images into one. In addition to making it possible to add photos, PhotoSuite also lets you add what it calls props (and what I think of more as stock images along the line of Windows clipart but a great deal classier) to your photos.

To superimpose a photo on top of the photo you're currently editing, you follow these steps:

1. **In the All Edit Features task pane, click the Add Photos button and then click Add Photos & Cutouts at the top of the button's pop-up menu.**

   The Add dialog box (which works just like the Open dialog box) appears where you select the folder or collection containing the photo or the cutout saved in its own file (see "Now, cut that out!" earlier in this chapter) you want to add and then click the photo's filename before clicking the Add button.

2. **Open the collection or file folder that contains the file with the photo or cutout you want to add, then click the graphic file's icon before you click the Add button.**

   When the Add dialog box closes, the added photo appears selected (indicated by its sizing and rotation handles) in the center of the photo you're currently editing. Next, you can reposition and, if necessary, resize and rotate the added photo.

3. **Resize and rotate the added image and then drag it to its final position on the background photo.**

   You can also edit this added photo with any of the features available on the Overall Quality, Facial Flaws, Damaged Photos, and Effects button in the All Edit Features task pane.

4. **(Optional) Making any needed editing changes to the added photo, including improving its overall quality, removing red eye and dust, or adding special effects, changing the transparency, or adding a shadow.**

   Now you're ready to save your changes either in the original graphics file, or, more likely in a new graphics file.

5. **Choose File⇨Save on the PhotoSuite menu bar to save your combined photos in the original photo's file or choose File⇨Save As and modify the folder location and/or filename before you click the Save button in the Save As dialog box to save your photo montage in a new graphics file.**

When you add one photo to another, PhotoSuite opens a Gallery pane which shows you thumbnails of each of the photos you're working with. You can use this Gallery to easily select the photo you want to edit: simply click its thumbnail in the Gallery pane. PhotoSuite shows you that the photo you click is now selected in the work area by enclosing the photo in dashed lines and adding sizing and rotation handles to it.

As I mention at the beginning of this section, instead of superimposing just photos on top of the photo you're editing, you can also add what the program likes to call props, which are small pictures of different isolated objects such as animals, vegetables, musical instruments, and the like.

To superimpose one of PhotoSuite's props on the photo you're currently editing, you follow these steps:

1. **Click Add Photos & Cutouts button in the All Edit Features task pane and then click Add Props on its pop-up menu.**

   The Add Props task pane opens showing a list of all the Prop collections included with the program.

2. **Click the drop-down button in the Select a Prop drop-down list box and then the name of the Prop category you want to use.**

   If you click the All item at the very top of the list, PhotoSuite displays thumbnails of all its prop photos in one huge list. You can also have a

better gander at these thumbnails by clicking the pop-up Palette button
(the one with the arrowhead pointing towards the right).

3. **Double-click the thumbnail of the prop you want to add or drag it
over to the photo in the work area and drop it anywhere.**

   PhotoSuite superimposes a copy of the prop in the exact center of the
   background photo. Now you're ready to resize it and put the prop in its
   proper position (I dare you to say that twenty times really fast).

4. **If needed, resize the prop and rotate it before you drag it to the
desired position in relation to the background photo.**

   To see how your prop fits in with the background, you may want to
   select it (especially if you reduced its size) to remove all the selection
   hash marks and sizing and rotation handles. You can do this by clicking
   the background photo anywhere outside of the prop or by clicking the
   thumbnail image of the background photo in the Gallery pane.

5. **Click the Done button and then save the changes to the file in the All
Edit Features task pane with File➪Save or in a new file with File➪
Save As.**

Figure 6-13 shows my photo of Columbus Street with the Transamerica
Pyramid after adding the Hot Air Balloon prop and positioning it up in the
sky. (I sure hope that that balloon doesn't end up coming down on the top of
that Pyramid building's spike — ouch!)

Figure 6-13:
Adding the
Hot Air
Balloon
prop from
the Add
Props task
pane to a
photo of
San
Francisco.

Playing with PhotoSuite Project Templates

PhotoSuite goes out of its way to make it easy to use your digital photos to create fun and interesting photo projects. These projects run the gamut from the ever-popular photo collage to posters. All are based on adding your own digital photos to project templates that give you ready-made background and, in many cases, stock text that you can adapt to your own needs.

To get a list of the various types of projects that PhotoSuite supports, launch PhotoSuite and then click the Projects link in the Edit & Create area of its Home Page. PhotoSuite opens the Create a Project task pane where you can select any of the following projects in the Project Type list box:

- ✔ **Collage** to make a collage with your photos using either a blank collage background or any of a number of pre-designed backgrounds including those for the new baby, birthdays, Christmas, weddings, and so on

- ✔ **Albums** to put your photos into the pages of photo albums using pre-designed pages dedicated to subjects such as the new baby, your wedding, the latest vacation, and the like

- ✔ **Calendars** to make calendars with your own photos using any of a wide variety of different calendar designs

- ✔ **Cards** to make greeting cards with your own photos for almost all the major holidays and occasions (including birthdays, anniversaries, graduation, and so on)

- ✔ **Gift Tags** to make gift tags carrying your photos for decorating anniversary, birthday, and Christmas presents

- ✔ **Magazines** to add your photos to pre-designed magazine covers for subjects as diverse as Cooking, Computer, Health & Beauty, Teen, Sports, Outdoor Adventure, and Home Décor (to name a few)

- ✔ **Postcards** to add your vacation photos to any of the various travel postcard designs

- ✔ **Posters** to make a poster using your own photos for events such as the Book Club, Concert, Birthday, and so on

In all categories, PhotoSuite makes it as easy as possible to create your new photo project by walking you through the steps. In most cases, all you have to do is select the project template you want to use, choose the photos you want to add to that template, and then make a few changes to modify the arrangement of the photos and customize the stock text.

Bring on the Borders

PhotoSuite's Borders feature enables you to give your photos a finished look by surrounding them with some sort of decorative border. When you click the Borders link in the PhotoSuite Home Page, The Borders task pane opens giving you a choice between three different types of borders:

- **Frame** to surround the photo in any of a wide variety of frame-type graphics
- **Mat** to mat the photo either with a solid color or colored texture
- **Edge** to select a type of edging that you then combine with a mat color or pattern

When you select the Frame option (the default), PhotoSuite then lets you choose a particular frame style and size (3.5x5, 4x6, 5x7, or 8x10). After you select the frame to use, PhotoSuite then lets you move and, if necessary, resize the photo in the frame in the program's work area. To help you in moving and resizing the photo in its frame, PhotoSuite indicates the edges of the image by showing its perimeter as a dotted line with round sizing handles at the corners and midpoints. Most often these edges image extend beyond the cutout portion of the frame. Moving and/or resizing the photo in the frame therefore displays different parts of the image in the cutout region (the frame actually ends up cropping parts of the image). Be careful when manipulating the image in the frame that you don't expose the white background behind the photo or crop a part of the image that you want displayed.

When you select the Mat option, PhotoSuite lets you select the proper mat among a wide variety of solid colored and textured (patterned) mats, or even enables you to select a photo as the textured mat. After selecting the mat color or texture, you then designate the size of the mat and can adjust the width of the mat as well as control whether or not to display beveling on the mat's edges and include v-groove (and adjust its offset from the inside of the mat). At the end of the process of adding a mat, PhotoSuite even gives you the opportunity to add a frame to surround the mat before you save your masterpiece.

When you select the Edge option, PhotoSuite lets you select an edging style to use with the matting. Immediately after you select the Edge style to use, you're given the opportunity to select the mat color or texture that you want to use with that style. After you select the mat color or texture, its size, and thickness, you are then given the chance to select a frame to surround the mat before you save your work of art.

Stitching It All Together

PhotoSuite's Photo Stitch feature makes it possible to create a single photo with a sweeping panorama from sequential and overlapping individual photos that you take of the same view. This feature is great provided that you've done your homework and the photos that you're trying to stitch together match up and overlap correctly. Accordingly, Roxio has set up some important guidelines for you to follow before attempting to stitch together your favorite photos of the Grand Canyon:

- Use a tripod when taking the photos to stitch together (if you don't have a tripod, try to keep the camera level and in same position when taking the pictures by rotating your body around the camera rather than rotating the camera around your body)

- Overlap each photo that you take in the sequence (Roxio recommends between 20% to 40% overlap on each shot)

- Don't change any of the settings on your camera between the shots you take

- Use only optical zoom when taking the picture: if your camera has a digital zoom, don't use it in shooting the photo sequence

- Take your photos in sequence from left to right or if you're scanning in developed photos, scan them in left-to-right order to ensure that their filenames appear in order

- Do not edit your photos in PhotoSuite before you stitch them together: instead, edit the final panorama produced by Photo Stitch

- Rotate your camera 90 degrees to take portrait shots of the panorama: doing this requires more shots but results in a much taller panorama with more detail

In addition to following these guidelines when taking the shots you would later like to stitch together, you must have one more piece of information at your fingertips when using Photo Stitch and that is the *focal length* used in taking the photos. Now focal length as any photographer will tell you is distance between the film (or CCD in a digital camera) and the optical center of the lens when the lens is set on infinity (this distance is usually given in millimeters and marked on the side of the fixed lenses on a standard 35mm camera).

Trying to determine the focal length for digital cameras, even real fancy ones like my Sony that are equipped with an optical zoom lens, can be difficult. Determining this information is complicated by the fact that the actual focal length for digital cameras is much less than for a standard 35mm camera because their CCDs are much smaller than 35mm film.

If your digital camera has an optical zoom lens, check and see if the camera records the focal length at the time you take your photos. If your camera doesn't record this information (I know that mine doesn't), check your camera manual. If you can't find that or it doesn't give you a clue as to the focal length of your lens when set at infinity, you'll just have to guess when it comes time to give Photo Stitch that information.

The procedure for stitching two or more sequential photos together to create a single panoramic photo is as follows:

1. **Launch PhotoSuite and then click the Photo Stitch link on the PhotoSuite Home Page.**

   Next you need to select the photos to stitch together. You must select a minimum of two photos although most panoramas (especially those taken in portrait mode) require more.

2. **Click the photos you want to stitch together in the Most Recently Used Photos list box or click the Add More Photos button and select them in the Add dialog box and then click the Next button.**

   Photo Stitch now gives you an opportunity to make any adjustments to the rotation or order of the photos you added to the work area. If they're not in order, you need to use the Sort Ascending button or drag them into order (don't forget to select the Fit to Page setting at the very bottom of the Select Zoom Level drop-down list box to display all the photos together in the work area).

3. **Make any necessary adjustments to the orientation or order of the photos so that they're all in portrait or landscape mode and are left-to-right order for stitching and then click the Next button.**

   Photo Stitch now attempts to automatically determine the focal length of your photos. If it can't determine this value (which is true for most of the digital photos you take), you need to select this value by dragging the Focal Length slider until the correct number (in millimeters) appears immediately above the right end of the Focal Length slider (see Figure 6-14).

4. **(Optional) If Photo Stitch can't automatically determine the focal length for your photos; select the correct length (or your best guess) with the Focal Length slider.**

   Now you're ready to have Photo Stitch do its magic.

Figure 6-14:
Using Photo
Stitch to
combine
three
overlapping
photos of a
single
sweeping
view into a
single
panorama.

5. **Click the Auto Align button.**

   Photo Stitch stitches together your photos, showing you a preview of the new panorama in the work area. If you notice some problems, try clicking the Fine Tuning button to see if Photo Stitch can detect and fix the problem. If this doesn't do it, click and manually drag the photos into final position (remember that you can use the arrow keys to nudge the selected photo into place).

6. **If necessary, fine-tune the positioning of the photos and then click the Next button.**

   Photo Stitch shows you the final product ready for you to save or print (see Figure 6-15). Be sure to save your photo before you click the Done button to return to the PhotoSuite Home Page.

7. **Click the Save button and then save your new panoramic photo in the DMSP file format in the Save As dialog box.**

After saving your panorama, you can edit its graphics file in PhotoSuite as you would any other digital photo that you at your disposal. Now is the time to use Overall Quality features to improve any exposure or color balance problems.

Figure 6-15:
The final
panoramic
photo after
Photo Stitch
did its
magic.

Group Editing

The last PhotoSuite feature to look at is the Multi Photo Enhance feature. This one enables you to do group editing to a bunch of photos that all need the same kind of modifications or enhancements. It's a real timesaver when you have a lot of photos that all need the same kind of changes made to them.

The modifications and enhancements that you can perform at one time on a group of photos include:

✔ **Fix** to take care of any of the exposure, color saturation, sharpness, or red eye problems in the group (you can even use the PhotoDoctor on them)

✔ **Transform** to rotate, flip, or resize all the photos in the group in the same way

✔ **Special Effects** to apply the Black and White, Invert, or Sepia special effects to all the photos in the group

✔ **Rename** to give new filenames made up of a keyword and a sequential number (such as Newbaby00, Newbaby01, Newbaby02, and so on)

✔ **Convert** to convert the group from one type of graphics file to another (such as DMSP to JPEG for use on the Internet)

Among the most important and unique modifications that you can perform with the Multi Photo Enhance feature are surely the Rename and Convert options. The Rename option enables you to name of group of related photo files so that they all show up together in a preset order in any file listing you do. The Convert option enables you to move a batch of photos from one file format to another in a fraction of the time it would take to convert them individually.

Printing and Sharing Your Photos

The Print option at the top of the Print & Share area at the bottom of the PhotoSuite Home Page enables you to print photos individually, in groups arranged for different types of photo paper, or even altogether as a contact sheet. You can use the E-mail link in the Print & Share area to e-mail photos to your friends and family. When sending photos, you have a choice between sending them as attachments to your messages or in the body of the message itself.

You can also use the E-mail link to assemble a bunch of photos together, add in a favorite tune as background music and package the whole thing up as a Windows WMV multimedia video file that you can then send to friends and family as an e-mail attachment. Your e-mail recipients can then open and play the resulting multimedia file as an automated slideshow complete with music using the Windows Media Player on their computers.

Finally, you can use the Online Photo Services link at the very bottom of the Print & Share area of the PhotoSuite Home Page to connect to the Roxio Photo Center where you can get your favorite digital photos professionally printed or post them to a Web page which your friends and family can then visit to see your latest and greatest snapshots.

Printing your own photos

Printing your photos with PhotoSuite is a straightforward process. About the only thing that could be considered the least little bit challenging about it is figuring out which photos you want to group together when printing snap-shots at smaller sizes on paper that can accommodate multiple pictures together on the same page.

After you click the Print link on the PhotoSuite Home Page and select the photos you want to print, the Print task pane gives you the following printing options:

- ✔ **One Photo per Page** to print each of the selected photos on a separate sheet of paper

- ✔ **Multiple Photos per Page** to choose between a wide variety of layouts using different readily-available paper, card, and label stock for printing more than one photo per page

- ✔ **As a Contact Sheet** to print all the selected photos sequentially as thumbnails with their filenames for easy identification

After you select your printing option and in the cases of the Multiple Photos per Page and As a Contact Sheet options, the page layout, you are then given the opportunity to select the printer to use, the photo layout on the page, and the number of copies. Figure 6-16 shows these options as they appear when you select the **One Photo per Page** printing option.

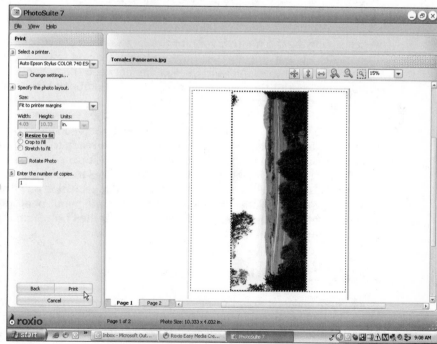

Figure 6-16:
Getting
ready to
print
multiple
photos
each on a
separate
page.

When specifying the photo layout for the One Photo per Page printing option, PhotoSuite gives you a choice among three different sizing options:

- ✔ **Resize to Fit** (the default) to reduce photos to the size required for them to print within the margins for the specified paper size
- ✔ **Crop to Fill** to crop the photos as required for them to fill the page and still print within the margins for the specified paper size
- ✔ **Stretch to Fit** to stretch the photos as required for them to fill the page and still print within the margins for the specified paper size

When specifying the photo layout for the Multiple Photos per Page printing option, PhotoSuite lets you decide between printing the same photo as many times on the same page as your selected photo size allows with the default Fill Each Page with Same Photo option button) and printing each of the selected photos only once per page with the Use Each Photo option button. Note that when you select the Use Each Photo option button, the Times text box (with 1 as the default value) becomes available. If you want to have each of the multiple photos that you've selected printed a set number of times (using as many pages as the photo size and layout require), you enter that number in this text box.

When specifying the photo layout for the As a Contact Sheet printing option, PhotoSuite lets you specify the number of columns and rows (with 4 columns in 5 rows being the default) and the spacing between them. You can also choose not to print the filenames beneath each thumbnail by clicking the Print Titles check box to remove its checkmark.

After specifying your print settings, be sure that you've loaded your printer with the right type of paper and that the printer is ready to go before you click the Print button at the bottom of the Print task pane to start the print job. During the brief moments that PhotoSuite takes to send your photo(s) to the printer, you can click the OK button in the Cancel dialog box if you decide to stop the printing. After PhotoSuite finishes printing your photo(s), click the Done button in the Print task pane to return to the PhotoSuite Home Page.

E-mailing your photos

PhotoSuite makes it easy to e-mail your edited photos to friends and family. When e-mailing photos, you can send them as attachments to an e-mail message or in the body of the message. To send your photos as part of a new e-mail message, you follow these steps:

1. **Launch PhotoSuite and then click the E-mail link in the Print & Share area of the PhotoSuite Home Page.**

   PhotoSuite opens the E-mail task pane that asks you to select the photo(s) you want to send. If these photos are among those shown in the Most Recently Used list box, you can select them by clicking their thumbnails in this list box. If the photo(s) are not listed here, click the Add More Files button and then select them by opening the appropriate file folder or collection and clicking them in the Add dialog box.

2. **Select the photo or photos you want to send either from the Most Recently Used list box or the Add dialog box opened by clicking the Add More Files button and then click the Next button.**

   The E-mail task pane that now appears enables you to choose between the default option, Send as Individual Files, and the option, Package All Files Into One Slideshow. Because you want to send your photos as individual files (either within the body of the e-mail message or as separate attachments, you leave the default option button selected).

   This task pane also contains an E-mail options button that you can select to modify the general options for sending your e-mail and getting your selected photos ready to send. By default, PhotoSuite is automatically set to warn when your total attachment file size exceeds a limit of 1Mb and to automatically convert your photos to the JPEG graphics file type optimized for a screen display set to a resolution of 800x600 pixels (many Internet service providers impose limits of 2Mb on e-mail attachments and large attachments not only take a really long time to send on a dial-up connection and forever to download on the other end but are more prone to errors that prevent successful transmission). If you want, you can make these options on the General and Photos tabs in the E-mail Options dialog box.

3. **Make any necessary changes in the E-mail Options dialog box (opened by clicking the E-mail Options button) to the e-mail options on the General and Photos tabs before you click the Next button.**

   The E-mail task pane that now appears enables you to either send your photos now using your current e-mail program (the default) or save the photos for sending later on. This task pane also contains a Format Photos as HTML Message check box that you select if you want your photo(s) placed inside the body of a new e-mail message rather than sent as file attachments. Note, however, that not all e-mail servers accept HTML e-mail (in which case, the photos get sent as attachments).

4. **Leave the Send Now Using My Default E-mail Client option button selected, but be sure to click the Format Photos as HTML Message check box if you want the photo(s) to appear in the body of the new e-mail message, before you click the Send button at the bottom of the E-mail task pane.**

When you click the Send button, PhotoSuite opens your computer's e-mail messaging program with a new e-mail message in which you then fill in the To and Subject lines and type in the message you want to accompany your photos (whose filenames are either listed in the Attach line of the new message or contents actually displayed at the very bottom of the new message).

5. **Click the Send button in your e-mail program to send the message.**

   After the e-mail program finishes sending your message with photos, its program window closes.

6. **Click the Done button at the bottom of the E-mail task pane to return to the PhotoSuite Home Page.**

Instead of sending your photos as standard e-mail attachments, you can have PhotoSuite package them into a slideshow complete with music that is sent as file attachment to a new e-mail message. When recipients receive the message, they can then play this slideshow with the Windows Media Player on their computers.

The procedure for putting your photos into a slideshow multimedia file and then sending that file as an e-mail attachment is almost identical to that for sending photos as regular file attachments. The big difference is that after selecting the files to be sent (in the order they should appear in the slideshow), then in the second E-mail task pane, you click the Package All Files into One Slideshow option button before you click the Next button (note that you can also click the E-mail Options button in this task pane and then modify the options for the slideshow on the Slideshows tab in the E-mail Options dialog box before clicking Next).

When you click the Next button after clicking the Package All Files into One Slideshow option button, PhotoSuite displays the Add a Background Sound dialog box. If you want to add music to play in the background as the slideshow plays, click the Yes button in this dialog box and then select the audio file to use in the Add a Background Sound dialog box. If you don't want to bother with music, just click the No button instead.

The next E-mail task pane that appears enables you to select a new screen size for the slideshow (the default is the medium size, 320 x 240 pixels) and then preview the slideshow before generating it and sending it:

1. **Click the SlideShow.DMSM thumbnail in the work area and then click the Preview button to play the slideshow in its own Preview window. When you finish viewing the slideshow preview, click this window's Close button.**

   When you click the Preview button, PhotoSuite generates a quick-and-dirty preview where the photo quality is not nearly as high as the finished product. If you want to take the time to have the program generate a high-quality preview using the Size setting you've chosen, click the Generate Preview button below the Size drop-down list box instead.

If you need to temporarily pause the playback of the slideshow preview, click the Pause button at the bottom of the Preview window. If you want to stop the slideshow entirely, click the Stop button instead. When you're finished playing the slideshow preview, click the window's Close button.

2. **If you're satisfied with the slideshow and ready to send it, click the Next button. If you need to make some changes to the music selection or the photos include, click the Back button and retrace your steps.**

   As soon as you click the Next button, PhotoSuite begins generating the slideshow, showing you its progress in the Generate Slideshow dialog box. When the program finishes generating the slideshow, a thumbnail for the file called SlideShow.WMV replaces that of SlideShow.DMSM. The WMV is the multimedia and video format used by the Windows Media Player.

3. **Click the Send button at the bottom of the E-mail to open a new e-mail message in your e-mail program with the SlideShow.WMV file attached to it.**

   Fill in the To and Subject lines and then type the text of the new e-mail message.

4. **Click the Send button in your e-mail program's window after filling the send To and subject information and typing the text for your new message.**

   After your e-mail program finishes sending the new message with your multimedia slideshow file attached, you can close the E-mail task pane.

5. **Click the Done button to close the E-mail task pane and return to the PhotoSuite Home Page.**

When the recipients open the slideshow attachment in your e-mail message on their computers, the Windows Media Player will automatically open and play the slideshow for them.

Using the Online Photo Services

When you click the Online Photo Services link at the very bottom of the Print & Share section of the PhotoSuite Home Page, PhotoSuite opens an Online Photo Services task pane where you select the photos that you want professionally developed or to upload to the Web. After you finish selecting the photos and you click the Next button, the Location of Photos to Share dialog box appears. This dialog box lets you know that copies of all your selected photos are ready to share, having been converted to the Internet-ready file format (JPEG) and placed in the For Sharing folder whose path is displayed both in this dialog box and in the Online Photo Services task pane.

After you click OK to close the Location of Photos to Share dialog box, you need to click the Launch Browser button in the Online Photos Services task pane to launch your Web browser and, if necessary, connect to the Internet. After your browser connects to the Internet, the Roxio Digital Media Services Web page similar to the one shown in Figure 6-17 appears.

Here, you must sign up for a new Roxio Photo Center, password-protected account (which is free) by clicking the Sign Up Free button and then filling out the new account form. After filling in your name, e-mail and physical address and picking a new password, you submit the account form by clicking the Get Started button. After submitting your account form, you can then start using the Online Photo Services (run by an outfit called Snapfish) by clicking the Start Using Snapfish button.

After you sign up for your Snapfish account, you can get right onto uploading photos for printing or viewing online by clicking the Log In button on the Roxio Digital Media Services Web page. This brings you to a Log In page where you enter your e-mail address and your password before you click the Log In button. Click the Remember Me Every Time I Visit Snapfish check box, if you want the site to automatically input your log in information each time you visit the site so that all you have to do is click the Log In button.

Figure 6-17:
Signing up
for the Roxio
online photo
services.

Uploading your photos to the Roxio Photo Center

Before you can have the Roxio Photo Center process prints from your digital photos or can share them on the Internet, you have to upload them to into a new album on the Roxio Media Center Web site. To do this, you need to log into your Snapfish account after selecting your photos and clicking the Launch Browser button in PhotoSuite's Online Photo Services task pane. Then click the Upload Photos link on your account page.

A new Web page opens with the icon for a new photo album given the title Album followed by the current day and month (you can change this album title by clicking the Album Title text box and replacing this automatic name. Next, you need to click the Upload to This Album button.

An Upload Photos Web page now opens where you click the Select Photos button to display an Open dialog box. In this dialog box, you need to select the path of the For Sharing folder where PhotoSuite placed the photos that you earlier selected. After you locate and open this For Sharing folder on your hard disk, select the photos that you want to upload. If you want to upload all the photos in the folder, press Ctrl+A to select them all before you click the Open button.

Snapfish then displays thumbnails of all the photos that you select in your For Sharing folder in the middle of the Upload Photos Web page. You can remove a particular photo from this list by clicking the Remove button that appears beneath it. If you need to rotate a photo, you can do so by clicking the Rotate Clockwise button (the one on the left side with the curved arrow rotating in a clockwise direction) or the Rotate Counterclockwise button (the one on the right side with the curved arrow rotating in a counterclockwise direction) that appear beneath the thumbnail on either side of the Remove button.

When you have the photos you want to upload properly displayed on the Upload Photos Web page, click the Upload button to have them copied onto the Roxio Photo Center's Web site. Once this uploading process is complete, you can then order prints of the photos or share them.

Ordering prints from the Roxio Photo Center

You can use the Roxio's online Photo Center to get high-quality prints of your favorite digital photos, develop and digitize rolls of standard photo film, and even upload and store your digital photos online for sharing on the Internet (see "Sharing photos online" later in this chapter for details). As an added bonus for you owners of the Roxio Easy Media Creator 7 suite, your subscription includes the printing 10 free 4x6 film-quality prints from digital photos that you upload to the Center as well as the developing and digitizing of one roll of photo film and all you pay is $1.99 for the return shipping and handling of your prints and negatives.

To get prints of the photos that you've uploaded to the Roxio Photo Center, follow the procedure for uploading the photos outlined in the previous section, and then click the Order Print button. You can then select the photos in your album that you want prints of. Note that if an orange triangle appears immediately above a photo's check box, this means that quality of your digital photo is not sufficient for the default 4x6 print size, and it's not recommended that you order professional prints (in other words, you need to upload high-resolution digital photos to get your money's worth when ordering prints from the Roxio Photo Center).

After selecting the photos in your album to print, click Choose These Photos to view the items you've ordered on Your Cart Web page. There, you can select the number of prints you want made of each photo as well as designate the print sizes before clicking the Check Out button. This takes you to the Billing and Shipping Web page where you need to give your credit card information and ship to address before placing your print order.

Sharing photos online

In addition to ordering high-quality prints of the digital photos that you upload to the Roxio Photo Center, you can also invite friends and family to view the photos that you've uploaded. To do this, you log onto the Roxio Photo Center, upload the photos into a new album (see "Uploading your photos to the Roxio Photo Center" earlier in this chapter) and then click the Share This Album link (this appears beneath the Share button when you click it). The Share an Album Web page opens where you can enter the e-mail addresses for all the people who you want to invite to view your photos online (when entering different e-mail addresses in the To list box, be sure to separate each address by a comma or press Enter after typing in each address to put it on its own line). You can then personalize the standard Subject line and stock message before clicking the Share Album Now button.

As soon as you click the Share Album Now button, Snapfish sends e-mail message to all the recipients you listed in the To list box inviting them to get online and come and see your works of art. The e-mail message that each person in the list receives contains a Snapfish window that shows the first photo in your uploaded album and that contains a View My Photos button. When recipients click this button, their Web browsers connect them to Internet and take them directly to the Roxio Photo Center Web site. There, after registering to use the Roxio Photo Center and then clicking the View the Album button, they can view thumbnails of all the photos in your album. To see any of the thumbnails full size, they simply click on the thumbnail, after which, they can view all the rest of the photos in the album full size either by clicking the Play link which automatically displays each photo in sequence as a slideshow or one at a time by clicking the Next link.

Chapter 7

Burning Audio CDs and MP3 Discs

* *

In This Chapter

▶ Starting a new Audio CD or MP3 Disc project in Creator Classic

▶ Adding online UPC and ISRC track information to your audio CD

▶ Creating an Enhanced CD with audio and data

▶ Creating a Mixed-CD with audio and data

▶ Burning your audio CD or MP3 disc

▶ Copying an audio CD

* *

Roxio Easy Media Creator makes it easy for you to compile your favorite
tunes and burn them onto CDs for playing on standalone audio CD players (such as the one in your car and the Walkman-variety you listen to at the
gym) as well as on the CD-ROM drive in your computer. The audio CDs that you
burn can be composed of music tracks that you've downloaded and purchased
from online music stores such as Napster, recorded from analog recordings
(such as LPs and audio cassettes) with the Sound Editor (see Chapter 5), or
ones that you rip from audio CDs that you already own.

As you find out in this chapter, with the Easy Media Creator you can create
not only standard audio CDs but MP3 discs, Enhanced CDs, and Mixed-mode
CDs as well. MP3 discs are audio CDs whose tracks are saved in the MP3 compressed file format. This file format enables you to fit many more tracks on
the CD than is possible on a standard CD-R disc (hundreds of tracks in MP3
versus about 20 maximum in the CD-R's normal WAVE format, which aren't
compressed at all). Besides being able to play the MP3 discs that you burn in
the Creator Classic application of Easy Media Creator on your computer's
CD-ROM drive, however, you can only play MP3 discs on standalone players
that support the MP3 file format. Fortunately, many of today's audio CD players, including the ever-popular Walkman-type, support the MP3 file format so
that this limitation may be no problem at all.

Enhanced and Mixed-mode CDs are CDs that mix computer data and audio files together. Enhanced CDs are multi-session CDs with the first session containing the audio tracks that can be played by any standard audio CD player and CD-ROM drive and the second session containing the data files that can be played only on the computer's CD-ROM drive. Mixed-mode CDs are also CDs that mix computer data and audio files. However, unlike the Enhanced CD which separates music tracks from data files in separate sessions, the Mixed-mode CD contains only one session with both the data and music (the data is laid down in the first track of the CD and all the audio tracks follow). This means that a Mixed-mode CD can only be played by your computer's CD-ROM drive (regular audio CD players like the one in your car can't play this kind of CD at all).

After exploring how to create all these types of audio CDs, this chapter ends with information on how to make copies of both the CDs that you burn with Easy Media Creator with the Roxio Disc Copier application.

Creating an Audio CD Project

Creator Classic is the Easy Media Creator application that you use for compiling and burning all your audio CDs. To launch Creator Classic from the Easy Media Creator Home window, click the Create New Audio CD link in the Music column or the Creator Classic link in the Applications area. If the Easy Media Creator Home window is not already open, you can launch Creator Classic by clicking the Start button on the Windows taskbar, highlighting All Programs on the Start submenu, Roxio on the All Programs submenu, and clicking Creator Classic on the Roxio submenu.

If you launched Creator Classic by clicking the Create New Audio CD link on the Easy Media Creator Home, the Creator Classic window with a new untitled Audio Project shown in Figure 7-1 appears. If, however, you started the application by clicking the Creator Classic link in the Easy Media Creator Home or from the Windows Start menu, you need to click the Audio CD link listed in the Common Tasks area of the Tasks pane.

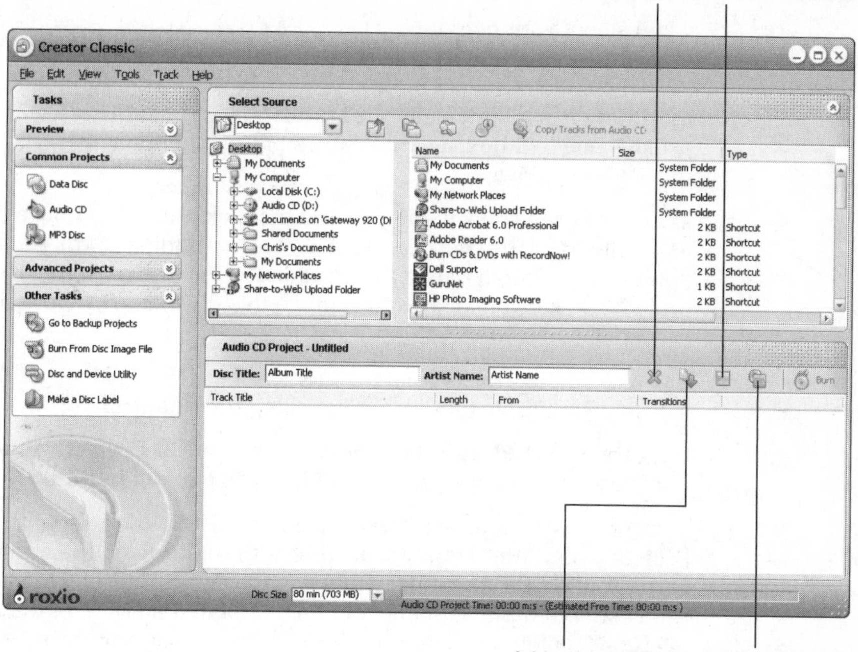

Remove Edit track transitions

Figure 7-1:
Starting a
new Audio
CD project
in Creator
Classic is
the first
step in
creating
your
audio CD.

Add selected files   Add selected files
to above project   to above project

Adding audio tracks to your project

After starting a new Audio CD project, you simply need to fill in your name for
the new disc in the Disc Title text box and the name of the artist(s) involved in
the Artist Name text box if you want this information to be included before
you add the music tracks to the project.

When adding your tracks to the Audio CD project, you follow these simple
steps:

1. **Open the folder or disc on your computer system with the Windows
   Explorer in the Select Source pane that contains the tracks you want
   to add.**

   If you've already copied the tracks you want to add to your computer's
   hard disk, these tracks are probably located in the My Music folder on
   your computer. If you're copying tracks from an audio CD in your computer's CD-ROM drive, select that drive's letter.

2. **Select the names of the track(s) you want to add.**

   If you select your computer's CD-ROM drive, Creator Classic attempts to obtain the track names and other album information of the CD it contains from the online Gracenote CD database. When this information is found, the album name appears in the Disc Title text box, the artist name in the Artist Name text box, and the names of the individual tracks appear in the list box below.

   In front of each track name you find a check box containing a checkmark indicating that the track is now selected for adding to the project. If you don't want to add a particular track in the list added to the audio CD project, click its check box to remove this checkmark before proceeding to Step 3.

   If you're adding tracks from a folder such as the My Music folder, you can select multiple files by Ctrl+clicking their names.

3. **Drag the selected tracks down to the Audio CD Project window or click the Add the Selected Files Above to Project button.**

   Creator Classic adds the names of all the selected tracks to the Audio CD Project pane. After adding your tracks to the project, their names appear in the Audio CD Project pane along with the number of tracks and their total estimated playing time and the estimated amount of total free playing time still left on the disc appear on the status bar at the bottom Project pane.

   If you find that you've added a track that you don't really want to include on the final CD, click the track and then press the Delete key or click the Remove from Project button on the Audio CD Project pane's toolbar and then click the Yes button in the Warning dialog box that appears.

If you try to add a track that you've downloaded to your computer's hard disk for playback but for which you don't have permission to copy by burning to a CD or MP3 disc, the Error alert dialog box appears. If this Error dialog box appears for a track that you've downloaded from an online music store without actually purchasing, you can rectify this situation by going back to the store and buying the track. When you purchase a music track from most online music centers such as Napster, you obtain both the play and burn rights to the song (although the burn rights may not enable you to make unlimited copies — you need to check this with the particular store).

So too, if you try to add an audio file to the project that's recorded in a file format not supported by the Easy Media Creator (that is, any format besides MP3, OGG, WAV, or WMA), Creator Classic displays a Warning Unsupported Files alert dialog box that tells you that the file you're trying to add carries an unrecognized file extension and that it will not be added to your project. This is what would happen, for example, if you tried to add a track that you'd purchased from Apple's online iTunes Music Store that uses Apple's AAC audio file format with the .M4P filename extension that's not supported by the Roxio Easy Media Creator software.

Accessing the online music database

If the disc information including the album title, artist's name, and track titles for a particular audio CD doesn't show up in the Select Source pane when you click the disc's CD or DVD drive in the Window Explorer, you can try to have this information located and downloaded from the online Gracenote CDDB (CD Database). The Gracenote CDDB is the world's largest online database of music information (listing about two and a half million CDs with just a little over 33 million songs!).

To get the vital statistics on the album you have in your computer's CD or DVD drive, click the Get Audio CD Info from the Gracenote CDDB Online Music Database button on the Select Source toolbar or choose Tools➪Get Audio CD Info from CDDB on the Creator Classic menu bar. Creator Classic then connects you to the Internet and the Gracenote CDDB to look for the CD's ISRC (International Standard Code) number in this humongous database. When it finds a match to the album's IRSC number in the Gracenote CDDB, it then downloads the information to the Select Source pane in the Creator Classic window.

Listening to tracks before you add them

You can listen to tracks with Creator Classic before you add them to the audio CD project you're building. To do this, click the track in the Select Source pane to select and then press the Enter key. As soon as you press the Enter key, Creator Classic opens the Preview pane shown in Figure 7-2 on the left side of the Creator Classic window and starts playing the selected track. As you can see in this figure, the Preview pane contains its own playback controls with buttons modeled on those on a standard CD and DVD remote control. Beneath this controller, you find a slider that you can drag to manually advance or rewind the playback, along with a volume-control slider that you can drag to increase or reduce the volume.

Previous

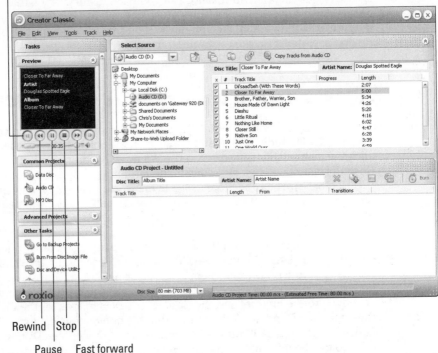

Figure 7-2:
Listening to
a track with
the Preview
pane before
adding it to
an audio CD
project.

Rewind Stop

Pause Fast forward

Rearranging tracks

When you add individual tracks from various sources that you copied on your computer's hard disk to your Audio CD Project (as opposed to a block of audio tracks from a single source such as a CD in your CD or DVD drive), Creator Classic automatically lists these tracks alphabetically by track title in the Project pane. You will not, however, always want to burn your audio CD with its tracks in this type of alphabetical order. More often than not, you'll end up arranging the tracks in the order in which you think you'd most prefer to listen to them (regardless of what havoc that inflicts upon the alphabetical track name order).

To modify the track order prior to burning the final audio CD disc, you need to drag the tracks in the Audio CD Project to their desired positions. To do this, click the track that you want to move to select it and then drag up or down to reposition it. As you drag, a dashed line appears right above the mouse pointer indicating where the track you're moving will be inserted if you release mouse button. Once you've positioned this dashed line in between the tracks in the Project pane where you want it to now appear, release the mouse button to move the selected track to that new position in the list. As soon as you release the mouse button, Creator Classic renumbers all the tracks to suit the new track order.

Although it is a little tedious to have to reposition each track in this manner, it is the only method that Creator Classic supports for rearranging the tracks you add so that they don't appear in alphabetical order by track name on the new CD.

Renaming tracks

Creator Classic enables you to rename the tracks that you add to your audio CD project. You might need to do this when Gracenote can't return the correct track name or when you're dealing with tracks that aren't registered with this database (as in the case of original music).

To rename one of the tracks, click its name in the Audio CD Project pane and press F2 (you can also do this by right-clicking the track name and then clicking the Rename item on the track's shortcut menu). Creator Classic then selects the track name within a text box waiting for you to make your changes to the name. To replace the name entirely, just start typing the new track name.

To edit the track name by inserting text, you can just click the Insertion point at the place in the track name where you need to start inserting characters. To delete just some of the characters in the name, drag through them with the arrowhead mouse pointer to select them and then press the Delete key. When you finish editing or replacing the track name, press the Enter key or click the mouse anywhere outside of the of the track name's text box.

Merging different tracks into one

Creator Classic makes it possible to merge the audio from different tracks that you've added to the Audio CD Project together so that they play as one continuous song track on the resulting CD that you burn. To merge song tracks, you simply Ctrl+click the tracks (if they're not sequential) in the Audio CD Project list or Shift+Click them (if they're sequentially listed in a block) and then choose Track⇨Merge Tracks on the Creator Classic menu bar or right-click the track selection and click Merge Tracks on its shortcut menu.

Creator Classic then joins the selected track together into one long track. This is indicated in the Project pane by the joining of the track titles so that the merged track now has a hyphenated track name (consisting of all the individual track names in the order in which you selected them for merging) and the presence of an Expand/Collapse button in front of the merged track. When you click the Expand button indicated by the plus sign (+), Creator

Classic expands to list the names of all the individual tracks of which it's now composed in outline form (see Figure 7-3). When you click the Collapse button (–) which replaces the Expand button, Creator Classic collapses the outline so that only the merged song track with its hyphenated track name is shown in the Audio CD Project pane.

Figure 7-3 illustrates the merging of two tracks in the track list of the Audio CD Project pane. For this particular example, I merged the first two tracks of Douglas Spotted Eagle's wonderful album, *Closer to Far Away*. I did this because the first track, "Dii'saad'beh (With These Words)" is actually a short introduction that flows quite naturally into the second song, "Closer to Far Away," the track that gives the album its name. When played as the merged track "Dii'saad'beh (With These Words)/ Closer to Far Away," there is no longer any gap between the end of the first song and the beginning of the second so that it plays one song (an edit which I think the producers of this album might well have made themselves in the studio when mixing this album).

In Figure 7-3, I've expanded the merged track by clicking its Expand button (+) so that the track names, track lengths, and sources of the two individual song tracks are now displayed in the track list in the Audio CD Project pane.

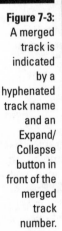

Figure 7-3: A merged track is indicated by a hyphenated track name and an Expand/ Collapse button in front of the merged track number.

After combining tracks into one merged track, you should listen to the merged track (to make sure you like the sound of it played back as one song). To do this, click the merged track name in the Audio CD Project pane and then press the Enter key. If you decide that it wasn't the greatest idea in the world to merge those particular individual tracks, you can split the merged track back into its individual tracks by choosing Track⇨Split Tracks on the Creator Classic menu bar or by right-clicking the merged track and then clicking Split Tracks on its short cut menu. Creator Classic immediately splits the merged track into its individual components, which are once again listed as individual tracks (with their original track names) in the Audio CD Project pane.

Adding audio transitions between tracks

You can control the types of transitions that occur between the song tracks in the list of tracks added to the Audio CD Project pane. When adding audio transitions between tracks, you can add a gap between the tracks that places so many seconds of silence between them or you can add a fade-in transition at the beginning of a track (so that the volume level gradually increases from silence to normal) and a fade-out transition at the end of the track (so that the volume level gradually decreases from normal to silence) of a particular duration of so many seconds.

To add an audio transition to a track that you've added to the Audio CD Project pane, follow these steps:

1. **Click the track to which you want to add some sort of audio transition in the Audio CD Project pane.**

   Now you're ready to open the Audio Transitions dialog box where you can select an audio transition for the start and end of the selected track.

2. **Click the Edit Track Transitions button on the Project pane's toolbar or choose Track⇨Transition Effects on the Creator Classic menu bar.**

   Creator Classic opens the Audio Transitions dialog box similar to the one shown in Figure 7-4. This dialog box shows a graphic display of the currently selected track beneath the Current Track drop-down list box. Below this graphic display of the track, you find two pairs of Play and Stop buttons, the first pair on the left side that you can use to start and stop playing the Start Transition you define and the other on the right that you can use to start and stop playing any End Transition that you define.

   Beneath the Play and Stop buttons, you find the controls for defining a Start Transition and a Stop Transition for the current track. When defining the Start Transition, you can select between a Fade-out at the end of the previous track and a Fade-in to the current track and set the number of seconds for the fade-out and fade-in effects, or you can choose between a Gap of silence and a Crossfade of so many seconds duration between the end of the previous track and the start of the current track.

   When defining the End Transition, you can select between a Fade-out at the end of the current track and a Fade-in to the next track and set the number of seconds for the fade-in and fade out effects, or you can choose between a Gap of silence and a Crossfade of so many seconds duration between the end of the current track and the start of the next track.

3. Select the desired Start Transition and/or End Transition effects and then test them with the appropriate pair of Play and Stop buttons.

Creator Classic depicts the particular fade-out, fade-in, gap, or cross-fade effects that you select in the graphic track display in the Audio Transitions dialog box. Fade-out effects appear as gray curves at the end of the track that extend from top to bottom of the track's thickness. Fade-in effects appear as gray curves at the beginning of the track that extend from the bottom to the top of the track's thickness. Gaps appear as gray spaces between the two tracks, and cross-fade effects appear as spaces in the color of the current track with tiny, vertical lines in the color of the preceding or following track.

Note that you can click the Apply to All button at the bottom of the Audio Transitions dialog box to apply the Start Transition and/or the End Transition you define to all the tracks listed in the Audio CD Project pane. Likewise, you can click the Clear All button to remove all start and end transitions between these tracks.

Be sure that you use the Start Transition Play and Stop buttons or the End Transition Play and Stop buttons to listen to the audio transitions to ensure that they are what you want on the CD you burn before go on to Step 4.

4. Click the OK button to apply your transitions to the current track and close the Audio Transitions dialog box.

Edit track transitions

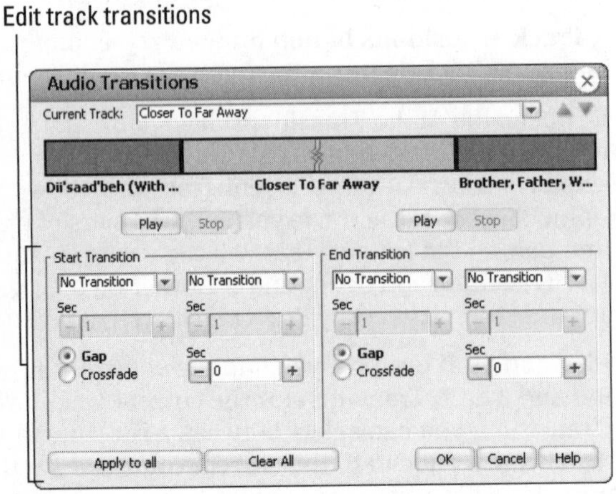

Figure 7-4:
You can use the controls in the Audio Transitions dialog box to add start and end transitions to the current track.

After you define start and end transitions for a track in the Audio Transitions dialog box, Creator Classic indicates their presence in the track listing in the Audio CD Project pane by representing the transition with back-to-back gray triangles (that together form a ramp with a gap between the triangles that Evel Knievel might want to jump) in the Transitions column of the track list.

To edit or remove an audio transition for a particular track in this listing in the Audio CD Project pane, you simply click the transition representation (the back-to-back triangles) for the track in question to open the Audio Transitions displaying its Start Transition and End Transition settings. To remove a particular transition, you select the No Transition setting in the appropriate Fade-in or Fade-out drop-down list box or reduce duration of the Gap or Crossfade effect to 0 in its particular Sec text box before you click the OK button.

Changing the Project and Track Settings

Prior to burning the tracks that you've added to the Audio CD Project pane, you can check and, if necessary, change the properties for the CD project. To do this, you open the Project Properties dialog box shown in Figure 7-6 by clicking the View and Edit Your Project Settings button on the Audio CD Project pane's toolbar, pressing Ctrl+R, or choosing File⇨Project Settings on the Creator Classic menu bar. A Project Properties dialog box appears.

The Project Properties dialog box contains two tabs, Audio and CD Text. The Audio lists the number of tracks and the total playing time. It also contains a UPC text box where you can enter the CD's 12-digit Universal Product Code if you've obtained one for your CD or are copying a CD and happen to know it. Beneath the UPC text box, you find the Normalize Audio (Applied at Time of Burn) check box. Click this check box when you've added audio tracks from different sources and want to have Creator Classic normalize their volume at the time that the tracks are burned onto the CD.

Beneath the Normalize Audio (Applied at Time of Burn) check box, you find the Automatically Save Artist/Title/Track Names After Recording check box that is automatically checked. When this box is checked, Creator Classic saves the artist, album name, and track names on your hard disk after burning the CD so that the next time you put the disc into your computer's CD or DVD drive to play it, these vital statistics will be available to the program you use to play the disc (such as the Windows Media Player or iTunes).

The CD Text tab of the Project Properties dialog box contains a list of different languages in which you can burn the CD Text at the beginning of the audio disc that contains the artist, title, and track names (many playback devices such as Walkman portable CD players can read this CD Text and show this information on the device's display screen). By default, only the English check box is selected, so this information is stored only in English. If you want to store this information in other languages (German, French, Spanish, Italian, or Dutch), click that language's check box on the CD Text tab before clicking the OK button to close the Project Properties dialog box.

In addition to getting information about the entire audio project you're creating, you can also get specific information on any track that you add to the Project pane. Simply right-click the track whose information you want displayed in the Audio CD Project pane and then click Properties at the bottom of the track's shortcut menu. When you do this, Creator Classic opens an Audio Track Properties dialog box.

The Audio Track Properties dialog box shows the selected track's track number and playing time along with the album's title, the artist's name, and the source on your computer for that track. In addition, beneath this information, you find an ISRC (International Standard Recording Code) text box where you can enter the 12-digit ISRC code for the track if you know it before you click the OK button to close the Audio Track Properties dialog box.

A music track's ISRC number serves as the recording's international identifier for the purposes of rights management. In other words, an ISRC number indicates who's entitled to the royalty payments for the distribution of that recording. If you're making a CD of your own music for distribution to various record companies and radio stations, you will definitely want to obtain ISRC numbers from an approved ISRC Agency and encode the tracks of the CD you're burning with Creator Classic for any type of distribution with those numbers.

Burning the CD

Once you've added all the tracks you want to your audio CD project and made any necessary adjustments to the tracks, including merging, audio transitions, track ISRC information, project settings, and the like, you're ready to burn the CD disc. Prior to starting the burn process, you may want to save your Audio CD Project so that you can use it again to burn future CDs. To save the project, press Ctrl+S or choose File➪Save Project on the Creator Classic menu bar; then select the appropriate folder and project name (Creator Classic automatically assigns .RCL file extension to all project files) in the Save As dialog box before you click the Save button.

To burn the audio project to CD, you then click the Burn button on the far right side of the Audio CD Project pane's toolbar or choose File➪Burn on the Creator Classic menu bar. Creator Classic then opens the Roxio Creator Classic - Burn Progress dialog box. To expand the dialog box so that this dialog box displays all of your options for burning the CD, you need to click the >>Details button in the lower-left corner of the dialog box.

Figure 7-5 shows the expanded version of the Burn Progress dialog box after clicking this button. In addition to the Project Summary and Device(s) Summary information, you also have access to the options offered in the Destinations, Record Methods, and Record Options areas as well.

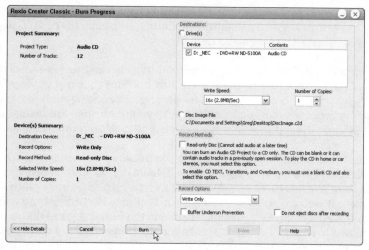

Figure 7-5:
Selecting
the settings
for burning
the CD
disc in the
expanded
Roxio
Creator
Classic -
Burn
Progress
dialog box.

The options that you can modify in these areas of the Burn Progress dialog box include:

- ✔ **Write Speed** drop-down list box may enable you to select another write speed (this depends upon what type of CD burner your computer is equipped with)

- ✔ **Number of Copies** text box to indicate the number of CD discs you want to burn

- ✔ **Disc Image File** option button to save a complete copy of the audio CD project on your hard disk which can then be burned to a CD disc at later time using Creator Classic

- ✔ **Read Only Disc (Cannot Add Data at a Later Time)** check box, which when selected prevents you from adding any more data files to this disc even when there's sufficient free space and you're using rewritable media (you must use this option if you want to be able to play your CD in standalone audio CD players such as the one in your car or on a portable Walkman-type player)

- ✔ **Record Options** drop-down to choose between Write Only to begin recording without doing any testing, Test Only to perform the recording test to determine whether or not files in the project can be successfully written to the disc, and Test and Write to perform the recording test and then, if the disc passes automatically, continue and burn the files to the disc

- ✔ **Buffer Underun Prevention** check box to enable or disable buffer prevention for your CD or DVD drive that creates a buffer in the memory to ensure that the data is recorded to the disc without any interruptions (note that check box will not be available when using an older CD recordable drive)

> ✔ **Do Not Eject Discs After Recording** check box to ensure or prevent Creator Classic from automatically ejecting each CD or DVD disc after it finishes recording all its data files

After making changes to any of these options in the Burn Progress dialog box, click the Burn button to begin recording burning your tracks. The Burn Progress dialog box then shows its progress in caching each of the tracks to your computer's hard disk (if the tracks you're burning are being taken from an existing CD and have not been copied onto your computer's hard disk).

After Creator Classic finishes caching the tracks from the existing CD, it then ejects that CD from your computer's CD-ROM drive and then displays an Insert Media dialog box that prompts you to insert a blank disc in its place. After you replace it with a blank disc and click the Continue Recording button in the Insert Media dialog box, the information in the Burn Progress dialog box is then updated to Disc 1 of 1, which shows you the progress of the data recording both in terms of the tracks and overall disc-recording progress. This updated Burn Progress dialog box contains a Start Label Creator button that you can click to launch the Label Creator application for creating a custom label for your new audio CD after its recording is completed (see Chapter 9 for details).

If you don't want to make a label for your new audio CD after all the tracks are burned onto it and Creator Classic ejects the disc, simply click the Close button to close the Roxio Creator Classic - Burn Progress dialog box and return to the Creator Classic window.

Creating an MP3 Disc Project

If you have a standalone or portable CD or DVD player capable of playing MP3 discs, instead of using Creator Classic to start an audio CD Project for burning standard audio CDs, you can start an MP3 disc project and burn an MP3 audio disc. The benefit of creating an MP3 audio disc instead of a standard CD is clear: because MP3 discs are composed only of audio files saved in the MPEG3 compressed file format, you can fit many, many more song tracks on your average MP3 disc than you ever can on a standard audio CD composed of tracks saved in the uncompressed WAVE file formats.

To start a new MP3 Disc Project from the Easy Media Creator Home window, click the Create New MP3 Disc link in the Music column of the Tasks area. To start a new MP3 Disc Project in Creator Classic, click the MP3 Disc link in the Common Projects area of the Tasks pane. Creator Classic then starts a new untitled MP3 Disc Project that contains a default playlist called (appropriately enough) PLAYLIST (see Figure 7-6).

Import data from appendable disc

Remove from project

Up one level

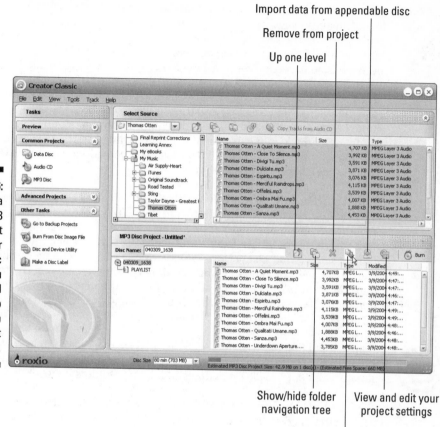

Figure 7-6:
Starting a
new MP3
Disc Project
in Creator
Classic
where you
can add
MP3 files to
folders in
the default
PLAYLIST.

Show/hide folder
navigation tree

View and edit your
project settings

Add selected files to project

After starting a new MP3 Disc Project, you can edit the volume name of the new disc and rename the default playlist. To change the volume name of the disc, click the Disc Name text box; then edit the default numeric name that Creator Classic assigns the disc and when finished, click somewhere outside of this text box. To rename the playlist, click PLAYLIST in the Folder Navigation Tree in the MP3 Disc Project pane to open the Playlist Editor dialog box and then replace PLAYLIST in the Playlist File Name text box before you click the OK button.

Adding MP3 files to a new MP3 Disc Project is much the same process as adding tracks to an Audio CD Project (simply select the files in the Select Source pane with Windows Explorer and then drag them into the MP3 Disc Project pane or click the Add Selected Files Above to Project button on the MP3 Disc Project pane's toolbar). The big difference is that instead of just adding individual songs as you do with an Audio CD Project, you can add entire folders of MP3 files to the Playlist (simply by dragging the folder from the Select Source pane down to MP3 Disc Project pane below the Playlist icon).

MP3 Disc Projects balk at any attempt to add anything but MP3 files. If you select an audio file saved in any other file format (WAVE, WMA, or OGG) and try to add it to the MP3 Disc Project pane, Creator Classic displays a Warning: Unsupported Files alert dialog box indicating that one or more files being added has an unrecognized file extension (that is, other than .MP3) and that these files will not be added to your MP3 disc project. If the audio file is saved as a WAVE file on an audio CD that you own, you can rip its track as MP3 files (see the sidebar that follows) and then add it to the MP3 Disc Project. If the audio file you want to add is saved on your hard disk and you have the burn rights to the track, you can open it in Sound Editor and then use its File⇔Save As command to save it as an MP3 file that you can add to your MP3 Disc Project (see Chapter 5 for details).

Note that when adding individual MP3 files to the MP3 Disc Project pane, you can create a new folder in which to add them. To create a new folder in the MP3 Disc Project pane, right-click the disc icon in the Navigation Tree and then click New Folder on its shortcut menu. Creator Classic then adds a new folder named (what else?) New Folder (which you can rename by clicking and then pressing F2 or right-clicking and then clicking Rename on the folder's shortcut menu). You can then add MP3 files to the new folder by clicking its icon in the Navigation Tree before you select and add individual MP3 files or groups of MP3 files in the Select Source pane.

Keep in mind that many simple MP3 disc players can't play tracks that you put into folders. When in doubt, keep all the tracks in the MP3 project in the root directory under PLAYLIST and don't add them to folders beneath this root level.

As you add MP3 files to your MP3 disc project, Creator Classic keeps track of them in the Playlist. To open the playlist to review or change the order of the songs in the playlist, click (no need to right-click) the playlist icon (named PLAYLIST until you rename it) in the Navigation Tree. Creator Classic then opens the Playlist Editor dialog box for the MP3 disc project similar to the one shown in Figure 7-7.

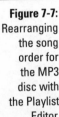

Figure 7-7:
Rearranging
the song
order for
the MP3
disc with
the Playlist
Editor.

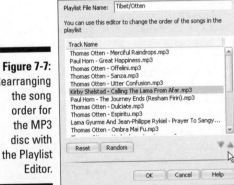

Ripping MP3 files from audio CDs with Creator Classic

Remember that you can use Creator Classic to rip tracks from the audio CDs that you own so that you can then, in turn, add them to an MP3 Disc Project that you create with the program. To rip MP3 from an audio CD, insert the CD into your computer's CD or DVD drive; then select that drive's letter in the Creator Classic's Select Source pane with the Windows Explorer and click the Copy Tracks from Audio CD button to open the Copy Tracks from Audio CD - Options dialog box. You can then designate the folder into which to copy the ripped MP3 tracks and adjust the compression slider for better quality audio or smaller MP3 files before clicking the Start button to start ripping the tracks. After Creator Classic finishes ripping the MP3 files, you can then add them to your MP3 Disc Project for burning onto a new MP3 disc.

You can use the controls in the Playlist Editor to arrange the order in which the MP3 normally plays in the final MP3 disc you burn. If you want a truly random order for the songs, simply click the Random button. If you want to manually determine where a particular song appears in the playlist, you can either drag its filename up or down the list or click the song filename and then click the Promote button (the one with triangle pointing upward) or Demote button (the one with the triangle pointing downward) to move the song up or down to the desired position.

After adding all the MP3 files that you want (or can fit) onto a new disc and arranging them in the order in which you want them to normally play, you're ready to burn the CD. To do this, you click the Burn button on the right side of the MP3 Disc Project pane's toolbar or choose File⇨Burn Project on the Creator Classic menu bar (see "Burning the CD" earlier in this chapter for details on the process of burning a new CD disc).

Creating an Enhanced CD

An Enhanced CD is a type of multi-session CD that combines data and audio together. The first session on the CD contains audio tracks (such as you add to a standard Audio CD Project — see "Creating an Audio CD Project" earlier in this chapter for details). The second session contains the data file such as you might add to a standard Data Disc Project in Creator Classic — see Chapter 3 for details).

When you play an Enhanced CD disc in a standalone CD player (such as the one in your car or a Walkman-type portable unit), the player plays the music session so that you can listen to its music tracks as you would any other audio CD. When, however, you play an Enhanced CD disc in your computer's CD-ROM or DVD drive, you cannot only play its music tracks with a software program such as the Windows Media Player, but you also have access to its data portion with the appropriate software program.

Enhanced CDs are a perfect solution when you've created an MTV-type music video (see Chapter 10 for details) that you want to package along with a bunch of music tracks. You can then add the music tracks to the first audio session and the music video file to the second data session of the Enhanced CD Project and then burn them together on a CD disc for distribution to friends, family, and, yes, that MTV producer who's about to discover you.

To start a new Enhanced CD Project, launch Creator Classic; then click the Advanced Projects Expand button (the one with two arrowheads pointing downward) in the Tasks pane on the left side of the Creator Classic window to display its three options and finally, click the Enhanced CD link at the top of the Advanced Projects area.

Creator Classic opens a new untitled Enhanced CD Project as shown in Figure 7-8. As you can see in this figure, in the Enhanced CD Project pane, two icons, an Audio Project and Data Disc icon (indicated by the numeric volume name) appear immediately below the Enhanced CD icon in the Navigation Tree. You add your audio tracks to the Audio Project portion of this tree (see "Adding audio tracks to your project" earlier in this chapter) and you then add your folders and data files to the Data Disc portion of the tree below (see Chapter 3).

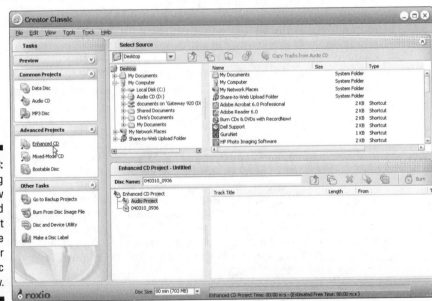

Figure 7-8:
Starting
a new
Enhanced
CD Project
in the
Creator
Classic
window.

After you finish adding your music tracks and data files to your Enhanced CD Project, you can save the project with the File⇨Save command and then burn the CD by clicking the Burn button on the Enhanced CD Project pane's toolbar or by choosing File⇨Burn on the Creator Classic menu bar (see "Burning the CD" earlier in this chapter for details on the burn process).

Creating a Mixed-CD

Like an Enhanced CD, a Mixed-mode CD also combines data files and music tracks on the same CD disc. Unlike the Enhanced CD, however, the Mixed-mode CD records both the computer data and music tracks in a single session and therefore can only be played back in your computer's CD or DVD drive using the appropriate software such as the Windows Media Player. Mixed-mode CDs are typically used to create multi-media projects for learning or entertainment (game) purposes that you can enjoy exclusively on the computer.

To start a new Mixed-Mode CD Project, launch Creator Classic; then click the Advanced Projects Expand button (the one with two arrowheads pointing downward) in the Tasks pane on the left side of the Creator Classic window to display its three options, and finally click the Mixed-Mode CD link in the middle of the Advanced Projects area.

Creator Classic opens a new untitled Mixed-Mode CD Project as shown in Figure 7-9. As you can see in this figure, in the Mixed-Mode CD Project pane two icons, a Data Disc icon (indicated by the numeric volume name) and an Audio Project icon appear immediately below the Mixed-Mode CD icon in the Navigation Tree. You add your folders and data files to the Data Disc portion of the tree (see Chapter 3) and then add your audio tracks to the Audio Project portion below (see "Adding audio tracks to your project" earlier in this chapter).

After you finish adding your data files and your music tracks to your Mixed-Mode CD Project, you can save the project with the File⇨Save command and then burn the CD by clicking the Burn button on the Mixed-Mode CD Project pane's toolbar or by choosing File⇨Burn on the Creator Classic menu bar (see "Burning the CD" earlier in this chapter for details on the burn process).

Figure 7-9:
Starting a
new Mixed-
mode CD
Project in
the Creator
Classic
window.

Copying an Audio CD

Although CD discs are long lived, they are by no means indestructible (see the end of Chapter 2 for information on the proper care and feeding of your CD and DVD discs). For that reason, you will be well-served to use the Roxio Disc Copier to make copies of the audio CDs and MP3 discs that you burn with Creator Classic.

To launch the Roxio Disc Copier application from the Easy Media Creator Home, click the Copy Audio CD link at the very top of the Music column of the upper Tasks area. You can also launch this application by clicking the Disc Copier link at the very top of the Applications column in the Home window. If you don't have the Easy Media Creator Home window open, you can launch this program by clicking the Start button on the Windows taskbar, highlighting All Programs on the Start menu and then Roxio on the All Programs submenu before you click Disc Copier on the Roxio submenu.

When you launch the Disc Copier application, the Roxio Disc Copier alert dialog box appears, warning you that unless you own the copyright to the material on the CD or have explicit permission to copy the disc from the copyright owner, you're in danger of violating copyright law and are subject to paying damages. You can go ahead and click the OK button to dismiss this alert box (on the presumption that you have said permission to burn the songs onto the original CD or MP3 disc). After you get rid of this annoying alert dialog box, the Roxio Disc copier window shown in Figure 7-10 appears.

Figure 7-10:
You can
make
backup
copies of
the CDs you
burn in
Creator
Classic with
the Roxio
Disc Copier
application.

With the audio CD or MP3 disc that you want to copy in your CD or DVD
drive (and a new blank disc on which to make the copy at hand), you can
then go ahead and click the Copy button on the right side of the Roxio Disc
Copier window to start the copy process. (For complete details on using the
Roxio Disc Copier, refer to the final section in Chapter 3.)

Chapter 8

Creating Disc Labels
and Case Inserts

In This Chapter

▶ The many ways of launching the Label Creator tool

▶ Choosing the proper disc template and disc project theme

▶ Automating the process of getting album and disc information for the new label

▶ Editing the image, graphic, and text objects in your label project

▶ Printing disc labels and case inserts

▶ Applying adhesive labels properly so you don't ruin your discs

*T*he Label Creator tool in the Roxio Easy Media Creator 7 Suite makes it a snap to create professional-looking disc labels, covers, booklet inserts and jewel case inserts for the audio CDs, MP3 discs, and DVD discs that you burn with various Easy Media Creator programs including Drag-to-Disc, Disc Copier, Creator Classic, and DVD Creator.

As you find out in this chapter, Label Creator makes the job of creating disc labels so easy through the combination of its standard templates and Smart Objects and Auto-Fill features that automate the filling in of vital information on the contents of your disc. This contents information can come either directly from the Gracenote CDDB in the case of audio CDs or from the Creator Classic and DVD Builder projects (see Chapters 3, 8, and 12) which you use in burning the discs in the case of both audio and DVD discs.

This chapter also covers how Label Creator can make short work of designing CD and DVD case covers, booklet inserts, and jewel case inserts. When designing these types of case inserts, you can make use the Smart Objects and Auto-Fill features you use to fill in disc label content as well as apply the same or new graphic themes. Finally, you find out how to print the labels and case inserts you create with Label Creator and how to properly apply the labels you print to the CD and DVD discs you burn.

Getting Familiar with the Label Creator Window

You can launch the Label Creator tool from Roxio Easy Media Creator Home window by clicking the Label Creator link in the Tools column. If the Home window is not open, launch the program from the Windows taskbar by clicking the Start button, then highlighting All Programs on the Start menu and Roxio on the All Programs submenu before clicking Label Creator on the Roxio submenu.

Figure 8-1 shows the Roxio Label Creator window that then opens. As you can see in this figure, this window contains two major panes:

✔ **Tasks** pane on the left side composed of the Edit Layout, Add Object, Tools, and Properties palettes, each containing the various tools you need in designing a new disc label and case inserts

✔ **Layout** pane on the right side that displays a preview of the disc label or case insert that you're currently designing

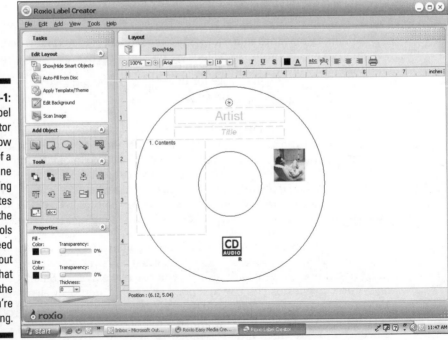

Figure 8-1:
The Label Creator window consists of a Tasks pane containing four palettes with the design tools you need and a Layout pane that previews the layout you're editing.

The Edit Layout palette

As you can see in Figure 8-1, the Tasks pane of the Label Creator window contains a whole bunch of design tools arranged into four palettes. The first one at the top of the Tasks pane is the Edit Layout palette consisting of the following links that you can click to perform common tasks for designing your disc labels and case inserts:

- **Show/Hide Smart Objects** link to display and hide the Show/Hide Smart Objects dialog box where you can select which type of information (such as Title, Track List, Disc Type, and so on) about the audio or data disc to include on the disc label on case inserts you're designing for the disc in Label Creator

- **Auto-Fill from Disc** link to add the name of the album, artist, and track list for the CD that you're burning or you have inserted into your computer's CD-ROM or DVD drive

- **Apply Template/Theme** link to open the Apply Template/Theme dialog box where you can select the type of layout template to use for the type of disc label you're creating (Audio, Backup, Game, MP3, Photos, Videos, and so on) and/or a graphic theme to apply to the design of both the label and the case inserts you're creating in Label Creator

- **Edit Background** link to open the Edit Smart Objects dialog box where you can select an image or a color to use for the background of the label or case insert you're currently designing in Label Creator

- **Scan Image** link to open a Scan dialog box where you can use your scanner to scan in a new image for use in the disc label or case inserts you're designing in Label Creator (if you get an error message when you click the Scan Image link, choose File➪Select Device on the Label Creator menu bar and make sure that your scanner is selected in the Select Source dialog box before you click this link again)

The Add Object palette

The Add Object palette (shown in Figure 8-2) contains the five following tools that you can use when you need to add images to or draw specific shapes in the disc labels or case inserts that you're creating in Label Creator. Label Creator recognizes three different types of objects that you can add to and manipulate in the labels and case inserts you're designing:

- **Image objects** which are graphics or photo images stored in separate files that you can bring into the label project

- **Graphic objects** which are rectangular or oval shapes or straight lines that you can size and place in the label project

✔ **Text objects** which are blocks of text inside text boxes that you can size and position on the label project

The Add Object palette contains the following buttons for adding image, graphic, or text objects to your label project:

✔ **Add an Image to the Current Layout** button to open the Add dialog box where you can select the file containing the graphic or photo image you want to add as an image object to the disc label or case insert you're designing in Label Creator

✔ **Add Rectangle Object** button to add a new rectangular graphic object to the disc label or case insert you're designing in Label Creator

✔ **Add Circle Object** button to add a new circular graphic object to the disc label or case insert you're designing in Label Creator

✔ **Add Line Object** button to add a straight line as a new graphic object to the disc label or case insert you're designing in Label Creator

✔ **Add Text Object** button to add a text object to the disc label or case insert you're designing in Label Creator where you can enter text that you want to appear on the label or insert

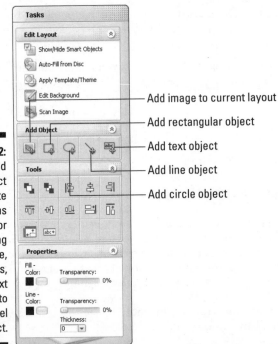

Figure 8-2:
The Add Object palette contains tools for adding image, graphics, and text objects to your label project.

Add image to current layout

Add rectangular object

Add text object

Add line object

Add circle object

The Tools palette

The Tools palette contains a whole cartload of useful stacking and alignment tools (see Figure 8-3) that you can use to control which image, graphic, or text objects are front and which are behind the others as well as how selected objects are aligned on the disc label or case insert layout you're editing. The buttons on the Tools palette include:

✔ **Bring Object to Front** button to bring the object you select in front all of the other objects that cover it in some way

✔ **Send Object to Back** button to place the object you select in back all of the other objects that its covers in some way

✔ **Align Selected Objects Left** button to left-align all the selected objects with the object you last select

✔ **Center Selected Objects Vertically** button to center all the selected objects on the vertical centerline of the disc label or case insert you're currently designing

✔ **Align Selected Objects Right** button to right-align all the selected objects with the object you last select

✔ **Align Selected Objects Top** button to align all the tops of the selected objects with the top of the object you last select

✔ **Center Selected Objects Horizontally** button to center all the selected objects on the horizontal centerline of the disc label or case insert you're currently designing

✔ **Align Selected Objects Bottom** button to align all the bottoms of the selected objects with the bottom of the object you last select

✔ **Match Object Width** button to match the width of all the selected objects to that of the object you last select

✔ **Match Object Height** button to match the height of all the selected objects to that of the object you last select

✔ **Match Object Width and Height** button to match the width and height of all the selected objects to that of the object you last select

✔ **Size to Text** button to resize the text box of a text graphic object so that all of its text is displayed

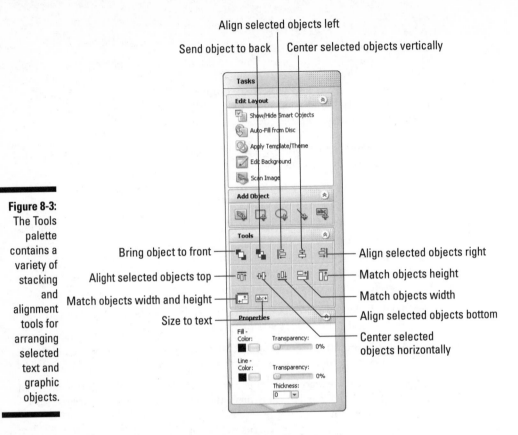

Figure 8-3:
The Tools palette contains a variety of stacking and alignment tools for arranging selected text and graphic objects.

The Properties palette

The Properties palette at the very bottom of the Tasks pane on the left side of the Label Creator window contains just two tools for selecting the fill color and outline color and thickness for selected image and graphic objects in the layout you're editing:

- ✔ **Fill-Color** button and Transparency slider to select the fill color and opacity for either the image or graphic objects that are currently selected in the label project

- ✔ **Line-Color** button, Transparency slider, and Thickness drop-down list box to select the outline color, opacity, and thickness for the graphic objects that are currently selected in the label project

Note that Fill-Color and Line-Color controls have no effect on any text objects that are selected in the layout at the time you change their settings.

Instant Disc Labels and Case Inserts

Label Creator 7 supports an Instant Label Creator Mode which enables you to whip up new disc labels, case inserts, and booklets in a jiff. You can access the Instant Label Creator Mode by clicking the Start Label Creator button in any Burn Progress dialog box or by choosing Tools⇨Instant Label Creator Mode from the Label Creator menu bar within the Label Creator window itself.

Label Creator responds by displaying the first page of the Instant Label Creator in the dialog box shown in Figure 8-4. Here, you select the type of layout(s) that you want to create by clicking the appropriate check box or boxes:

- ✔ **Disc** to create a standard CD or DVD disc label (the default already checked whenever you open the Instant Label Creator dialog box)

- ✔ **Mini Disc** to create a disc label for the smaller 3-inch diameter mini-CD (sometimes called a micro-CD)

- ✔ **Front** to design the front cover insert for a CD jewel case

- ✔ **Slim Case Insert** to create the front cover insert for a slim CD jewel case

- ✔ **Back** to create to the back cover insert for a CD jewel case

- ✔ **DVD Case** to create a front, back, and spine cover insert for a DVD case

- ✔ **Booklet** to create the front and back of a booklet insert for a CD jewel case

- ✔ **DVD Booklet** to create the front and back of a booklet insert for a DVD case

After you select all the check boxes for the layouts you want to include in the new label project and click the Next button, the second page of the Instant Label Creator similar to the one shown in Figure 8-5 appears. Here, you can select the template that you want to use for the selected layout in the Template drop-down list box and any theme that you want to apply to the entire label project in the Theme drop-down list box. In addition, you can indicate which Smart Objects to use in the new label project by selecting or deselecting their check boxes.

Click the Auto-Fill from Disc link that you find on the lower-right side of the Instant Label Creator dialog box to have Label Creator retrieve the information for the Smart Objects that are checked in this dialog box from the audio or data disc that's currently in your computer's CD-ROM or DVD drive. Label Creator then adds the appropriate statistics such as the album name, artist name, and track titles to the Preview section of the Instant Label Creator dialog box, depending upon which particular template and layout are selected.

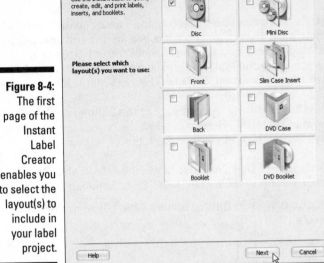

Figure 8-4:
The first page of the Instant Label Creator enables you to select the layout(s) to include in your label project.

Figure 8-5:
The second page of the Instant Label Creator enables you to select the template, theme, and the Smart Objects to apply to your label project.

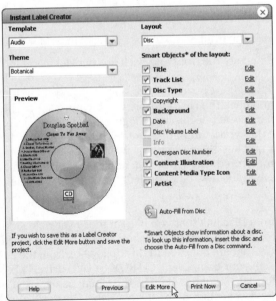

Note that you can edit any of the Smart Objects that you select in the Smart Objects of the Layout section of the second page of the Instant Label Creator by clicking the Edit link that appears after its name. For example, suppose that you want to replace the default CD Audio R icon that automatically appears at the bottom of a new disc label using the Audio template with CD Audio RW (because you've burned an audio disc that is rewritable). To make this change, you click the Edit link following the Disc Type check box to open the Edit Smart Objects dialog box (shown in Figure 8-6) where you click the CD_audio_RW.png graphic file in the Disc Type list box before clicking the OK button.

Figure 8-6:
Selecting a
new Disc
Type icon
for your
label project
in the Edit
Smart
Objects
dialog box.

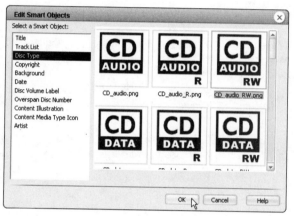

If you selected more than one layout check box in the dialog box with the first page of the Instant Label Creator, you can use the Layout drop-down list box on the second page to select any of those layouts. You can modify the theme for that particular layout or edit a particular Smart Object that the layout uses.

When you finish editing the elements for the different layouts in your label project in the second page of the Instant Label Creator, you can print the label project by clicking the Print Now button. If you want to save your label project and perhaps review its contents, checking for any further editing changes that you might need to do in the Label Creator's Layout pane, click the Edit More button to close the Instant Label Creator dialog box and return to the Label Creator window.

Always save your label project when you return to the Label Creator window so that you can reuse it if you later make more copies of the same CD or DVD disc. To save a label project, choose File⇨Save Project on the Label Creator menu bar or press Ctrl+S and then select the appropriate folder and filename (Label Creator automatically adds the .JWL extension to it) in the Save As dialog box before you click the Save button.

Editing Elements of the Label Project

Chances are that even after editing the contents of the layouts you select in the second page of the Instant Label Creator, you will still want to make some modifications to the layouts of the disc label and case inserts in your label project. As you see in Figure 8-7, you can do your further editing in Label Creator's Layout pane using both the two rows of buttons at the top of the Layout pane and the many controls in the Tasks pane (see "Getting Familiar with the Label Creator Window" earlier in this chapter for details on the controls in the Tasks pane).

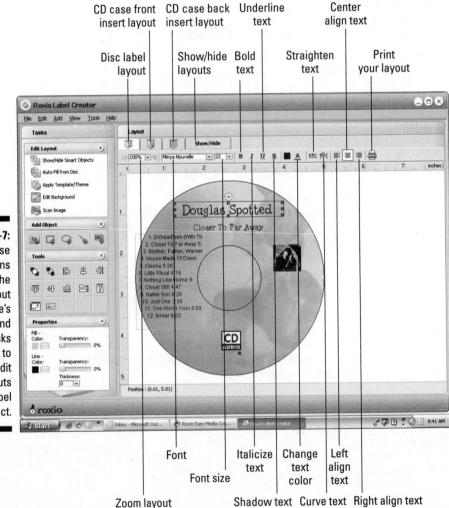

Figure 8-7: You can use the buttons on the Layout pane's toolbar and the Tasks pane to further edit the layouts in your label project.

CD case front insert layout

CD case back insert layout

Underline text

Center align text

Disc label layout

Show/hide layouts

Bold text

Straighten text

Print your layout

Font

Italicize text

Change text color

Left align text

Font size

Zoom layout

Shadow text

Curve text

Right align text

Displaying the layout you want to edit

The top row of buttons on the Layout pane enables you to display and edit the different layouts that you've included in your label project. The tab buttons that appear on this row depend upon which layouts you select for the label project on the first page of the Instant Label Creator dialog box.

For the particular example shown in Figure 8-7, I included three layouts in the label project: Disc, Front, and Back. Label Creator therefore created three tab buttons: Disc Label Layout, CD Case Front Insert Layout, and CD Case Back Insert Layout to jump to and display the Disc, Front, and Back layout, respectively.

Note that the Show/Hide Layouts button at the end of the first row is always displayed at the end of the first row of buttons regardless of which layout buttons you have. You click this button to display the Show/Hide Layouts dialog box. This dialog box includes all the disc label and case insert layouts that you selected from on the first page of the Instant Label Creator and enables you to add to or remove layouts from the current project that you're editing.

Editing the text objects in your layouts

The second row of buttons across the top of the Layout pane mostly enables you to make modifications to the text objects in your layouts. However, the very first button enables you to select zoom in and out on the layout you're editing by selecting a new magnification setting, and the very last button enables you to layout you're editing (or all the layouts in the label project, if you so desire).

The rest of the tools on this second row are used in modifying the text objects that you have selected in the layout you're editing. Most of these tools are the standard ones you're probably familiar with from using them in your word processing program. For example, you use the Font drop-down list box to select a new font for the selected text objects and the Font Size drop-down list box to select a new font size. So too, you click the Bold Text button to add or remove the boldface enhancement in the selected text objects, the Italicize Text button to add or remove italics, the Underline Text to add or remove underlining, and the Shadow Text to add or remove the shadow text enhancement (note that you can only apply the shadow enhancement to certain fonts).

The Change Text Color button enables you to select a new color for the text in the text objects you've selected by clicking its color square in the pop-up palette that appears when you click the button (you can also create new colors for the text using the Eyedropper tool, the Hue and/or Shades mixing boxes, or by entering new Red, Green, and Blue values or new Hue, Saturation, and Value percentages). You can use the Left Align Text, Center Text, and Right Align Text buttons to modify the text alignment within the text boxes of the selected text objects. Note that Center Text option is the default for all new text objects and that Label Creator automatically adjusts the text using whatever alignment option you select when you modify the size and shape of text object's text box.

The only two buttons that are definitely not standard in word processing programs are the Straighten Text and Curve Text buttons. These buttons are great, however, when editing the layout for your disc labels. Because of the round nature of disc labels, it often makes sense to put text like the album and artist's name on a curve rather than on a straight line.

To curve a particular text object in the Disc Label Layout, click the text object or objects (Ctrl+Click to select more than one) and then click the Curve Text button. After curving the text box of a particular text object, you can then rotate that text box around the disc label (Label Creator will modify the text to suit the new orientation on the disc). If you decide that a particular text object doesn't look so hot on the curve, you can convert it back to a standard text box with straight text by clicking the Straighten Text button.

When it comes to the text objects that contain track lists (automatically generated by clicking the Auto-Fill from Smart Objects link in the second page of the Instant Label Creator dialog box or by choosing Tools⇨Auto-Fill Smart Objects from Disc on the Label Creator menu bar), Label Creator automatically left-aligns their text in their text boxes. Further in the Disc Label Layout, the program also automatically indents the list to fit the curve of the label (both the curve of the inside hole and that of the outer diameter) when you position this list on the left or right side of the disc label.

Figure 8-8 shows my edited disc label after making modifications to all of its text objects. In this example, I used the Curve Text button to put both the album and artist name on the bias at the top of the label (I also used the Bold button to boldface their text and the Font drop-down list box to change the font from Minya Nouvelle to Arial). For the text object containing the track list, I manually resized its text box after selecting Arial Narrow in the Font drop-down list and reducing the font from 9 to 8 points by selecting 8 in the Font Size drop-down list. Then I dragged this text object to its final position on the right side of the label, making sure that all of the track list information was now displayed.

Remember that instead of having to manually resize each text box to suit a font or font size change, you can have Label Creator automatically do this for you by clicking the Size to Text button in the Tools palette in Tasks pane.

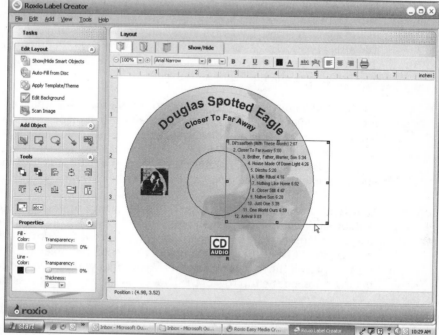

Figure 8-8:
The Disc
Label Layout
after editing
its text
objects with
the tools at
the top of
the Layout
pane.

Editing the image and graphic objects in your layouts

When editing the layouts for the disc label and case inserts in your label project, you may well have to edit their image and graphic objects. Remember that image objects contain any graphics files that you add to the layouts, whereas graphic objects are composed of the rectangles, circular shapes, and straight lines that you insert with the Add Rectangle Object, Add Circle Object, and Add Line Object tools on the Add Object palette.

When you click an image or graphic object in the layout, Label Creator indicates that it is selected by placing sizing handles around the perimeter of the object. You can then drag these sizing handles to make the selected image or graphic object larger or smaller.

To reposition the image or graphic object that you've selected, position the mouse pointer in the middle of the selected image or graphic and then use the hand pointer to drag the object to the desired position in the current layout.

The sizing and moving of line graphic objects present a little different story from all the rest. To select a line graphic for resizing, click one of its two ends to add a gray resizing handle. Then position the arrowhead mouse pointer over that sizing handle and drag the mouse (the pointer then becomes a hand) until the line is longer or shorter (you can also rotate the line around the opposite, unselected end which remains stationary).

To reposition a line graphic, drag the mouse to draw a bounding box around the line to select both ends. One end of the line then displays a gray sizing handle, while the other end displays a white repositioning handle. You position the arrowhead mouse pointer over the white repositioning handle and then drag the mouse (the pointer then becomes a hand) to move the entire line graphic object to the desired position in the current layout.

You can also delete and cut or copy a selected image or graphic object to the Windows Clipboard. To delete the object, press the Delete key. To cut the image (for later pasting in other layout), press Ctrl+X. To copy the object instead, press Ctrl+C. To paste the object you've cut or copied to the Clipboard in a new part of the layout (or another layout that you've selected by clicking its tab button on the top row of the Label Creator window), press Ctrl+V.

Keep in mind when editing the images and graphics in a particular layout that you can also select a new background image or color to use in that layout by clicking the Edit Background link in the Edit Layout palette in the Tasks pane. Label Creator then opens the Edit Smart Objects dialog box with the Background object selected (any color or image you select in this dialog box overrides any background graphic supplied to the current layout by the theme you've applied to the entire label project).

To add a new background color, click the color in the color palette in the Edit Smart Objects dialog box or click the More Colors button and create a custom color in the More Colors dialog box. To add a new background image instead, click the Use the Following Image as Background Image check box in the Edit Smart Objects dialog box and then click the Browse button. Label Creator then opens the Add dialog box where you can select the folder and graphics file that contains the image you want displayed as the background of the layout you're editing.

Figure 8-9 shows you my sample disc label in the Label Creator's Layout pane after modifying the two image objects: the one of the album cover that serves as the Content Illustration on the left side (this scanned image replaces the stock photo of the guy sitting in the chair listening to music with his headphones) and the default Disc Type graphic that identifies the disc as the CD Audio R type. I resized the Content Illustration so that it matches as closely as possible the size of the track list and then repositioned this image on the left side of the disc label. I then resized the Disc Type image, although I left it in its original position at the bottom of the label.

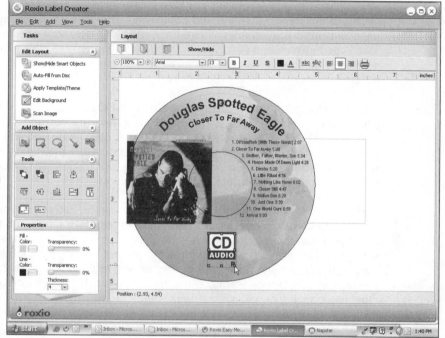

Figure 8-9:
Sample disc
label in
the Layout
pane after
resizing and
reposition-
ing its image
objects.

TIP

If you decide that you want to replace a particular image object in the layout, double-click the object. Doing this causes Label Creator to open the Edit Smart Objects dialog box with that image's smart object already selected. You can then use the controls in this dialog box to select the replacement graphic.

Printing Disc Labels and Case Inserts

After you have all the layouts in your label project edited the way you want them, you're ready to print the project (after you saved your changes with Ctrl+S, of course). Before you actually send the project to the printer, it's always a good idea to use the program's Print Preview feature to check each layout in the project and make sure that every detail is exactly as you want it (remember, generally speaking you're wasting special, fairly expensive paper with the adhesive disc labels and perforations for the case inserts and not just regular cheapo paper if you print your layouts with errors).

To check the layouts with Print Preview, click the tab button for the first layout at the top of the Layout pane and then choose File➪Print Preview on the Label Creator menu bar. Label Creator opens the first layout (usually the one with the disc label) in the Print Preview window (shown in Figure 8-10). You can then use the buttons in the Print Preview toolbar to display the next and previous pages (Next and Prev) in the project, zoom in and out on details in the layout (Zoom In and Zoom Out), or even switch between two-page and single-page displays (Two Page and One Page, which replaces the Two Page button when you click it). Note that you can also click a particular section of the layout with the Magnifying Glass mouse pointer to zoom in on it in the display.

When you finish checking your layouts in Print Preview, you can load your printer with special label paper and then click the Print button to open the Print dialog box and then send the job to the printer. If you find some details that need further modification or you want to check the page setup settings before you print the project, click the Close button to close the Print Preview window and to return to the Label Creator window.

Because you want to use special paper in printing the different layouts in a typical label project (high-gloss adhesive label paper for labels and matte finish perforated paper for case inserts), you often need to change the page settings before printing each layout in the project separately, each time putting the right paper into your printer as well as making sure that you've put the paper in the right way (some printers want the glossy side of the label paper facing down, while others want it facing up).

Figure 8-10:
Checking the layouts in your label project in the Print Preview window.

Open the Page Setup dialog box (shown in Figure 8-11) where you can select the Paper Type to use in printing each layout in the label project as well as make any necessary adjustments to where the printing starts. To select a different paper type besides Generic (plain paper), the default setting for all the layouts in your project, click the Current Paper Type drop-down list button for that layout and select the type and size of paper you're using (this list contains a wide range of paper types and sizes from different manufacturers). To select a new layout for which to select a new paper type, click that layout's tab at the top of the Page Setup dialog box (click the button at the right of the last tab with the blue triangle pointing right to display more tabs for the other layouts in your label project).

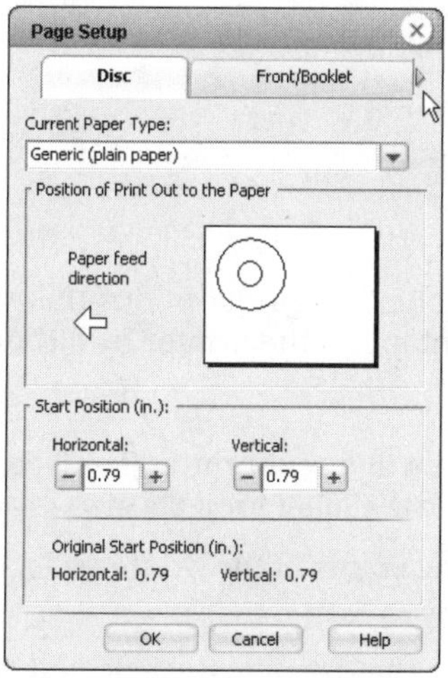

Figure 8-11:
Modifying
the Paper
Type and
Start
Position
settings
in the
Page Setup
dialog box.

The Page Setup dialog box also enables you to adjust the start positioning of the printout on the particular paper you select. To adjust how far the printing starts from the left edge of the paper (relative to the orientation of the diagram of the sheet shown in the Position to Print Out to the Paper area of the Page Setup dialog box), enter a new value into the Horizontal text box or select a new value with its plus (+) or minus (–) buttons. To adjust how far down the printing starts from the top of the paper (relative to the way it's shown in the diagram), enter a new value into the Vertical text box or select a new value with its plus (+) or minus (–) buttons.

After you finish selecting the paper type for the various layouts in your label project, you're ready to print each one. To do this, close the Page Setup dialog box by clicking OK and then choose File➪Print or press Ctrl+P to open the Print dialog box like the one shown in Figure 8-12.

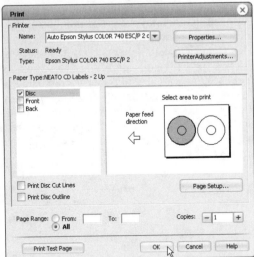

Figure 8-12:
Getting
ready to
print the
first layout
in the label
project in
the Print
dialog box.

The Print dialog box contains a whole bunch of print options that you can modify before actually sending the print job to the printer by clicking the OK button:

✔ **Name** drop-down list box to select a different printer installed on your computer system to use in printing the label project

✔ **Status** displays the current printing status of the printer selected in the Name drop-down list box

✔ **Type** displays the model of printer that is currently selected in the Name drop-down list box

✔ **Properties** button to open the Properties dialog box for the type of printer currently selected where you can change certain advanced settings (which are entirely printer dependent) such as the paper orientation (Portrait or Landscape), the page order in printing, the paper source, and the printer quality, among other things

✔ **Printer Adjustments** button to open the Printer Adjustments dialog box (see Figure 8-13) where you can tweak where the printer starts printing on each page and increase or decrease the height and width of the printing

✔ **Paper Type** displays a description of the type of paper along with its diagram for the layout which is currently selected in the area with the check boxes below. Click the check box before the name of each layout you want included the print job. Click the name of the layout following the check box to display a description and diagram of the type of paper selected for that particular layout in central sections of the Print dialog box (click the Page Setup button to open the Page Setup dialog box where you can modify the paper type for the selected layout)

✔ **Print Disc Cut Lines** check box to print dotted lines indicated where the label or case inserts should be cut in the printout

✔ **Print Disc Outline** check box to print the outline of the disc (when printing the Disc layout) in the printout

✔ **Page Setup** button to open the Page Setup dialog box where you can select a new type of paper for the currently selected layout and modify the start position for the printing on that type of paper

✔ **Page Range** option button to print only the range of pages you indicate in the From and To text boxes rather than all the pages needed for each layout you've selected for printing in the Paper Type area of the Print dialog box

✔ **Copies** text box to indicate the number of copies to print of each layout whose check box is selected in the Print dialog

✔ **Print Test Page** button to obtain a quick and dirty printout just showing part of the outline of the disc label or case insert you're printing: you can then use this test page to compare with the outlines of the labels on the actual label paper or perforations of the case inserts on the actual insert paper to see if you need to make any adjustments to where the printing starts before actually returning to the Print dialog box and printing the real disc labels and case inserts

After you finish modifying the necessary print settings in the Print dialog box, you can start the printing by clicking the OK button to send the print job to the printer. If your printer requires manual feeding of the type of paper you selected for printing one or more of the selected layouts, you will be prompted to insert the paper before the printing actually begins.

After printing your label project, you may find that you still need to make slight adjustments to where the print area begins or to the overall size of the print area. To make these adjustments before trying to print the label project again, choose File➪Printer Adjustments on the Label Creator menu bar or, if you have the Print dialog box open, click the Printer Adjustments button. Label Creator opens the Printer Adjustments dialog box shown in Figure 8-13.

Here, you can adjust the left edge of the print area (relative to the left edge of the paper as it's fed into the printer as shown in the Preview Area of this dialog box) by entering a new value between –5.00 and 5.00 in the Horizontal text box or by selecting the value with its plus (+) and minus (–) buttons — a positive value moves the print area slightly to the right, while a negative value moves it slightly to the left (relative to the default print area for the type of printer you've selected).

So too, you can adjust the top edge of the print area (relative to the top edge of the paper as it's fed into the printer as shown in the Preview Area of this dialog box) by entering a new value between –5.00 and 5.00 in the Vertical text box or by selecting the value with its plus (+) and minus (–) buttons — a positive value moves the print area slightly down, while a negative value moves it slightly up (relative to the default print area for the type of printer you've selected).

In addition to adjusting where the print area starts in relation to left and top edge of the paper, you can also increase or decrease the size of the printing area (and thereby the size of the disc labels and case inserts that are being printing within it) by adjusting the scaling in the Height and Width text boxes in the Printer Adjustments dialog box.

Note that as long as the Keep Aspect Ratio check box has a checkmark, any adjustment you make to the scaling of the height in the print area in the Height text box is automatically echoed in the Width text box as well. So, for example, if you enter 90 into the Height text box, Label Creator immediately changes the value in the Width text box to 90 as well (and because this 90 represents a percentage of the overall height and width of the print area and not an actual dimension, the physical length and width change proportionally).

If you want to be able to adjust the Height and Width percentages independently, you need to click the Keep Aspect Ratio check box to remove its checkmark before you enter a new percentage value in either of these text boxes or select one with their respective plus (+) and minus (–) buttons.

After making any necessary adjustments to paper alignments or print area scaling in the Printer Adjustments dialog box and clicking the OK button, you're ready to try printing all or just some of the layouts in your label projects.

Applying Labels to Discs

Applying the disc label to the actual CD or DVD disc is, perhaps, one of the most daunting tasks that a body can perform because if you mess up and get any wrinkles or bubbles in the label, you might as well toss the CD or DVD disc in the trash, cause it'll never play properly (if at all).

So too, you must never, never, ever try to remove and reapply a disc label that you've only got partially applied to a disc, as the adhesive in the label will undoubtedly rip off part of the coating on the top of the disc (the one that's not read by the laser) and as a result the disc is dead meat and will never play again.

In other words, the application of disc labels to your CD or DVD discs is a one-shot deal during which you cannot afford any flub-ups (enough to make you sweat bullets). In fact, because it's such a delicate practice that I've screwed up plenty in my time, I won't even attempt to apply a disc label without the aid of one of the those applicators which consists of a spindle for centering the disc and label and a base for holding the label (adhesive side up and printed side down) with a spring-loaded plunger-type spindle in the middle, with the button in the middle for pushing down the disc (with the top, coated side facing down and the shiny, data side that you never touch facing up) to meet and bond with the adhesive on the label. (The particular model I favor is a sweet Italian number by Neato that has a felt pad on the bottom of the base so it won't slide during the crucial punch-down phase where the top, coated side of the CD or DVD disc meets the adhesive of the disc label.) You can also find other models by manufacturers such as DYMO and USDM that you can use to do the same thing.

Part IV
Creating Projects for DVDs

The 5th Wave   By Rich Tennant

"I ran this Bob Dylan CD through our voice recognition system, and he really is just saying, 'Manaama-manaaabadhaabadha...' "

In this part . . .

*I*t seems to me that the heart of the Easy Media Creator 7 suite lies in its two major applications for video productions: VideoWave, which provides you with an easy-to-use but robust video editor; and DVD Builder, which provides you with both an easy-to-use DVD project builder and Roxio's great burn engine for burning both your video and DVD projects to disc. Part IV not only covers the complete use of these two applications (in Chapters 10 and 11) but also covers, in Chapter 9, Easy Media Creator's Capture program, a tool that you'll come to rely on heavily for acquiring the various types of digital media you use in your projects destined for DVD.

Chapter 9

Acquiring Digital Media

· ·

In This Chapter

▶ Launching the Capture tool and selecting the devices from which to acquire media

▶ Scanning photos or copying them directly from your digital camera

▶ Capturing live video or video clips from your Web camera or digital camcorder

▶ Capturing live audio and copying tracks from an Audio CD

▶ Copying movie titles from unencrypted DVD discs to your computer's hard disk

▶ Moving and copying captured media files to new media collection files

· ·

*B*efore you can get down to making your own videos and movies with either the Easy Media Creator's VideoWave program or its DVD builder, you have to acquire the digital media files that you need in putting together your final multimedia productions. These media files can include video clips taken from your digital camcorder, still images from your digital camera and scanner, audio files recorded with your computer's microphone or taken through a line into your computer from an analog device like a LP record player or audio cassette as well as audio tracks from an audio CD and, if all that's not enough for you, DVD movie titles that you've saved on your computer's hard disk as well.

This chapter gives you the lowdown on how to use Roxio Easy Media Creator's Capture utility to acquire all these different types of digital media for your video and DVD movie productions. It also gives you pointers on how to organize the media files that you acquire and save to your hard disk with the Capture utility into media collections that are ready to use when you go on to make your multimedia productions with VideoWave (see Chapter 10) and the DVD Builder (see Chapter 11).

Using the Capture Tool

In acquiring media for your video and DVD movie productions, you will come to rely heavily on the Roxio Capture tool. To launch Capture from the Roxio Easy Media Creator Home window, click the Capture link in the Tools column. To launch Capture from the Windows taskbar, click the Start button on the taskbar; highlight the All Programs option on the Start menu followed by the Roxio option on the All Programs submenu before you click the Capture option at the very top of the Roxio submenu.

Capture is also supposed to automatically launch whenever you use Windows XP's plug-and-play feature to an external digital device such as a scanner, digital camera, or digital camcorder to your computer using the cable and port appropriate to that device. Note, however, that this feature may not work if you've installed another graphics or video editing program after installing Roxio Easy Media Creator 7 on your computer. In such a case, you have to manually launch Capture after connecting the device.

The initial Capture window similar to the one shown in Figure 9-1 appears. This window contains links to all the digital devices along with all the other sources for acquiring different types of digital media that you have available to your computer in the Detected Devices pane on the left. When you position the mouse pointer over a particular link in the Detected Devices pane, a description of what kind of media you can acquire from that device appears.

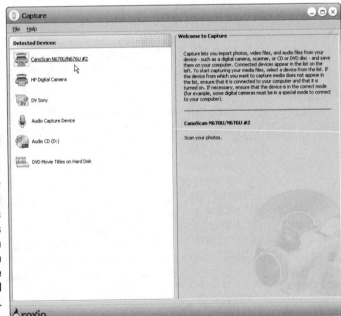

Figure 9-1:
The Capture window shows all the sources and devices from which you can acquire digital media.

To start the process of acquiring data from a particular device (such as your digital camera or camcorder) or source (such as DVD movie titles saved on your hard disk), you click its link in the Detected Devices.

Connecting digital devices to use in Capture

Before an external device such as your scanner, digital camera, or camcorder will appear in the Detected Devices pane of the Capture window, you must have it properly installed and connected to your computer. Note that most digital devices such as digital cameras and scanners connect to your computer through a free USB (Universal Serial Bus) port using a special USB cable. Others devices such as digital video cameras (also known as camcorders) usually connect to your computer via the faster, IEEE1394 FireWire connection necessary to handle streaming video (note, however, that some of the newer digital cameras that take video as well as still pictures also support FireWire).

When dealing with external digital devices such as scanners and digital still cameras, there are two standards (both of which are supported by Capture) for acquiring still images and streaming video: the so-called TWAIN (as in Kipling's "Never the twain shall meet . . .") standard and Microsoft's WIA (Windows Image Acquisition) standard developed for Windows XP. In order for Capture to recognize your TWAIN or WIA device, you must have installed the TWAIN or WIA device drivers on your computer (these drivers are supplied on the CDs that come with your devices — if you don't have the CD readily available, check the manufacturer's Web site for them).

To install the drivers for a new digital device, you may need to open the Scanners and Cameras control panel dialog box (do this by clicking the Control Panel item on the Windows Start menu, the Printers and Other Hardware link in the Pick a Category area of the Control Panel dialog box, and then clicking Scanners and Cameras link in the Or Pick a Control Panel Icon area of the Printers and Other Hardware dialog box). In the Scanners and Cameras dialog box, click the Add an Imaging Device link in Imaging Tasks pane on the left and then follow the steps in the Scanner and Camera Installation Wizard that appears. When prompted for the name of the scanner or camera you want to install, either select the name of the manufacturer and model in the Manufacturer and Model list boxes or click the Have Disk button and then select the letter of your computer's CD drive in the Copy Manufacturer's Files From drop-down list box before you click the OK button.

After Windows finishes copying the device drivers from the manufacturer's CD, an icon with the name of the new digital scanner or camera appears in the Scanners and Cameras dialog box. If you close this dialog box and then launch Capture, the name of the scanner or camera you just installed with the Windows Scanner and Camera Installation Wizard appears in the Detected Devices. This happens as soon as you connect the scanner or camera to your computer with the proper USB or IEEE1394 FireWire cable and turn the device on (the name of the device appears behind a WIA or TWAIN icon depending upon which type of driver it uses). You can then start acquiring images from these digital devices in Capture by clicking the links associated with their names in the Detected Devices pane.

Customizing the Capture options

Before you start working with Capture to acquire your favorite media files, you may want to modify the default locations where the program automatically saves different types of media files in the Options dialog box. To do this, choose File⇨Options to open the Options dialog box similar to the one shown in Figure 9-2. As you can see in this figure, the top portion of this dialog box contains a Temporary Working Folders list box that shows you the path and the name of the folder where Photo, Video, Audio, and DVD media files are automatically saved when you acquire them with Capture.

Figure 9-2:
You can modify the folders where different types of media files are automatically saved in the Options dialog box.

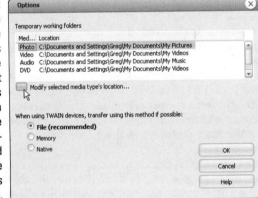

To change any of these default folder locations, click the type of media and its pathname in this list box and then click the Modify Selected Media Type's Location button (that becomes active only after you click one of the media types in the Temporary Working Folders list box). The Browse Location dialog box then appears with a list box containing a Navigation Tree that shows the selected media type's current default folder location. Use the Navigation Tree in this list box to select a new folder location (you can also use the New Folder button at the bottom of the Browse Location dialog box to create a new folder to use) and then click the OK button.

The lower portion of the Options dialog box contains three option buttons, File (Recommended), Memory, and Native, which determine how devices using the TWAIN-type drivers transfer their files. The File (Recommended) option button is the default and the Roxio people highly advocate leaving this option selected. Should you connect a TWAIN device that can't use the File transfer option, Capture is programmed to talk to the device and automatically select either the Memory or Native transfer option. You would only manually change to one of these two other options if Capture proved unable to automatically detect which of these two other transfer methods to use.

Acquiring Digital Photos

Most of the time, you will acquire the digital photos that you use in your various photo and DVD productions either from your scanner or directly from your digital camera. You use the scanner to acquire and simultaneously convert developed photos into digital media. Photos taken with a digital camera, of course, require no analog-to-digital conversion and don't have to be acquired through Capture (you may prefer to acquire digital photos from your camera and save them on your computer using the software that came with the camera or using Windows Scanner and Camera Wizard).

The next two sections cover how to use Capture to acquire digital photos from these two types of devices. First, you find out how to acquire photos that you scan via Capture and then you find out how to acquire photos when your digital camera is connected to your computer using either a TWAIN or WIA device driver.

Scanning images into Capture

To scan a photo into Capture, you follow these steps:

1. **Launch Capture and then connect the scanner to your computer and turn it on if you haven't already done so.**

   Place the photo that you want to acquire in Capture in the proper position on the scanner's glass plate. If you're using a scanner in which you feed the sheet, get the paper ready to feed. If you're using a handheld scanner, position the scanner at the top of the sheet.

2. **Click the link associated with the scanner's name in the Detected Devices pane.**

   Capture opens a Capture window which contains two panes: a Capture From pane on the left showing the name the scanner and a Contents Of pane on the right that shows the preview of the photo you're scanning after you click the Preview button.

3. **Click the Preview button to have the scanner preview the photo you're scanning.**

   After the scanner finishes previewing the image you're scanning, its preview appears in the Contents pane. You can then adjust the scan rectangle in the Contents pane so that it surrounds only the photo (if it's smaller than the platen) or the part of the photo you want scanned. To adjust the scanning area, you drag the sizing handles on the scan rectangle until it encloses just the area you want included (see Figure 9-3).

4. **Drag the sizing handles on the scan rectangle until this rectangle encloses the area of the photo you want scanned.**

You can adjust the scan quality by selecting among the Good (100 dpi), Better (150 dpi), Best (300 dpi), and Other option buttons — when you select Other, you can choose between 600 x 600 dpi (dots per inch) and 1200 x 1200 dpi, in the Scan Quality drop-down list box, assuming that your scanner supports these very high resolution settings. Of course, the higher the scan resolution, the more detail you get and the larger the resulting graphics file.

5. **(Optional) Select the desired scan quality option button and then click the Next > button to proceed to the next Capture window.**

The Capture task pane enables you to designate the folder where you want to save the scanned digital photo file as well as the descriptive name you want to assign to the photo (Capture automatically appends the next available sequential number starting with 00000 to this name) and allows you to associate the photo with one of the collections that you've already set up in Media Manager or with a new collection that you create.

6. **(Optional) To save the photo in a folder other than default folder for Photo media, click the Browse Folders button and then select the desired destination folder using the Navigation Tree in the Browse Location dialog box.**

You can change the descriptive part of the photo name in the Name the Photo text box. If you don't select a new photo name, Capture automatically uses Captured Photos as the descriptive name to which it appends the next available sequential number, as in Captured Photos 00000, Captured Photos 00001, and so on.

7. **(Optional) Click the Name the Photo text box and replace Captured Photos with your own descriptive name.**

You may associate the photo you're about to scan with an existing or a new collection (see the section "Adding Media Files to Collections" later in this chapter for more on file collections).

8. **(Optional) Click the Browse Collections button and then click the name of the collection file to which you want to make the scanned photo a part in the Browse Collection dialog box or click its New button and enter the name for the new collection in the Browse Collection Navigation Tree before you click OK.**

Now that you've made all your desired changes to the settings in the Capture task pane, you're ready to have Capture actually scan the photo and save it on your hard disk.

9. **Click the Capture > button at the bottom of the Capture Settings pane to scan the photo.**

   After Capture finishes scanning and saving your photo, the program displays the Photo Successfully Captured alert dialog box.

10. **Click OK to close the Photo Successfully Captured alert dialog box.**

    After you close this alert dialog box, Capture displays its final Capture task pane (shown in Figure 9-4) where you can select an Easy Media Creator application (Media Manager, DVD Builder, PhotoSuite 7, or VideoWave 7) in which to use the scanned photo (Capture opens the program whose option button is selected as soon as you click the Done button). You can also elect to do more media capturing by clicking the Capture More option button (which takes you back to the initial Capture window when you click the Done button), or you can indicate that you're finished capturing media by leaving the default Finished Capturing option button selected when you click the Done button.

11. **Select the appropriate activity option button in the Capture task pane and then click the Done button at the very bottom of the Capture window.**

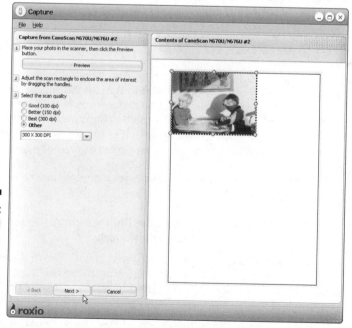

Figure 9-3:
Adjusting
the area
to be
scanned and
selecting the
scan quality.

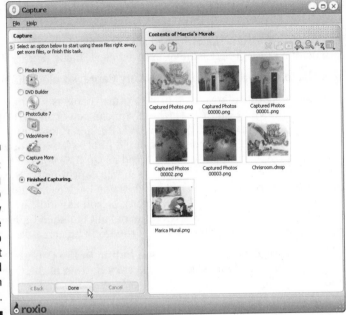

Copying photos directly from your camera

The procedure for capturing photos directly from a digital camera that you've connected to your computer is very similar to that for capturing scanned images. The big difference between the two procedures is the amount of photos that you capture: normally, when you use Capture to copy photos from your digital camera, you import a whole bunch of photos at one time rather than copying just a single image as when capturing from your scanner.

The general steps for copying the photos on your digital camera onto your hard disk are as follows:

1. **Launch Capture and then connect the digital camera to your computer and turn it on if you haven't already done so.**

   Note that connecting your camera may well cause the Windows XP Photo Wizard or some other photo editing software that came with your camera to automatically start up. If that happens, click the program's close box to return to the Capture program.

   You have to click the link in the Detected Devices pane of the initial Capture window for your camera.

2. **Click the link with your camera's name in the Detected Devices pane.**

   Capture opens a Capture window which contains two panes: a Capture From pane on the left showing the name the camera and a Contents Of pane on the right that shows thumbnails of all the photos on your camera, all of which are automatically selected for copying.

Depending upon the make of your camera, the Capture From task pane may contain more than one folder from which you can import files (this is especially true in the case of digital cameras that take video as well as still images). If, after selecting the folder which contains the images to import, you decide that you don't want to copy all the images onto your hard disk, click the Deselect All Files button and then hold down the Ctrl key as you click the thumbnails of just the photos you do want to import.

3. **(Optional) Select the folder that contains the images you want to import. If you don't want all the images in a folder, click the Deselect All Files button and then Ctrl+click the thumbnails of the images you do want to copy.**

After selecting the images to import, you're ready to proceed to the next window where you select a destination folder, specify a group name for the photos, and, if you wish, make the imported photos part of a media collection.

4. **Click the Next > button to proceed to the next Capture window.**

You can change the folder on your hard disk where the digital photos are saved.

5. **(Optional) To save the photos in a folder other than the default folder for Photo media, click the Browse Folders button and then select the desired destination folder using the Navigation Tree in the Browse Location dialog box.**

You can assign a descriptive group name to the photos in the Group Files Name text box. If you don't select a new photo name, Capture automatically uses the filenames that the camera assigns to the photos. If you do enter a group filename, Capture then automatically appends the next available sequential number starting with 00000 whatever group name you assign.

6. **(Optional) Click the Group File Name text box and type in a descriptive name for the group of photos you're about to import.**

You may associate the photos you're about to copy with an existing or a new collection (see "Adding Media Files to Collections" later in this chapter for more on file collections).

7. **(Optional) Click the Browse Collections button and then click the name of the collection file to which you want to make the imported photos a part in the Browse Collection dialog box or click its New button and enter the name for the new collection in the Browse Collection Navigation Tree before you click OK.**

You may want to have Capture remove the selected photos from the camera after copying them to your hard disk.

8. **(Optional) Click the Delete Photos from Camera After Capture check box if you want Capture to remove the selected photos from the camera's storage after it copies them onto your hard disk.**

   Now you're ready to have Capture import the selected photos to the destination folder that you've specified.

9. **Click the Capture > button at the bottom of the Capture Settings pane to scan the photo.**

   After Capture finishes copying and saving your photo, the program displays the Files Successfully Captured alert dialog box and thumbnails of the imported photos appear in the Contents pane on the right side of the Capture window.

10. **Click OK to close the Files Successfully Captured alert dialog box.**

    After you close this alert dialog box, Capture displays its final Capture task pane where you can select an Easy Media Creator application (Media Manager, DVD Builder, PhotoSuite 7, or VideoWave 7) in which to use the scanned photo (Capture opens the program whose option button is selected as soon as you click the Done button). You can also elect to do more media capturing by clicking the Capture More option button (which takes you back to the initial Capture window when you click the Done button), or you can indicate that you're finished capturing media by leaving the default Finished Capturing option button selected when you click the Done button.

11. **Select the appropriate activity option button in the Capture task pane and then click the Done button at the very bottom of the Capture window.**

Acquiring Digital Video

Capture is perhaps most useful when you use it to capture digital video that you've taken with your DV (digital video) camera (also known affectionately as a camcorder). Note that although you will mostly use capture to import video clips from footage that you've already taken, you can also use Capture to capture live video taken with your camcorder (which, of course, must remain connected to your computer throughout the shoot) or with a Web camera.

When importing previously recorded video clips from your DV camera, you can choose between importing the video with Manual Capture or SmartScan Capture. When you capture clips with Manual Capture (the only mode available when you're capturing live footage with your DV or Web camera), you decide which video to capture by manually operating a Start Capturing and Stop

Capturing button. When you capture clips with SmartScan Capture, Capture scans the entire video tape, using the time-code information stored on the tape to automatically divide it into discrete scenes which you can then import.

Figure 9-5 shows the type of Capture window that appears after you connect your camera to you computer, turn the camera on in Video mode (sometimes abbreviated VTR) and then click the link for your DV Camera in the initial Capture window. This DV Capture window contains a Capture Preview pane where you can see the video footage that you're capturing on the left side and a Media Selector pane where you can select the media collection file into which you want to add the captured video.

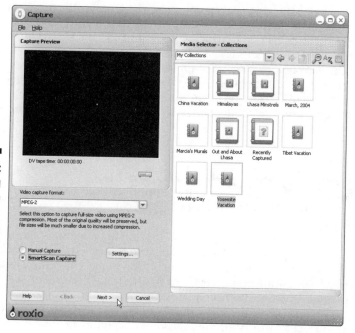

Figure 9-5:
Selecting
the Capture
settings you
want to use
in importing
video from
your digital
video
camera.

Beneath the Preview Pane, you see the following three controls that enable you to select the Capture settings that you now want to use in capturing your video:

- ✔ **Video Capture Format** drop-down list box that enables you to choose between the default DV mode, which captures full-size video in the AVI uncompressed file format that eats up hard disk space like nobody's business, and MPEG-2 mode, which captures full-size video using the MPEG-2 compressed file format (which still gives you good quality video along with smaller files sizes)

✔ **Manual Capture** and **SmartScan Capture** option buttons that enable you to choose between manually capturing the video with the Start Capturing and Stop Capturing buttons (Manual Capture) and having the Capture program scan the video tape and divide it up into scenes that you can then import (SmartScan)

✔ **Settings** button that enables you to select new video settings for your DV camera (the actual options offered on the Source and Preference tabs of the Capture Settings dialog box that appears when you click the Settings button depend upon the type and model DV camera you're using — settings that you can change appear in bold, while settings that you can only review appear in normal type

After specifying the video capture format, mode, and settings, select All Collections in the Media Selector drop-down list box and then click the name of the of media collection to which you want to add the video clips that you import before you click the Next > button. Selecting the collection in which to put the clips before you start capturing them saves you from having to organize them later with Media Manager. Note, however, that you must have created the media collection file in Media Manager (see Chapter 4) before you launch Capture and select the name of your DV camera in the Detected Devices pane.

Capturing recorded video with SmartScan Capture

When you click the SmartScan Capture button to have the program scan your tape for scenes, a Capture Window similar to the one shown in Figure 9-6 appears. Here, you click the Start Scan button (which then turns into a Stop Scan button). Capture responds by rewinding the video tape if necessary and then scanning the tape for potential scenes.

As Capture fast forwards through the video, scanning its time code, the program lists the scenes it locates in the SmartScan – Scenes pane on the right. Each scene listed in the SmartScan – Scenes pane displays the thumbnail of the first frame in the scene, is sequentially numbered (Scene 1, Scene 2, and so on), and lists the duration of the scene in minutes and seconds (as in 5m42s for a scene that is five minutes and 42 seconds long).

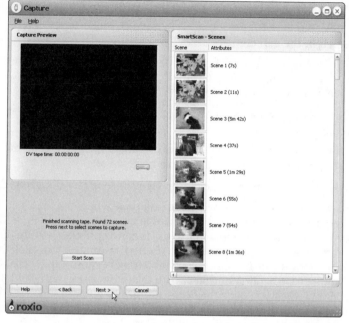

Figure 9-6:
Scanning
the video
tape for
scenes in
SmartScan
mode.

After Capture finishes scanning your video tape and identifying all the scenes it contains, you need to click the Next > button to advance to the next Capture window (shown in Figure 9-7) where you indicate which scenes to capture and where to capture them to:

1. **Ctrl+Click all the individual scenes in the SmartScan – Scenes pane that you want to import or press Ctrl+A to select all the scenes identified on the tape.**

   After selecting the scenes to capture in the SmartScan – Scenes pane, you can select the descriptive part of the video filename into which the individual video scenes are saved. If you don't modify this option, Capture gives these video files the default filename of VideoCap followed by the next available sequential number as in VideoCap0, VideoCap1, and so on.

2. **(Optional) Click the Video File text box and replace the descriptive part of the default video file name with one of your own.**

   Before you begin capturing video in the selected scenes, you need to select the folder in which the video is automatically saved (usually this default folder is the My Videos folder in the My Documents folder on your hard disk).

3. **Click the Default Folder button and then select the folder in which you want the video files saved using the Navigation Tree in the Folder Location dialog box or click the New button to create a new folder before you click OK.**

Now you're ready to start capturing the video in the selected scenes.

4. **Click the Start Capture button to have Capture locate and record the video in the selected scenes.**

   The moment you click the Start Capture button to start recording the video, it becomes a Stop Capture button that you can click to stop the recording before all the selected scenes are captured.

5. **Click the Done button when Capture finishes capturing all the selected scenes.**

   Capture then displays a Files Successfully Captured alert dialog box indicating where your video files have been saved.

6. **Click the OK button to close the Files Successfully Captured dialog box.**

   Capture displays its final Capture task pane where you can select an Easy Media Creator application (Media Manager, DVD Builder, PhotoSuite 7, or VideoWave 7) in which to use the scanned photo (Capture opens the program whose option button is selected as soon as you click the Done button). You can also elect to do more media capturing by clicking the Capture More option button (which takes you back to the initial Capture window when you click the Done button), or you can indicate that you're finished capturing media by leaving the default Finished Capturing option button selected when you click the Done button.

7. **Select the appropriate activity option button in the Capture task pane and then click the Done button at the very bottom of the Capture window.**

Figure 9-7:
Capturing
selected
scenes with
Capture in
SmartScan
mode.

Capturing recorded video with Manual Capture

Instead of having Capture decide where the scenes are in your video tape, you can identify the scenes yourself and determine what video you want to import using the Manual Capture mode. To manually capture video, make sure that the Manual Capture option button is selected in the initial Capture task pane before you click the Next > button. Capture then displays a window similar to the one shown in Figure 9-8 where you can use the standard controls at the bottom of the Preview pane (the same as you find on your video remote) to preview the video and find that place where you want to start recording.

Figure 9-8:
You use the controls at the bottom of the Preview pane in Manual Capture mode to find the scenes you want recorded.

As with SmartScan, you can indicate the group filename you want your video clips to have, specify the folder where these video files are saved, and specify the media collection file with which they are associated before you begin capturing the video.

To capture a video clip, locate the place in the tape where you want to begin recording the clip and then click the Pause button to pause the playback. Next, click the Start Capturing button to begin recording a new scene. When you reach the place in the tape where you want to stop the recording, click the Stop Capturing button (which replaces the Start Capturing button the moment you click it). Note that Capture may automatically divide your video clip into sequentially numbered scenes starting with Scene_000000 depending upon the Limit Capture setting in effect for your video camera before you actually click the Stop Capturing button.

If you want to record all the video on the tape, simply click the Capture Full Tape button. Capture then rewinds the tape and records all its video from beginning to end.

When you finish manually capturing video clips, click the Done button. As with SmartScan Capture, the program displays the Files Successfully Captured alert dialog box followed by the final Capture task pane that contains the next activity option buttons (Media Manager, DVD Builder, PhotoSuite 7, VideoWave 7, Capture More, or Finished Capturing) that you can select before clicking its Done button.

Recording live video with Manual Capture

Instead of importing video clips from the video you've already recorded on tape, you can use Capture's Manual Capture mode to import live video as you're actually recording it. To record live video in Capture, you have to make sure that you switch your DV camera to Camera or Record mode rather than Video mode before you select the DV camera in the Detected Devices pane in the initial Capture window. When you select your camcorder in the initial Capture window and the camera is set to Camera or Record mode, Manual Capture is the only capture mode available (the SmartScan Capture option button is grayed out).

When you click the Next > button, the familiar Manual Capture window appears (like the one shown earlier in Figure 9-8) where you can select the standard part of the video filenames and the folder where the clips are saved as well as the media collection with which the video files are to be associated. You'll find the biggest difference in the Capture Preview pane, which now shows you what your video camera's lens is actually seeing at the time rather than a key frame recorded on the tape.

To start capturing what the camera is seeing (even if the video camera is in standby mode), click the Start Capturing button in the Capture window. Capture then records what the camera sees in real time. To get the shot you want, you can then pan the camera and use its zoom lens to zoom in and out on objects around you. When you're finished recording a clip in real time, click the Stop Capturing button (which replaces the Start Capturing button as soon as you click it).

When you finish recording live video clips, click the Done button. As with SmartScan Capture and Manual Capture with previously recorded video, the program displays the Files Successfully Captured alert dialog box followed by the final Capture task pane that contains the next activity option buttons (Media Manager, DVD Builder, PhotoSuite 7, VideoWave 7, Capture More, or Finished Capturing) that you can select before clicking its Done button).

Acquiring Audio Files

Capture enables you not only to import images (both still and video) for use in other Easy Media Creator projects but your audio as well. When using Capture to import audio, you have a choice between recording the audio live, that is, capturing it in real time as the audio is playing or copying audio tracks from a pre-recorded audio CD.

To acquire live audio, you click the Audio Capture Device link in the Detected Devices pane of the initial Capture window. This audio-capture device can be your computer's built-in microphone or some analog audio device such as an amplifier with a record player playing an LP or audio cassette connected to your computer's line-in connection (see Chapter 5 for details).

To acquire audio tracks from a CD, you click the Audio CD link in the Detected Devices pane of the initial Capture window. This audio CD can be one that you've purchased or one that you've burned with the Easy Media Creator's Creator Classic program (see Chapter 8).

Capturing live audio

To record an audio file with Capture, connect the external analog audio device to your computer (usually through its external microphone jack). Turn on the analog audio device and cue up the LP record or audio cassette you want to record. Then launch Capture and click the Audio Capture Device link in the Detected Devices pane of the initial Capture window.

Capture then opens a Capture window similar to the one shown in Figure 9-9. This window is divided into a Capture from Audio Capture Device pane on the left side and a Contents Of pane that displays the contents of the media collection that is currently selected.

In the Capture from Audio Capture Device pane, you can select a new folder in which to save the audio file you're about to record. To do this, click the Browse Folders button beneath the Capture Files To heading and then click the desired folder name. You can also select a group name for the audio files in Name of Group Files text box, associate the files with a particular media collection with the Browse Collections button beneath the Add Files to Collection heading, and choose the recording quality in the Select a Recording Quality drop-down list box.

Figure 9-9:
Selecting
the
recording
settings for
recording
live audio
with
Capture.

When it comes to selecting the recording quality in this drop-down list box, you can choose among the following three options:

- **CD Quality** (the default) that produces a WAV audio file of the highest quality and the largest size

- **Radio Quality** that produces a WAV audio file of the medium quality and average size

- **Telephone Quality** that produces a WAV audio file of the lowest quality and smallest size

After selecting the desired recording settings in the Capture from Audio Capture Device pane, you're ready to record the live audio by following these steps:

1. **If the source of the audio is an analog playback device, cue up the track on that device.**

   For example, if you're about to record a track on the audio cassette, you need to find the silence right before the track on the tape. If you're recording live audio with a microphone connected to your computer, you need to make sure that the mike is on and positioned correctly for recording the sound.

2. **Click the Record button at the bottom of the Capture from Audio Device pane in the Capture window.**

Right after you click the Record button, you need to start the playback of the analog recording that you're saving. If you're recording live audio through a microphone, you don't perform Step 2 until the live audio you want to record starts playing.

3. **If the source of the audio is an analog playback device, start playing the recording that you want to capture with that device.**

    As Capture records the live audio, its recording light blinks red and gray and the Recorded Length indicator keeps you informed of how long the program has been recording.

4. **When the audio source stops playing, click the Stop button (which replaces the Record button as soon as you click it).**

As soon as you click the Stop button, Capture adds a WAV audio file using the Group Filename and the next available sequential number (starting with 00000 as in Captured Sounds 00000.wav, Captured Sounds 00001.wav, and so on). The program saves the WAV audio file in the folder that you selected with the Browse Files button and associates it with the media collection that you selected with the Browse Collections button.

After clicking the Stop button, you can then immediately start recording another live recording with Capture simply by clicking the Record button again. When you're finished recording with Capture, click the Next > button at the bottom of the Capture from Audio Device pane.

The Capture program then displays the final Capture task pane that contains the next activity option buttons (Media Manager, DVD Builder, PhotoSuite 7, VideoWave 7, Capture More, or Finished Capturing) that you can select before clicking its Done button.

Remember that you can edit the WAV files that you record in Capture with Easy Media Creator's Sound Editor tool where you can use its many features to enhance the raw audio that you've captured (see Chapter 5 for details).

Copying tracks from an audio CD

To copy tracks from an audio CD, place the CD in your computer's CD or DVD drive and then click the Audio CD link in the Detected Devices pane of the initial Capture window.

Capture then opens a Capture window similar to the one shown in Figure 9-10. This window is divided into a Capture from Audio CD pane on the left side and a Contents Of pane on the right side showing the contents of the media collection that is currently selected.

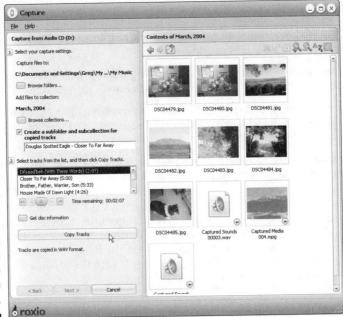

Figure 9-10:
Specifying
the settings
for copying
tracks from
an audio
CD with
Capture.

In the Capture from Audio CD pane, you can select a new folder in which to
save the tracks you're about to record with the Browse Folders button beneath
the Capture Files To heading. You can also associate the audio tracks with a
particular media collection with the Browse Collections button beneath the
Add Files to Collection heading, and specify the name of a subfolder in which
the tracks are stored in the Create a Subfolder and Subcollection for the Copied
Tracks text box. Note that if you don't specify your own subfolder name,
Capture automatically creates a composite name for this folder and new collection that is composed of Copied Tracks followed by the current date and time
(when you opened the Capture from Audio CD pane) as in Copied Tracks
[2004-3-17] [09_50am].

The Capture from Audio CD pane also contains a Select Tracks list box that
contains a listing of all the tracks on the audio CD (indicated by track number
only as in Track 1, Track 2, and the like). If you want Capture to replace the
track numbers with the appropriate track names, click the Get Disc Information
button immediately beneath the Select Tracks list box. Capture then connects
to the Gracenote CDDB Web site from which it attempts to obtain the track
information. If the program finds this information online, Capture then replaces
the track numbers in the Select Tracks list box with their corresponding names
and playing time.

If you want to listen to a particular track on the CD before selecting it for
copying in the Select Tracks list box, click its track number or name in this
list box. Then, click the triangular Play button in the playback controls that

appear at the bottom of the Select Tracks list box (these controls only appear when one track is selected in this list box). When you finish listening to the track, click the square Stop button in the playback controls (which replaces the Play button as soon as you click it).

To select only certain tracks from the list in the Select Tracks list box, hold down the Ctrl key as you click it. To select all the tracks in the list, click the first one at the top of the box; then drag the scroll button down and hold down the Shift key as you click the final track.

Once you've selected the tracks that you want Capture to copy to your hard disk in the Select Tracks list box, click the Copy Tracks button at the bottom of the Capture from Audio CD pane. Capture displays the Copying Audio Tracks dialog box that shows you the progress of the track copying. When Capture finishes copying the selected tracks, this dialog box disappears and thumbnails of the copied track(s) appear in the Contents Of pane that now shows the contents of the subfolder (and new collection) that was created as part of the copy process.

If you're finished copying tracks from the CD, you can replace it with another and continue copying in Capture from Audio CD pane or, if you're done, you can click the Next > button. The program then displays the final Capture task pane that contains the next activity option buttons (Media Manager, DVD Builder, PhotoSuite 7, VideoWave 7, Capture More, or Finished Capturing) that you can select before clicking its Done button.

Use Sound Editor to convert the audio CD tracks that you've just copied to your hard disk in the WAV audio file format to MP3 files if you want to be able to download them onto your portable MP3 player or add them to a playlist on an MP3 disc that you create with Creator Classic (see Chapter 8). To do this, you open the WAV file form of the track in Sound Editor and then choose its File⇨Save command. Then click the MPEG Layer 3 (*.mp3) item in the Save as Type drop-down list box before you click the Save button in the Save dialog box.

Copying DVD Movie Titles

If you've created DVD discs with the Easy Media Creator's VideoWave or DVD Builder applications, you can use Capture to copy particular movie titles from the disc to your computer's hard disk (note that you can't use Capture to copy movie titles from professionally recorded DVDs that you rent or purchase, as these discs are encrypted).

To copy movie titles from a DVD disc that you've prepared, you follow these steps:

1. **Place the DVD disc that contains the movie titles you want to copy to your hard disk in your computer's DVD drive.**

   Now you're ready to launch the Capture tool.

2. **Launch Capture and then click the link with the volume name of your DVD disc in the Detected Devices pane of the initial Capture window.**

   A new Capture window appears with a Capture From pane (followed by the name of the disc) on the left and a The Titles Of pane (followed by the name of the disc) on the right. This pane displays thumbnails of all the movie titles on your DVD disc. By default, all the thumbnails are selected so that all the movie titles on the DVD disc are copied.

3. **(Optional) If you don't want all the movie titles copied, click the Deselect All Titles button in Capture From pane and then hold down the Ctrl key as you click the individual thumbnails of all the titles you do want to copy.**

   Now you're ready to copy the selected movie titles.

4. **Click the Next > button at the bottom of the Capture From pane.**

   A Capture window with a new Capture From pane and Contents Of pane appears. In the Capture From pane, you can specify a different folder that is to contain the copied movie titles with the Browse Folders button (Capture uses your My Videos folder by default), change the group name for the copied files in the Name of Group Files text box (Captures uses Captured Media followed by the next available sequential number starting with 00000 by default), or select a different media collection with which to associate the copied movie titles with the Browse Collections button.

5. **(Optional) Make any necessary changes to the destination folder, the group filename, and/or the media collection settings in the Capture From pane.**

   Now you're ready to have Capture copy the selected movie titles to your hard disk.

6. **Click the Copy> button at the bottom of the Capture From pane to begin copying the selected movie titles.**

   Captures displays the DVD Copy dialog box that keeps you informed of the progress in copying the selected movie titles. When Capture finishes making the copies, the DVD Copy dialog box closes and the Files Successfully Captured alert dialog box appears.

7. **Click the OK button in the Files Successfully Captured dialog box to close it.**

   In the Contents Of pane of the Capture window on the right, thumbnails of the copied movie titles with the group filename and the next available sequential number appear (and the .mpg for MPEG filename extension).

The Capture pane on the left contains the activity option buttons: Media Manager, DVD Builder, PhotoSuite 7, VideoWave 7, Capture More, or Finished Capturing. You can select one of these before you click the Done button.

8. **Click the option button of application you want to launch next or click the Capture More button (if you want to do more copying) or the Finished Capturing button (if you're done capturing) before you click the Done button at the bottom of the Capture From pane.**

Moving and Copying Files to New Collections

As discussed in Chapter 4, media collections enable you to associate different types of media with one another even when the files are physically stored across different folders and on different drives spread out over your computer system. The Capture program heavily encourages the use of media collections when capturing the different types of media files it supports (photos, audio files, video clips, and movie titles) by including collections as part of the Capture program's setup for each media type.

Sometimes after using Capture to copy a particular type of media files, you may decide that you want to move the files you've captured and associated with one collection to another, better-suited collection. You may also decide that you want to copy files from the collection to which you originally added the files during the capture process to an additional collection file which also needs to make use of the same media.

In these cases, you need to return to the Easy Media Creator Home window after you finish with Capture and click its Media Manager link at the very top of the Tools column. Then, when the Media Manager window opens, you need to follow these general steps for moving or copying media files already apart from one collection to another:

1. **Click the Organize Your Collections button (the one on the end of the toolbar immediately above Folders pane on the left side of the Media Manager window).**

   Media Manager splits the window into four panes.

2. **Click the name of the collection that contains the media files that you want to move or copy to another collection in the Collections pane in the upper-left of the Media Manager.**

   Thumbnails of all the media files added to the collection you select appear in the upper Media Manager Contents pane on the right.

3. **Click the name of the collection into which you want to move or copy the media files from the upper Contents pane in the lower Collections pane.**

   Media Manager now displays the contents of the collection you selected as the destination collection in the lower Contents pane.

4. **Select all the media files you want to move or copy in the upper Contents pane.**

   Remember that you can Click, Shift+Click to select a series of thumbnails (click the first one in the series and then Shift+Click the last one to select all of them in between) or Ctrl+Click to select multiple, individual thumbnails.

   Now you're ready either to move or copy the selected media files in the collection displayed in the upper Contents pane to the collection displayed in lower Contents pane. To move the files from the upper to lower pane, you click the Move Selected Collection Item(s) Above to Collection Below button (the one with downward-pointing arrow to the left of the word Move).

   To copy the files from the upper to lower pane, you click the Copy Selected Collection Item(s) Above to Collection Below button (the one with downward-pointing arrow to the left of the word Copy) instead.

5. **Click the Move Selected Collection Item(s) Above to Collection Below button to move the selected media files. Otherwise, click the Copy Selected Collection Item(s) Above to Collection Below button to copy them.**

After you finish moving or copying the selected media files, you can return the Media Manager window to its normal Folders view by clicking the Browse Folders button (the first one on the left on the toolbar right below the Media Manager menu bar) or to a single Collections view by clicking the Browse Collections button (the second from the left on the same toolbar).

Keep in mind that moving and copying media files to different collections in the Media Manager when the Organize Your Collections button is selected is a two-way street. Although the preceding steps outline how to move or copy files from the source collection in the upper Contents pane to a destination in the lower Contents pane, you can just as well reverse this process, making the collection displayed in the lower Contents pane the source and the collection displayed in the upper Contents pane the destination.

To do this, make sure no media files are selected in the upper Contents pane (you can do this by clicking anywhere in the upper pane in the space between the media files thumbnails) and then select the media files that you want to move or copy in the lower Contents pane. To move the selected media files from the collection in the lower Contents pane to the one in the upper pane, click Move Selected Collection Item(s) Below to Collection Above button (the one with upward-pointing arrow to the immediate right of the word Move). To copy the selected media files from the collection in the lower Contents pane to the one in the upper pane instead, click Copy Selected Collection Item(s) Below to Collection Above button (the one with upward-pointing arrow to the immediate right of the word Copy).

Chapter 10

Creating and Editing Video Productions

In This Chapter

▶ Getting familiar and comfortable with the VideoWave window and components

▶ Using CineMagic to quickly turn your video clips into music videos

▶ Using StoryBuilder to make easy work of turning your video clips into finished videos

▶ Assembling and editing videos using the VideoWave Production Editor

▶ Adding audio, transitions, and special effects to your video

▶ Outputting your finished video in various file formats or burning it to a DVD disc

*V*ideoWave is a powerful video editing program which enables you to quickly assemble your digital video clips, audio tracks, and photo images (which you can capture with the Easy Media Creator Capture utility as described in Chapter 10) into professional-looking finished video productions. You can then output the finished VideoWave video productions into a variety of file formats or burn the video on a DVD disc for distribution to your friends and family. You can also use your VideoWave video productions as movie titles in the next DVD project that you create with Easy Media Creator's DVD Builder application (see Chapter 13).

This chapter covers all the major aspects of using VideoWave to create a wide variety of video productions. It begins by familiarizing you with the features and components of the VideoWave window, and then goes on to introduce you the use of the program's new CineMagic component, a nifty little feature for turning your favorite video clips into instant music videos using music of your own choice. Next, the chapter covers the use of VideoWave's new StoryBuilder component, a Wizard-like feature that enables you to create thematic videos which play your video clips as part of pre-designed themes that include ready-made graphic backdrops and stock background music.

If CineMagic and StoryBuilder aren't enough for your video needs, the chapter then introduces you to the use of VideoWave's full-featured Production Editor. Here, you discover how to edit your videos in both the standard storyline and the more advanced timeline view. As part of this process, you also find out how to add audio to your video and apply any of a variety of scene transitions and special video effects.

The chapter concludes with information on your options for outputting your final video productions into a variety of different formats. These include formats for playback on your computer with programs like Windows Media Player, playback on your TV or camcorder, as well as for uploading to the Web or e-mailing to your friends and family. You also find out how to burn your final video productions to DVD disc for playback on your computer's DVD drive and standalone DVD players.

Getting Cozy with VideoWave

You can launch VideoWave from the Easy Media Creator Home window either by clicking the Edit Video link in the Video column in the row at the top or clicking the VideoWave link in the Applications column in the middle of the window. If Easy Media Creator isn't running, you can also launch VideoWave from the Windows taskbar by clicking the Start button, then highlighting All Programs on the Start menu and Roxio on the All Programs submenu before you click VideoWave on the Roxio submenu.

When you first launch VideoWave, a VideoWave 7 – Production Window appears. This window is divided into three panes:

- **Production Preview** pane in the upper left where you can preview the video clips, transitions, and special effects you add to your video production

- **Media Selector** pane in the upper right where you can select the folder or media collection that contains the video, audio, or still images you want to add to your video production

- **Production Editor** pane in Storyline view in the lower third of the Video-Wave window where you can add and edit video clips, background audio or narration, scene transitions, and special effects for your video production

The Production Preview pane

The Production Preview pane enables you to review your video at any stage as you build and edit its content. As you see in Figure 10-1, beneath the preview display, this pane shows the time code of your current position in the video review as well as that of the very last frame. By checking out the time code of the last frame (which gives you the hours, minutes, seconds, and tenths of a second), you can immediately tell how long the video is.

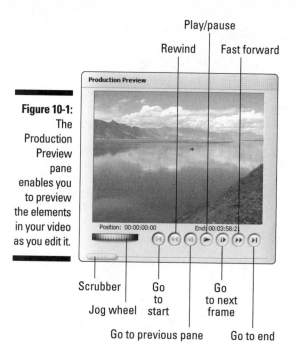

Play/pause

Rewind   Fast forward

Production Preview

Position: 00:00:00:00   End: 00:03:58:2

Figure 10-1:
The
Production
Preview
pane
enables you
to preview
the elements
in your video
as you edit it.

Scrubber   Go   Go
to   to next
Jog wheel   start   frame

Go to previous pane   Go to end

Beneath the current and ending time code, this pane displays the playback buttons and controls that you find on your standard DVD controller. To advance to the first frame of the video, you click the Go to Start button. To then play the video, you click the Play button (which immediately changes to a Pause button).

To advance through the video quickly to find a particular frame to review, you click the Fast Forward button. So too, if you want to go back through the video to find an earlier frame, you click the Rewind button. If you're reviewing a really long video and you want to increase the fast forward or rewind speed, you simply click the Fast Forward or Rewind button again.

To manually advance forward or backward in the video to find a particular frame, you drag the Scrubber button right or left along the bottom of the Production Preview pane. If you want to move forward or backward through the frames in equal increments to find a specific place, drag the Jog Wheel control to the right or left instead.

Keep in mind that the Production Preview pane is only for reviewing the video that you're building in the Production Editor. You can't use this pane to review the video clips or previously made videos in the Media Selector pane that you might possibly want to add to the current video production. (For information on how to preview the video clips and movies displayed in the Media Selector pane, see "Previewing video in the Media Selector pane" later in this chapter.)

The Media Selector pane

The Media Selector pane enables you to locate the different types of digital media files (video, audio, and still graphic images such as photos) that you might want to use in your final video production. This pane can display the contents of any of the folders on your computer system or any of the media collection files that you've created (see Chapter 4 for details).

Figure 10-2 shows you the Media Selector – Folders pane (the default) after choosing the My Videos folder that resides in the Windows' My Documents folder in Navigation Tree displayed on the Select Folder drop-down list. To switch the Media Selector to Collections, click the Browse Collections on the left side of the toolbar at the bottom of the Media Selector pane. To switch back to Folders (the default view), you click the Browse Folders on Your Computer button at the very beginning of this lower toolbar.

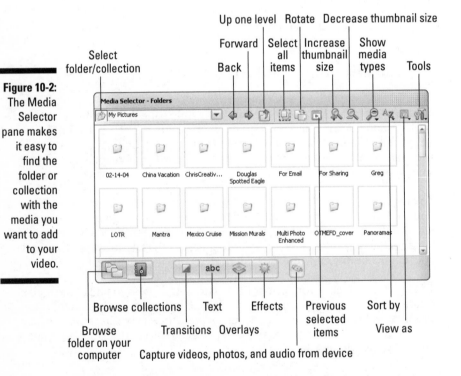

Figure 10-2: The Media Selector pane makes it easy to find the folder or collection with the media you want to add to your video.

Previewing video files displayed in the Media Selector pane

Video clips and finished movie files displayed in the Media Selector pane can't be played in the Production Preview pane. To preview these video files before you add them to your video production, you can either click the video file's thumbnail(s) and then click the Preview Selected Item(s) button on Media Selector's toolbar or you can click the Play button in the lower-right corner of each video clip's or movie's thumbnail.

When you click the Preview Selected Item(s) button to play selected thumbnails, VideoWave opens a separate Preview Window where the selected video plays (similar to the one shown in Figure 10-3). This window appears in the middle of the VideoWave screen. At the bottom of this window, you find a Pause button (that changes to a Play button when you click it) and a Stop button that you can use to start and stop the video playback. Immediately following the Pause and Stop buttons, you find the time code for your current position in the video that's playing along with the time code for the video's duration (indicating the total length of the video clip or finished movie).

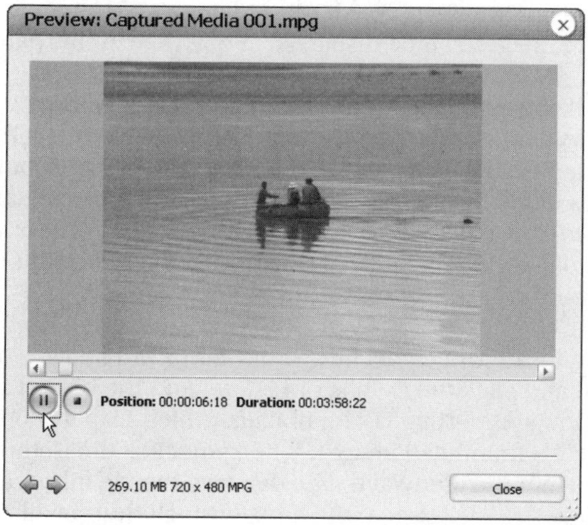

Figure 10-3:
Previewing
video files
listed in the
Media
Selector
pane before
adding them
to the
Production
Editor pane.

If you select more multiple video file thumbnails before you click Preview Selected Item(s) button, this Preview window contains a Previous and a Back button that you can use to advance to the next selected video or return to the previous one. Immediately below the Preview window's display, you find a horizontal scroll bar that you can use to move back and forth through the frames of the video without playing it. Drag the scroll button to move back and forth to particular key frames in the video file. Click the left or right scroll-arrow button to scrub through the video (like you do with Scrubber button in the Production Preview pane).

If you click the tiny Play button that appears in the lower-right of a particular video file's thumbnail image, VideoWave then plays the file's video in place in the Media Selector pane, that is, at the very same size and position as its original thumbnail image. As soon as VideoWave starts playing the video, a Pause button and a progress indicator appears below the thumbnail video display. You can click the Pause to pause the playback of the video at any time. When you're finished previewing the video, click anywhere outside of the thumbnail video display to remove the video's Pause button and progress indicator, returning the file's thumbnail to its original still image.

Controlling how folders and files are displayed in Media Selector pane

After you open the folder or collection in the Media Selector pane that contains the media files you're potentially interested in using in your new video, you can then use the buttons on the right half of the toolbar at the top of the Media Selector pane to modify how its folders and files are displayed.

You can click the Increase Thumbnail Size button to make the thumbnail images larger so that you can make out more detail on each (although fewer images will then be displayed at one time in the Media Selector pane). You can also click the Decrease Thumbnail Size button to make the thumbnail images smaller so that more images can be displayed at one time in this pane.

By default, the Media Selector pane shows all types of media files contained within the current folder or collection that you have open in the pane. To make the file list more manageable, you can use the Show Media Types button to control which types of files are displayed. To filter all but a particular media file type in the open folder or collection, click the Show Media Types button and then click the type of file (Video, Photo, or Audio) that you do want displayed on the button's pop-up menu.

To further help you locate the media files you want to work with, you can click the View As button and click the Details or List item on the button's pop-up menu (the default View As setting is Thumbnails, which displays only the file-name below each file's thumbnail image). When you click the Details item on the View As pop-up menu, VideoWave then displays the file information in columns that include the File Name (with a really small thumbnail image), File Size, Date Created, Date Modified, and Attributes. When you click the List item on the View As pop-up menu, VideoWave displays the file information in the Media Selector pane as a simple, multi-columnar list that displays only the file-name following the file's thumbnail image.

In addition to modifying how folders and file attributes are displayed in the Media Selector pane, you can also can modify the order in which they are displayed in this pane by clicking the Sort By button. By default, VideoWave displays the folders and files by name. If you prefer to see the folder and files arranged in another order, you can have VideoWave reorder the contents of the Media Selector pane by selecting a new attribute on which to sort (Date Created, Date Modified, or Size) in the Sort By pop-up menu.

When you view the contents of the Media Selector pane in Detail view (by selecting Details on the View As button's pop-up menu), you can have Video-Wave resort the folder and files list simply by clicking the column heading at the top of the pane. Click the column heading (such as File Size) once to have the list sorted by that column in ascending order (from A to Z alphabetically and smaller to larger numerically). Click the same column heading a second time to have VideoWave sort the list on that column this time in descending order (from Z to A alphabetically and larger to smaller numerically).

Editing the video files in Media Selector pane

The Tools button, the very last one at the far right of the Media Selector tool-bar, contains a pop-up menu full of options that you can use to perform a variety of important edits on the media files in the Media Selector pane (you can also display these options on a shortcut menu by right-clicking a particular media file's thumbnail in the Media Selector pane).

The options on the Tools pop-up menu include common ones associated with file editing, including an option for previewing the file, adding the file to collection automatically created for the current video production, cutting, copying and pasting the file to the Windows Clipboard as well as deleting and renaming the file. In addition to these general editing options, you also find the following options that are targeted specifically to the video files found in the Media Selector pane:

- ✔ **Scene Detect** to have VideoWave use the video's time code to find and mark individual scenes in the video

- ✔ **Extract Image** to open the Extract Image dialog box where you can preview the video until you find the frame you want to save as still photo in any of the graphic file formats (such as BMP, JPG, or PNG) that Easy Media Creator supports

- ✔ **Extract Audio** to have VideoWave save the audio track in the video in a separate WAV audio file

- ✔ **Export to TV** to open VideoWave's Output to TV/VCR window where you can you can play the video file on your TV or save it on video cassette on your VCR (assuming that these devices are connected to your computer)

- ✔ **Export to Internet** to open VideoWave's Output to Internet window where you can upload the video to a particular Web page (note that this option is only available for movies that you've already output to the Internet by saving it as a compressed WMV file — see "Outputting the Video Production" later in this chapter for details)

- ✔ **Export to DV Recorder** to open VideoWave's Output to DV Camcorder window where you can transfer your finished movie to playback on your digital camcorder for playback (assuming that the camcorder's connected to your computer with an IEEE 1394 FireWire cable and that the recorder is set to its VCR/VTR mode).

The final option on the Tools pop-up menu is the Properties option. Click this option to open a Properties dialog box with a General and a Details tab that give you file statistics and specific file information appropriate to its particular type of media file (video, audio, or photo).

Use the Extract Image option on the Tools menu to pull out still images from the key frames in your videos that you want to save as individual photos. You can then edit your extracted photos with PhotoSuite's many features (see Chapter 6) as you would any other of your digital photos. Extracted photos can make wonderful introductory screens to the video portion of your digital movies, especially when you use PhotoSuite's Add or Edit Text feature to annotate them with general information about the movie or with the movie's credits (see Chapter 11 for more ideas on designing DVD movies with DVD Builder).

The Production Editor pane

The Production Editor pane is the area where all the VideoWave designing action takes place. This is the spot where you add and sequence the video clips, audio track, still photos and other graphics that you want played in your finished movie production. When designing and sequencing a movie in the Production Editor pane, you can work in one of two modes:

- ✔ **Storyline** mode (the default) which presents the movie in storyboard fashion by showing the sequence of video clips and still images that you add to the movie in the order in which they play, along with all the scene transitions you add to take you from one video or still image to another (see "Working in Storyline mode" later in this chapter for details)

- ✔ **Timeline** mode which presents the movie as individual video, audio, effects, text, and overlay tracks along a time line that indicates when particular elements on each track play in the movie (see "Working in Timeline mode" later in this chapter for details)

Most of the time, you want to construct the basic elements for your new movie in Storyline mode, including the video clips, still images, and the transitions you want between them. Then, if you add background audio or narration, or any text, overlays, and special effects to your production, you will want to switch over to Timeline mode so that you can check up and adjust their timing in relation to the movie's video.

Instant Music Videos with CineMagic

CineMagic is a nifty new feature of VideoWave 7 for creating instant music videos, that is, videos that have no other sound than the music track that you choose to play (the wizard automatically suppresses the audio track recorded by your camcorder). One way of thinking about CineMagic music videos is to consider the music as setting the right mood and enhancing the action contained in the video. The only caveat when using CineMagic to create a new music video is that the length of the video clip that you select has to be at least twice as long as the length of the song track that you select to accompany it. In other words, if the song you want to use is 2:22 (two minute, twenty-two seconds) long, your video clip needs to be at the very least 4:44 (four minutes, forty-four seconds) long.

The best way to understand how easy it is to create a new music video with CineMagic is to follow along with the steps for creating one. For this example, I'm creating a music video using vacation video of my recent boat trip down the Yang-tze River in central China with the music provided by Vivaldi's *Fantasmi* from his *Concerto No. 2 in G Minor.*

To begin the new CineMagic music video production, I begin by launching the Easy Media Creator Home window and then clicking its Auto Edit with CineMagic link in the Video column (you can also launch it from within VideoWave by choosing File⇨New CineMagic Production on the VideoWave menu bar). The initial CineMagic window opens similar to the one shown in Figure 10-4. This window is divided into panes: the pane on the left with the instructions for creating a new video that keeps you informed of what step you're completing, the pane in the middle with the Production Preview display and the controls that you use in defining elements for the video and the pane on the right with the Media Selector which you use to select the video clips and audio track that you want your new music video to play.

Figure 10-4:
The initial CineMagic window is where you designate the name for your new music video production.

CineMagic

1. Name Production
2. Select Video
3. Select Audio
4. Select a Style
5. Processing
6. Finish

Name your new production.

To use the CineMagic wizard to create a new music video, follow these steps:

1. **Click the Name for Your New Production text box and then replace the temporary CineMagic1 name with one of your own.**

   Next, you may want to select a new folder into which you save the new video (by default VideoWave saves all videos in the My Videos folder in the My Documents folder on your hard disk).

2. **If you want to save the video in a new folder, click the Browse button and then select the new folder in Save Production As dialog box and click the Save button before you click the Next > button at the bottom of the CineMagic window.**

   In the second CineMagic window (similar to the one shown in Figure 10-5, you select the video clips that you want to use in your video. Keep in mind that you can add as many different video clips as you'd like to the production (just make sure that all total they take at least twice as long to play as your music selection) and that CineMagic will follow the general order in which the video is played but that when it comes to ordering the different scenes within each clip, CineMagic is completely in charge.

3. **Select the folder or collection that contains the video files that you want to add to the music video in Media Selector pane and then select the their thumbnails and drag them to the Add Video list box below the Production Preview display in the middle pane and then click the Next > button.**

   As you add your various video clips, VideoWave keeps you informed of the total video duration with the indicator below the Add Video list box. Make sure that this duration is at least twice as long as that of the music you're about to select in the next step (you should check the length of the music track you intend to use in a program such as the Windows Media Player before you launch the CineMagic wizard).

   In the third CineMagic window (similar to the one shown in Figure 10-6), you select the audio track that you want the new video to play in the Media Selector pane and then drag it to the Audio text box in the middle pane.

4. **Select the folder or collection that contains the video files that you want to add to the music video in Media Selector pane; then select the their thumbnails and drag them to the Add Video list box below the Production Preview display in the middle pane. Click Next >.**

   VideoWave displays the duration of the audio track you select above the duration of your video clip(s): remember that the video duration must be at least twice that of the audio or you will get an error message when you click the Next > button and then have to retrace your steps by rese-lecting the audio or selecting few or different video clips.

   The fourth CineMagic window is where you select a style for your new music video. Each style uses slightly different cuts, transitions, and backgrounds. In deciding which style to select, click the name in the

Video Style list box and then read the description of that style beneath the list box. For my Yang-tze Fantasy music video, I selected the Fun and Fast style described as being "fast paced with cuts timed to the music." Keep in mind that all these CineMagic styles scramble the order of the scenes in your original video a little differently.

5. **Click the name of the style of music video you want to create in the Video Styles list box and then click the Next> button.**

   The CineMagic wizard begins processing your music video by analyzing your video and audio selections and then generating the production. When the wizard finishes processing the music video, the Edit Production and Output To options appear in middle pane and the Play button in the playback controls beneath the Production Preview display becomes active. You can then preview the finished video (see Figure 10-7), save it to disk by clicking the Finish button (because the Output To option is automatically selected), or you can edit the video in VideoWave using the Production Editor (see "Video Editing with the Production Editor" later in this chapter) by clicking the Edit Production option before you click the Finish button.

6. **Click the Play button to preview the music video and then click the Finish button save the production.**

   When you click Finish when the Output To option is selected, the Video-Wave Output To window opens. Here, you select the destination for your finished video: Video File for playback on your computer, Internet for uploading your movie to a Web site, TV/VCR for playback on your TV, VCR, or analog camcorder, DV Camcorder for playback on your digital camcorder, or E-mail to send the movie as an attachment to an e-mail message.

7. **Click the appropriate destination option in the Select Destination list box and then click the Next > button.**

   The options that appear in the Output To window when you click the Next > button depend upon which destination option you select. For some destinations, you must select a purpose and video quality for your finished movie. For others, you select the file type and video quality. (When you select DV Camcorder as the destination, you are taken right to the step for designating the filename in Step 9).

8. **Select the purpose, quality, and file type associated with your destination in the appropriate drop-down list boxes and then click the Next > button.**

   In the next Output To window, VideoWave lets you modify the name you give the finished movie and where it's saved on your computer. By default, VideoWave gives the new movie file the same name as you gave to the video production and saves it in the My Videos folder in My Docume. on your hard disk.

9. **If you want, modify the movie's file name in the Choose a File Name for the Finished Movie text box and select a new folder in which to save the file in the Save Movie As dialog box (opened by clicking the Browse button). Then click Next >.**

10. **Click the Render File button.**

   As VideoWave renders the frames in the new movie, it previews them in the Production Preview pane while showing you the overall progress in the Completed indicator below. When VideoWave finishes rendering the entire movie, the View Movie button appears in the window along with Video Complete message and you can preview the movie by clicking the View Movie button.

11. **Click the View Movie button beneath the Production Preview pane to see and hear your finished music video masterpiece.**

   The finished music video plays in its own Preview window in the middle of your computer screen. Click the Pause to temporarily pause the movie's playback. Click the Stop button to stop the playback and rewind the movie to the start. Use the scroll bar arrow buttons or scroll button to scrub through the video or select a new place from which to start the playback. When you finish previewing the music video, click its Close button to get rid of the preview window.

12. **Click the Close button in the Preview window to close it and then click the Finish button in the Output To button to close it.**

Figure 10-5:
The second CineMagic window is where you select and add the video clips to be used in your new music video.

1. Name Production
2. **Select Video**
3. Select Audio
4. Select a Style
5. Processing
6. Finish

Add video by dragging clips from the Media Selector.

The total length of video must be at least twice as long as the audio you select in the next step.

Figure 10-6:
The third
CineMagic
window is
where you
select the
audio track
to be used
in your new
music video.

Figure 10-7:
When
CineMagic
finishes
generating
the music
video you
can preview
it, edit it,
or save it
to disk.

When you close the Output To window, the normal VideoWave window appears. This window contains your new video production displayed in the Timeline view. You can then do further editing to the video production (see "Video Editing with the Production Editor" later in this chapter) or use VideoWave's Output Your Production in Different Forms or File⇨Output Production To command to save your music video in another file suited for playback on a different device or from a different destination (see "Outputting the Video Production" later in this chapter for details).

Instant Themed Videos with StoryBuilder

VideoWave's new StoryBuilder wizard makes it fun and easy to create movies that use pre-designed themes and templates. Unlike when creating a music video with the program's CineMagic wizard where you have to pair video clips with your own music track, when creating a movie with StoryBuilder, you have only to select a video category and template to use before you select the video clips to play and you're done (the only other thing you can possibly do is edit the introductory and end text that the template uses in the first and last frames of the movie and this step is purely optional).

To get an idea of how easy it is to create a themed video with StoryBuilder, follow along with the steps I used to create a video of my youngest dog's first birthday, which, of course, makes use of StoryBuilder's readymade birthday template.

To begin the new StoryBuilder video production, I begin by launching the Easy Media Creator Home window and then clicking its Guided Edit with StoryBuilder link in the Video column (you can also launch it from within VideoWave by choosing File⇨New Storybuilder Production on the VideoWave menu bar). The initial StoryBuilder window opens similarly to the one shown in Figure 10-8 . This window is divided into panes: the pane on the left contains instructions for creating a new video that keeps you informed of what step you're completing; the pane in the middle has the Production Preview display and the controls that you use in defining elements for your movie; the pane on the right includes the Media Selector which you use to select the video clips that you want to add to your new movie.

StoryBuilder

1. **Name Production**
2. Select Category
3. Select Template
4. Create Intro Text
5. Add Video Clips
6. Create End Text
7. Finish

Name your new StoryBuilder production.

Figure 10-8:
Selecting
the name for
the new
birthday-
themed
video
production
in the initial
StoryBuilder
window.

To use the StoryBuilder wizard to create a themed video, follow these steps:

1. **Click the Name for Your New Production text box and then replace the temporary StoryBuilder1 name with one of your own.**

   You may want to select a new folder into which you save the new video (by default VideoWave saves all videos in the My Videos folder in the My Documents folder on your hard disk).

2. **If you want to save the video in a new folder, click the Browse button and then select the new folder in Save Production As dialog box and click the Save button before you click the Next > button at the bottom of the StoryBuilder window.**

   In the second StoryBuilder window, you select the category of your video. StoryBuilder lets you choose Birthday, Contemporary Concepts, Holidays, Moments in Time, Sports, or Travel as the video's category. Of course, for this example, I chose Birthday at the very top of the Select a Category list box as the category for my new video production.

3. **Click the most appropriate category for your new video production in the Select a Category list box and then click the Next > button.**

Each video category has different templates with their own backgrounds and transitions associated with it. In the third StoryBuilder window, you select the template that you want to use. For my particular video, I selected first template thumbnail called Balloons in the Select a Template list box.

If you can't find a template that you want to use for the category you've selected, click the < Back button and then select a different category in the Select a Category list box before you click the Next > button to return to the window with the Select a Template list box.

4. Click the thumbnail of the template you want to use in the Select a Template list box and then click the Next > button.

The fourth StoryBuilder window shows you the text that the template that you've selected uses as an introduction in the first few frames of the finished video (in the case of the Balloons template, this introductory text is Happy Birthday!). You can, if you want, edit this default text in the Enter the Text to Appear for the Introduction list box. You can also select a new font size for the text from the Font Size drop-down list box and change the default center justification to left- or right-aligned on the movie display.

To preview any changes that you make to the introductory text or just to see the introduction for the particular template you've selected, click the Play button in the controls that appear beneath the Production Preview display before you click the Next > button to display the fifth StoryBuilder window.

5. (Optional) Edit the introductory text in the Enter the Text to Appear for the Introduction list box, its font size in the Font Size drop-down list box, and/or click a new Justification option button (Left or Right) and then click the Next > button.

In the fifth StoryBuilder window (similar to the one shown in Figure 10-9), you select all video clips that you want in new your video production. Select the folder or collection that contains the video clips to be added to the movie in the Media Selector pane. Then drag the thumbnails of each video clip you want to add from the Media Selector to the Drag Clips To list box.

After you add the clips, you can do any of the following things to them:

• To preview how the video clips you've added will play in the final movie, click the Play button in the controls beneath the Production Preview pane. To shorten a particular clip by trimming its start and/or end point, select it in the Drag Clips To list box and then click the Adjust the Duration of the Selected Item button (the one with the alarm clock). VideoWave opens a Video Trimmer dialog box similar to the one shown in Figure 10-10. Drag the Start Jog Wheel until you come to the frame at which you want the clip to begin and then click the Set the Start Point at the Current Position button. Next, drag the End Jog Wheel to the frame on which the clip is to end and then click the Set the End Point at the Current Position button before you click OK.

- To change the order in which the clips play, click the clip in the Drag Clips To list whose play you want to promote so that is plays earlier in the sequence and then click the Move Selected Item Up button (the one with the green arrow pointing up) until it's in its proper position. To demote a clip so that it plays later in the sequence, select it and then click the Move Selected Item Down button (the one with the green arrow pointing down) until it's properly positioned.

- To remove a video clip from the movie, click its thumbnail in the Drag Clips To list box and then click the Remove the Selected Item button (the one with the big red X).

- To remove the background music from the final movie (some of it is pretty chintzy), click the Play Background Music check box that appears right below the Drag Clips To list box to remove its checkmark before you click the Next > button. Note that if you don't disable the Play Background Music option and your video clips have their own sound tracks (which almost all do), both the background music and sound tracks will play against each other in the finished production.

6. **Open the folder or collection in the Media Selector pane that contains the video clips you want to add and then drag their thumbnails to the Drag Clips to List Box Below list box, then adjust their order and length as needed before you click the Next > button.**

   In the sixth StoryBuilder builder, you have a chance to edit the text that's displayed in the last frames of the video. As with the introductory text, you can edit this end text in the Enter the Text to Appear for the Ending list box, change its font size in the Font Size drop-down list box, and/or change its justification on the screen. To preview any changes you make to the ending text, click the Play button in the playback controls at the bottom of the Production Preview pane.

7. **(Optional) Edit the ending text in the Enter the Text to Appear for the Ending list box, its font size in the Font Size drop-down list box, and/ or click a new Justification option button (Left or Right) before you click the Next > button.**

   The seventh and last StoryBuilder window appears. There, you can preview the entire production and select between outputting it to a movie file and editing it further in VideoWave's Production Editor.

   When you click the Finish button and the default Output To option is selected, VideoWave opens an Output To window with the same wizard that you use in CineMagic. This wizard enables you to select the playback destination, video quality, movie filename and folder and to have VideoWave render your finished movie (see Steps 7–12 in the previous section, "Instant music videos with CineMagic" for details).

8. **Click the Play button to preview the complete video and then click the Finish button save the production and follow the prompts in VideoWave's Output To wizard to save and render the final movie.**

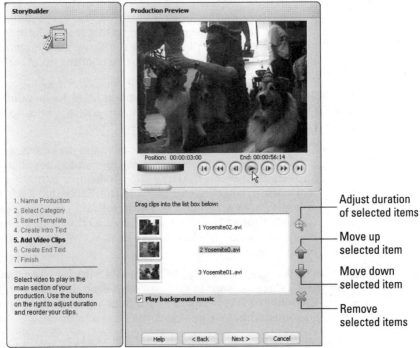

Figure 10-9:
Adding and editing the video clips to include in the new StoryBuilder video production.

Adjust duration of selected items

Move up selected item

Move down selected item

Remove selected items

Figure 10-10:
Trimming a video clip that's been added to the new StoryBuilder video production.

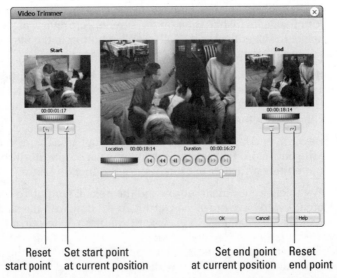

Reset start point

Set start point at current position

Set end point at current position

Reset end point

Video Editing in the Production Editor

As great as CineMagic and StoryBuilder are for quickly putting together finished videos, by their very automation of common video tasks they can put a damper on your own creativity. If you want to be free to make your own decisions when it comes to what goes into a particular scene, how long a scene lasts, or what transition to use when going on to the next scene, you need to be familiar and comfortable using VideoWave's Production Editor.

Fortunately, Roxio has made using the Production Editor to design your own video movies as easy as pie. Both its Storyline and Timeline modes are intuitive and take very little getting used to make you feel like you're ready to video editing with the "big boys."

Working in Storyline mode

Figure 10-11 shows the Production Editor pane in the VideoWave window as it first opens in Storyline mode after adding some video clips and transitions. In Storyline mode, individual scenes are represented by panels that are sequentially numbered and arranged in rows (a kind of digital storyboarding). Each scene panel can contain a particular photo, video clip, or color panel that you add from the Media Selector pane to the Production Editor pane by dragging it to its numbered panel square.

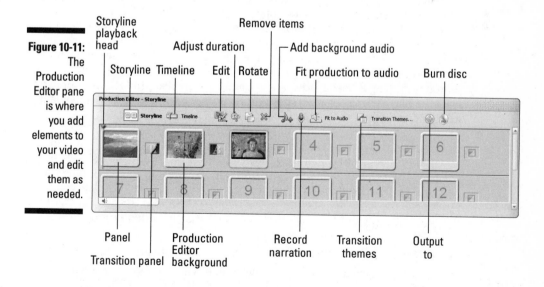

Figure 10-11: The Production Editor pane is where you add elements to your video and edit them as needed.

Storyline playback head

Adjust duration

Remove items

Add background audio

Storyline   Timeline   Edit   Rotate   Fit production to audio   Burn disc

Panel

Transition panel   Production Editor background

Record narration

Transition themes

Output to

In between each scene panel, you find a transition panel that you can use to add a particular scene transition, determining how one scene leads into the next. VideoWave gives you a choice among hundreds of different transitions, the most widely used one being the Dissolve transition whereby the last frames of the current scene literally dissolve into the first frames of the next scene (the duration of the Dissolve transition being the determining factor in how much information from the current scene remains visible as the beginning of the next scene takes over).

Note that you don't have to add any transition between scene panels in your video production, but keep in mind that if you don't use add transitions, your finished movie will have a jumpy feel to it if it contains multiple video clips and still images. This is because the moment one scene ends, the next one abruptly starts up. Depending upon how different the visual information at the end of one clip is from that of the beginning of the next, the effect can be jarring to the eye and very disrupting to the flow of your story. Therefore, I highly recommend the use of transitions to smooth the changeover from one scene to the next, while at the same time, I caution against using a whole bunch of different transitions in the same movie. Be careful with your transition selections because using a variety of different transitions to make scene changes can be almost as distracting as using none.

The Storyline Playback Head keeps your place in the Production Editor as you preview the video production using the playback controls at the bottom of the Production Preview pane. As you review your video production, the Storyline Playback Head moves through the scene and transition panels in the Production Editor pane, keeping track of your present position in the current video clip, still image, or transition as its images appear in the Production Preview pane above. Note that you can't move the Storyline Playback Head directly in the Production Editor: to move it to a new place in this pane, you need to use the playback controls in the Production Preview pane. For example, to find the place in the movie where you want to start playing back the production, you drag the Scrubber button or the Jog Wheel to advance to frame in the video production where you want the playback to begin and then click the Play button to start the playback from that position.

Note that when working on a video production in Storyline mode, you can add audio, special effects, and overlays for the entire production simply by dragging their thumbnails to Production Editor pane and then dropping them anywhere on the Production Editor Background (just make sure that you don't drop the icon on a specific scene pane or the audio, special effect, or overlay will apply only to that scene, not to the entire video production).

The different kinds of files you can add to your movie

Most of the movies that you'll make with VideoWave will consist of video clips that you've acquired with the Capture application (see Chapter 10 for details). Some of the movies you make may also include the use of digital still photos that you've acquired with the Capture program and then edited with the PhotoSuite application (as described in Chapter 7).

In addition to standard video clips and still photos, you may also want to add color panels to the first and last scenes of the movie. These color panels, usually in black, enable you to transition from a black matt screen into the first frames of the initial video clip and then from last frames of the final video clip to another black matt (when you use the Dissolve transition between the final video clip and the final black matt, in Hollywood lingo, your movie is said to fade to black).

Note that you can also add finished movies created with VideoWave and output to the MPG file format to scene panels in a new VideoWave video production. When you add a finished movie to a panel, VideoWave then plays that movie (with all of its scenes, transitions, audio, and so on) as soon as the Storyline Playback Head reaches it during playback.

Don't forget that you can use VideoWave to make a really effective slideshow out of your digital photos. All you have to do is add your digital photos to the sequential scene panels in the Production Editor pane in the order you want them to appear in the slideshow, add the type of transition you want between each photo, and then add any background audio or narration that you want your audience to hear.

Table 10-1 shows a list of all the files types that you can add to your video production. Note that the graphic file formats supported include the BMP, JPEG, and PNG graphics file formats. Bitmap graphics are most often used for storing simple images such as Clip Art. The JPEG graphics format is most often used for storing digital still photos as well as more complex graphic images. The PNG graphics file format is mostly used for Web graphics (where it's attempting to replace the older, GIF (Graphics Information File) format.

The video and audio file formats supported by VideoWave include all the major formats that you're likely to run into. In terms of the video file formats, the Easy Media Creator applications are only able to save its video productions in the MPEG2 and WMV compressed video formats. The Windows AVI and MOV video files that you use in your VideoWave productions must be produced in programs not part of the Easy Media Creator suite and then imported into VideoWave.

Table 10-1 File Formats Supported in VideoWave Video Productions

Category	File type (file extension)	Description
Graphics files	BMP (.bmp, .rle, .dib)	Bitmap graphics
	TIF (.tif, .tiff)	Tagged Information Graphics
	PNG (.png)	Portable Network Graphics

(continued)

Table 10-1 (continued)

Category	File type (file extension)	Description
	JPEG (.jpg, .jpeg, .jpe)	Joint Photographic Experts Group
Video files	MPEG (.mpg, .mpeg, .m2s)	Moving Pictures Experts Group
	AVI (.avi)	Audio Video Interleave
	MOV (.mov)	QuickTime Movie
	WMV (.wmv)	Windows Media Video
Audio files	WAV (.wav)	WAVE or PCM (Pulse Code Modulation) files
	MP3 (.mp3)	MPEG Layer 3
	WMA (.wma)	Windows Media Audio

In addition to the standard graphics, video, and audio file formats listed in Table 10-1, VideoWave also lets you add Roxio project files created with the PhotoSuite application and saved in its native file format to a new video production. These project files carry the .dmsp filename extension. Note, however, that you cannot add VideoWave project files (that carry the .dmsm filename extension) directly to a new VideoWave video production. Before you can add movies that you create with VideoWave to new VideoWave video productions, you must first output them and save them as MPG files (see "Outputting the Video Production" later in this chapter for details).

Adding color panels and text to your movie

As stated earlier, you can add black color panels to the beginning and end of your movies and then with the help of the Dissolve transition start the video production by fading in from black and then end it by fading to black. Because you can add text to your color panels, you can also use them to introduce new scenes in the movie, to create general introductions to the movie as well as to provide the credits for production (with you, of course, as the director).

You follow these two steps to create a new color panel in your video production:

1. **Right-click the blank scene panel in the Production Editor pane where the color panel is to appear and then click Insert Color Panel on the shortcut menu.**

    The Color Picker dialog box appears where you select the color for the new panel. If none of the pre-defined colors will do, click the Create

Colors >> button to expand the Color Picker dialog box. Here, you can create a new color by dragging through the Hues and Shades boxes, clicking the Eyedropper mouse pointer on some color in the Production Preview pane, or entering new values in the Hue, Saturation, and Values or the Red, Green, and Blue text boxes.

2. **Select the color for the new color panel in the Color Picker dialog box and then click the OK button.**

   VideoWave inserts a panel in the color you selected in the Color Picker in the scene panel you right-clicked.

After inserting a color panel in your video production, you can, if you want, add text to the panel that explains the upcoming scene in the vein of those old silent movies or gives your audience some important information about the video clip that they're about to witness. To add text to a color panel you added, you follow these steps:

1. **Click the scene panel in the Production Editor pane that contains the color panel to which you want to add your text.**

   After selecting the color panel, you need to select the Text samples in the Media Selector pane above.

2. **Click the Text button at the bottom of the Media Selector pane (the one with the abc icon).**

   VideoWave displays the first of many text samples in the Media Selector. To narrow the samples to a particular category, click the drop-down button on the right of the drop-down list box at the top of Media Selector pane and then click the category (see Figure 10-12).

   If you want to animate your text so that moves onto and off the color panel (like some Hollywood movie credits do), click the Motion category. VideoWave then displays ten different animated text samples from which to choose. To get an idea of how your text will move onto the color panel and in some cases move off, click the animated sample's tiny Play button in its lower-right corner.

3. **Click the text sample in the Media Selector- Text pane that you want to follow in creating your own text and then drag the sample to the Production Editor pane and drop it on color panel to which the text is to be affixed.**

   VideoWave opens its Text Editor window similar to the one shown in Figure 10-12. This window contains a preview display on the left side with Text tab options on the right where you can enter the text and define its basic attributes. In addition, this window contains four other tabs of options (Style, Path, Frame, and 3-D) which you can use to further enhance the text.

   Enter the text you want to appear on color panel in the list box at the top of the Text tab. Press the Enter key to insert line breaks in the text.

Use the options on the Font, Size, Style, and Justification drop-down list boxes to select a new font, font size, style other than Bold, and justification other than Center. You can also increase or decrease the spacing between the letters in the text by entering a new value in the Letter Spacing text box or selecting one with its Plus (+) or Minus (–) keys. Likewise, you can increase or decrease the spacing between lines when the text spans multiple lines by entering a new value in the Line Spacing text box or selecting one with its Plus (+) or Minus (–) keys.

You can use the options on the Style tab to customize such items as the fill of the text characters, their outline, and shadow. You can use the options on the Path tab to animate the text and control how it appears and disappears on the color panel. You can use the options on the Frame tab to add a custom frame that appears around the text. You can use the options on the 3-D tab to create custom 3-D effects for the text characters as well as their outlines, frames, and the frame edges.

When defining the settings for animated text, you can preview the animation in the Preview display by clicking its Play button before you close the Text Editor window by clicking its OK button.

4. **Enter the text you want to appear on color panel in the list box at the top of the Text tab and then use the options on this tab as well as the other four tabs to customize its settings before you click the OK button.**

VideoWave closes the Text Editor window while building a preview of the color panel with your text, which now appears on the color panel in the Production Editor pane of the VideoWave window (unless you've selected animated text). If your text is animated, you can preview it by clicking the Play button in the Production Preview pane.

You may want to adjust the time that color panel and its text stays on the screen when your movie plays. By default, VideoWave displays all still images including scanned graphics, digital photos, and color panels that you add to a video production, and these panels are given a duration of five seconds. If you have a lot of text on your color panel, you may want to increase this duration. If you have just a simple one- or two-line title, you may want to decrease this duration.

5. **(Optional) To increase or decrease the time the color panel stays onscreen in your movie, right-click the color panel and then click Adjust Duration on the shortcut menu.**

The Adjust Duration dialog box appears where you can increase or decrease the time that the panel is displayed by entering a new value (in seconds) in the Duration text box or by selecting one with its Plus (+) or Minus (–) keys.

If you want to make the new value you enter in the Duration text box the default for all still images (including photos and color panels) that you add to your VideoWave video productions, click the Save as Default check box. If you want to apply the new value to all other still images (photos and color panels) that you've already added to the current VideoWave video production, click the Apply Duration to All Still Images in the Current Production check box.

6. **(Optional) Enter a new value (in seconds) in the Duration text box in the Adjust Duration dialog box before you click the OK button.**

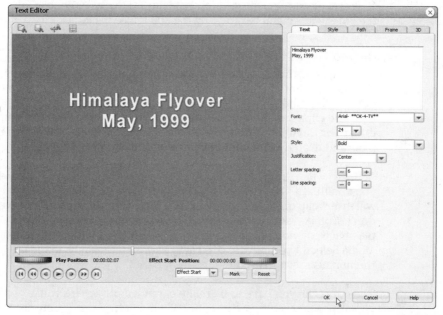

Figure 10-12:
You enter
the text for
your color
panel,
specify its
enhance-
ments, and
preview it
in the
Text Editor
window.

Note that in addition to color panels, you can also add text to photos or any other kinds of still graphic image as well as to the video clips in your video production. In fact, you can even add text to the entire video production which is displayed during the entire playing of the movie (to do this, you have to drag the text thumbnail from the Media Selector pane and drop it on the Production Editor Background in the Production Editor pane rather than a specific scene panel). When adding text to a still image, video clip, or entire video production, you may have to use the Enter key to insert a number of line returns in order to get the text down low enough on the screen so that it doesn't obscure some important part of the still or video image that is playing.

If you decide that you want to get rid of the text that you've added to a particular photo or color panel, you can remove the text without removing the image by right-clicking its scene panel in the Production Editor pane and then clicking Remove➪Text on its shortcut menu.

If you decide that you want to delete the color panel from the video production (along with any text that you've added to it), you can just click its scene panel in the Production Editor pane to select it and then press the Delete key (you can also do this by right-clicking the pane and then clicking Delete on its short-cut menu). VideoWave immediately eliminates the still image along with any text the image contains and closes any gap its removal has caused in the video production without asking you to confirm the deletion. If you get a case of "Deleters angst," you must immediately press Ctrl+Z or choose Edit⇔Undo on the VideoWave menu bar to bring the still image back.

Adding video clips and still images to your movie

The basic technique for adding video clips or still images such as scanned graphics or photos that you've captured to your VideoWave video productions couldn't be simpler: you open the folder or media collection that contains the clips or photos you want to use in the Media Selector pane and then drag their thumbnails from the Media Selector pane to Production Editor pane and drop them on the next unused scene panel.

Actually, when dragging a video clip or photo into the Production Editor pane, you don't even have to be that careful with where you drop it as VideoWave will insert clip or image in the next available unused scene panel even if you don't drop it exactly on that panel. Also keep in mind that you can add multiple images or video clips at one time by selecting all their thumbnails in the Media Selector pane (with Ctrl+click) and then dragging all the selected thumbnails down to Production Editor pane.

The only time you have to be really careful about where you drop the video clip or photo is when you intentionally mean to insert it between two already occupied scene panels. Suppose, for example, that you discover a new video clip that you want played in between the clips currently occupying Panel 4 and Panel 5 of your video production. All you have to do to insert the new video clip in between them is drop the new one right on top of Panel 5. When you release the mouse button, instead of the new clip replacing the clip that previously occupied Panel 5, the new clip takes over its position in Panel 5 and the previous owner of Panel 5 moves over to Panel 6 (and the rest of the occupied panels from 6 on are adjusted one to the right as well).

You can also play musical scene panels by rearranging the still images and video clips that you've added to the Production Editor pane. Just click the panel with the image or clip that you want to move and then drag it to and then drop it on the panel where it should go. VideoWave will then insert the image or clip you moved in the panel where you dropped it and adjust the panel position of all the remaining images and clips in the production as needed.

To duplicate an image or clip that you've added to the production, right-click its panel in the Production Editor pane and then click Copy on the panel's shortcut menu. Then, to insert the copied image or clip, right-click the panel in the Production Editor pane in front of which the duplicate image or clip is to go and then click Paste on that panel's shortcut menu. VideoWave then inserts the copied image or clip into a new panel at the place in the production, moving the panel you originally right-clicked and all the panels that come after it down one.

If you want to remove an image or clip from the video production, click its panel in the Production Editor pane and then press the Delete key (or you can right-click the panel and click the Delete item on its shortcut menu. As with deleting color panels, VideoWave deletes your photos and video clips without asking for your confirmation. The only way to bring them back to the production if you made a boo-boo is to press Ctrl+Z or choose Edit⇔Undo on the VideoWave menu bar right away.

Use the Tools⇔Find Panel command on the VideoWave to quickly locate and select a particular clip or still image that you've added to your production. When you select this command, VideoWave opens a Find Panel dialog box that sequentially lists the names of all the scene and transition panels in your production along with a short description and the scene or transition's starting and ending time. To go directly to a particular panel or transition in the Production Editor pane, click in the Find Panel dialog box and then click the OK button. VideoWave then closes the Find Panel dialog box and then goes to the selected panel or transition in the Production Editor pane. VideoWave also positions the Storyline Playback Head right in front of the panel so that you can review the scene or transition in the Production Preview pane simply by clicking that pane's Play button.

Trimming your video clips

Some of the video clips that you add to a production may require some trimming to make them just the right length and to ensure that clip starts and ends on just the frames that you want included. To trim a video clip that you've added to your video production, right-click its panel in the Production Editor pane and then click the Adjust Duration option on its shortcut menu.

VideoWave then opens a Video Trimmer dialog box similar to the one shown in Figure 10-13. Here, you can reset either the starting or the ending frame of the video clip or reset both the starting and ending frames. To reset the starting frame, use the playback controls under the center preview area to display the frame where you want to clip to begin playing and then click the Set the Start Point at the Current Position button. To reset the ending frame, use the playback controls to display the frame where you want to clip to stop playing and then click the Set the End Point at the Current Position button.

To preview the trimmed clip from start to end, click the Go to Start button in the playback controls and then click its Play button. If you're happy with how the clip now plays, click the OK button to close the Video Trimmer dialog box and return to the VideoWave window. If you're not happy with where the clip now starts or ends, click the Reset Start Point or Reset End Point button and then readjust where the video clip starts or ends.

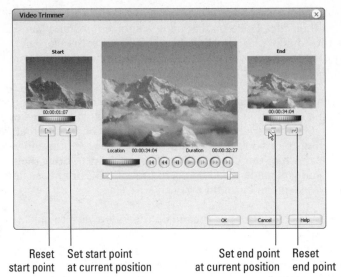

Figure 10-13:
You can trim the start and/or ending of any video clip in your production in the Video Trimmer dialog box.

Reset start point   Set start point at current position   Set end point at current position   Reset end point

Adjusting the quality of your video clips and still images

Not all the video clips and still images that you add to your video production will be of the highest quality. If you need to, you can tweak the overall brightness, contrast, and color balance and tint of any video clip or still image in the Production Editor pane. When dealing with video clips, you can also fine-tune the speed at which the video plays (this feature, of course, is not available when editing still images).

To make any of these adjustments to the video clip or still image you've added to the Production Editor pane, simply right-click its panel and then click Edit⇨Adjust on its shortcut menu. VideoWave opens the Video Adjust Editor dialog box similar to the one shown in Figure 10-14. If the panel you right-clicked contains a still image, the image appears in the preview area of the dialog box and the Speed adjustment slider is grayed out and only the Color Adjust sliders (Brightness, Contrast, Color, Red, Green, and Blue) are available to you. If the panel you right-clicked contains a video clip (as does the one in Figure 10-14), the first frame of the clip appears in the preview area and the Speed slider as well as all the Color Adjust sliders are available to you.

To adjust a particular visual aspect of still image or video, drag the appropriate slider to the right or left or click Plus (+) or Minus (–) buttons to change its settings. If you want to return to a default speed or color setting, click the Default button to the immediate right of its slider.

If you're adjusting the speed of a video clip by tweaking its Speed slider, you can click the Play button to review the speed adjustment in the Preview area before putting the change into effect. When everything is as you want it for the edited clip or image, click the OK button to close the Video Trimmer dialog box and return to the VideoWave window where the program puts your adjusted settings into effect.

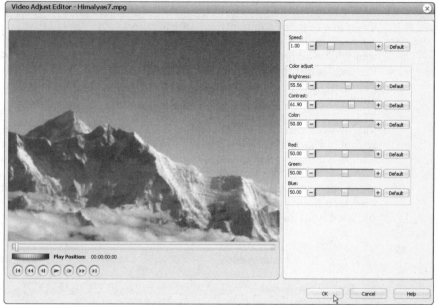

Figure 10-14:
You can
adjust the
quality of
any video
clip or still
image
in your
production
in the Video
Adjust Editor
dialog box.

If you're dealing with a digital photo and find that you need to make adjustments to it such as cropping, rotating, removing red eye, or resizing it, you can subject it to this type of photo editing in the Photo Editor window. To open the Photo Editor, right-click the photo's panel in the Production Editor pane and then click the Edit⇨Photo options on its shortcut menu. The Photo Editor contains four tabs (Crop, Rotate, Red Eye, and Resize) of options for editing your photo (see Chapter 7 if you need help using any of these photo editing options).

Automatically panning and zooming your still images

VideoWave has this really cool Auto Motion feature that you can apply to the still images such as scanned graphics and digital photos that you add to a new video production. When you apply the Auto Motion feature to a photo, VideoWave gives the illusion of animating it by panning and/or zooming in or out on the image.

To apply this feature to a still image that you've added to the Production Editor pane, right-click its panel and then click the Auto Motion option on its shortcut menu. VideoWave then applies the feature to the image and immediately positions the Storyline Playback Head immediately in front of the still image in the video production. You can then preview actual panning and zooming applied to your still image by then clicking the Play button in Production Preview pane. If you don't happen to like the Auto Motion effect that VideoWave has applied, press Ctrl+Z or choose Edit⇨Undo on the VideoWave menu bar immediately to remove it and return it to its original completely static image.

Adding panning and zooming to still images and video clips

If you like to remain in control of any pan-and-zoom effects that you add to your still images or would like to control the camera motion in a video clip that you've added to video production, you can use VideoWave's Motion Pictures editor to do this. Right-click the panel with the image or video clip you want to pan and zoom and then click Edit⇨Motion Pictures on its shortcut menu.

VideoWave opens the Motion Pictures Editor window similar to the one shown in Figure 10-15. Here, you create panning effect by defining a smaller Visible Window within in the still image or video clip and then defining a path upon which this window moves at different key points in the playback of the video clip or the still image's duration. To zoom in and out on key frames of the video or on portions of the image, you simply modify the size of the visible window at any given key point in time.

Visible window   Size slider

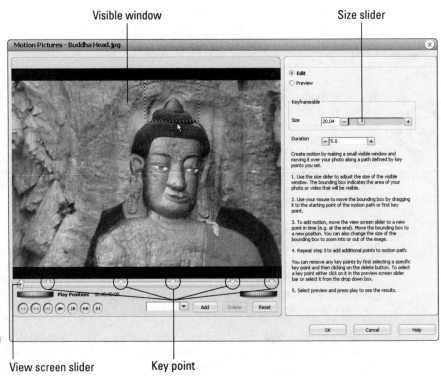

Figure 10-15:
You can create pan and zoom motion effects for a still image or video clip in the Motion Pictures Editor.

View screen slider   Key point

To get an idea of how you can use the Motion Picture Editor to create pan and zoom motion effects, follow along with the steps I followed for slowly zooming out from the top of Buddha's crown in the still photo shown in Figure 10-15 to reveal the entire Buddha image at the end of the still image's five-second duration:

1. **Right-click the panel where you add the pan and zoom effect and then click the Edit⇨Motion Pictures options on its shortcut menu.**

   VideoWave opens the Motion Pictures Editor window just like the one shown in Figure 10-15. Note that the Edit option button is automatically selected at the top of the right pane in this window (you must select the Edit option button in order to be able to resize the view window and define its path).

   When you first open the Motion Pictures Editor, the Visible Window (indicated by the bounding box with a dashed outline) is as large as the still image or the first frame of the video clip. The first step in defining any pan or zoom motion effect is to reduce the size of this window. (In other words, before you can zoom out on this photo, I must zoom in.)

   For this example, I reduced the Visible Window until it was only big enough to display the very top of Buddha's head.

2. **Drag the Size slider in the Keyframeable area to the left until the Visible Window is the size that you want it at the first frame of the video clip or at the beginning of the still image's duration.**

   After resizing the Visible Window, you can now drag its bounding box into position within the image or first frame of the video.

3. **Drag the bounding box representing the View Window to the place in the first video frame or the start of the image's duration where you want VideoWave to zoom in.**

   For this example, I repositioned the Visible Window so that it encloses just the top of Buddha's crown. Keep in mind that if I were now to play the Motions Picture effect I've added to my photo of Buddha, VideoWave would start the playback as though it had zoomed in on just Buddha's crown that's displayed within the Visible Window. In other words, the crown portion of the Buddha image would zoom up so that it fills the entire preview screen if I were to click the Play button!

   To pan to a new area or zoom out further in the video or still image, I now need to establish another key point in its timeline (the key points that you add define the motion path). To establish the next key point, I drag the View Screen Slider to that place in the timeline where I want to make my next adjustment to the position or size of the Visible Window and then click the Add button at the bottom of the Preview display.

 4. **Drag the View Screen Slider to the place in the clip's or image's time-line and then click the Add button.**

 As soon as you click the Add button, VideoWave adds a new key point whose indicator appears on the timeline. The next step is to resize and reposition the Visible Window to display the portion of the video frame or clip that you want displayed on the screen at this new key point.

 In my case, I only need to increase the size of the Visible Window's bounding box and move it slightly so that it's still centered on the Buddha image and now encloses both his crown and forehead.

 5. **Adjust the size of the Visible Window using the Size slider as required at this key point and then drag its bounding box into the desired position.**

 For this example, I established four additional key points for the zoom out effect. At each key point, I slightly enlarged the Visible Window so that it encompassed more and more of the Buddha image, each time reposition-ing the bounding box so that it remained centered on his image.

 6. **Repeat Steps 4 and 5 until you have established all the key points on the timeline for the pan-and-zoom effect you want.**

 After you finish establishing your key points, you're ready to see what you've got. To preview the motion effect, you must first click the Preview option button (automatically deselecting the Edit option button) and then click the Play button in the playback controls.

 7. **Click the Preview option button on the right side of the Motions Pictures window and then click the Play button in the playback controls below the preview area.**

 If, upon reviewing the pan-and-zoom motion effects, you're happy with what you've got, you click the OK button to apply the motion effect to the video clip or still image.

 If you still need to fine-tune the effect, you can do so by clicking the Edit option button again. To change the effect at a particular key point, click its indicator in the timeline and then adjust the size and position of the Visible Window as required. If you find that you don't really need a par-ticular key, you can remove it by clicking its indicator and then clicking the Delete button.

 8. **Click the OK button to close the Motion Pictures window and apply the effect to the clip or image in the VideoWave window.**

Adding transitions to the scenes in your movie

VideoWave offers you a wide choice in transitions that can smooth the changeover from one scene to the next in your movie. To add a transition between the scene panels in the Production Editor pane, you follow these steps in the VideoWave window:

1. **Click the Transitions button at the bottom of the Media Selector pane (the one with the rectangle that is divided diagonally).**

   VideoWave displays thumbnails for the first two rows of its all transitions in the Media Selector - Transitions pane as shown in Figure 10-16. To reduce the display to only the transitions in a particular category, click the drop-down list button to the right of All and click the desired category (Basic, Simple Reveals, Theme Reveals, Page Turns, Particles, Slab, 3-D, or SMPTE Wipes) in the drop-down list box.

   To get an idea of how the transition works, click the tiny Play button in the lower-right corner of its thumbnail. The thumbnail demonstrates the transition from A (in dark blue) to B (in gold) with A representing the current scene in the panel to the immediate left of the transition panel in the Production Editor pane where you set this transition and B representing the very next scene in the panel to the immediate right.

2. **Drag the thumbnail of the transition you want to use from the Media Selector pane to the Production Editor pane and then drop it on the blank transition panel between the two scene panels that are to use that transition.**

   After setting a transition between scenes, VideoWave automatically positions the Storyline Playback Head right before the new transition so that you can then test it out in the Production Preview pane by simply clicking its Play button.

3. **Click the Play button in the Production Preview pane's controls to review the new transition.**

   Sometimes the transition will play so quickly that your audience doesn't get the full visual effect when the movie goes from one scene to the next. If this is the case, you can lengthen the duration of the transition to slow it down.

4. **(Optional) To adjust the length of the new transition, right-click it in its transition panel, click the Set Transition Duration option on its shortcut menu, and then enter or select a new length (in seconds) in the Duration text box before clicking the Set Transition Duration dialog box's OK button.**

Instead of repeating the previous steps to individually add the same transition over and over again to the rest of the transition panels in your video production, you can apply the first transition that you add manually to all the other transition panels. Right-click the transition panel containing the first transition that you added by hand and then click the Apply Transition to All option that appears on its shortcut menu. VideoWave then displays an alert dialog box asking you to confirm the replacement of all transitions in your production. As soon as you click the Yes button in this dialog box, the program adds the first transition to the all the rest of the transition panels that occur between occupied scene panels.

Figure 10-16:
To add a
transition,
drag its
thumbnail
from the
Media
Selector -
Transitions
pane to the
transition
panel in the
Production
Editor pane.

If you don't really want to use the exact same transition between every scene
in the video production, instead of selecting the Apply Transition to All option
on the transition panel's shortcut menu, try using the Apply Transition Theme
option instead. When you click this option, VideoWave opens the Apply
Transition Theme dialog box where you can select among five different transition themes (Fast Dissolves, Slow Dissolves, Simple Transitions, Page Turns,
and Random). When you click one of these transition themes and then click
the OK button (and click the Yes button in the alert dialog box asking you to
confirm the replacement of all existing transitions in your production), the
program applies a progression of related transitions (that is, those in a similar
style) to all the rest of the transition panels between occupied scenes in the
production.

Adding special effects and overlays to your movie

VideoWave offers you a wide variety of special effects (that consist mostly of
filters with some cutouts) and overlays (that consist mostly of cutouts and
frames) that you can apply to the video clips and still images that you've
added to the scene panels of your production in the Production Editor pane.

To choose a particular filtering or cutout effect for your video production in
the Effects category, you click the Effects button (the one with the starburst)
at the end of the toolbar at the bottom of the Media Selector pane. VideoWave
opens the Media Selector - Effects pane displaying the thumbnails for the first

two rows of all the special effects you can choose from. To narrow the display to particular subcategories of effects, click the drop-down button to the right of the drop-down list box that currently contains All and then click the subcategory to display (Mirror, 3-D, Colorize, Fun Effects, Frames, Soften & Sharpen, Basic Effects, Emboss, or Noise) on this list.

To choose a particular cutout or frame for your video production in the Overlays category, click the Overlays button (the one with a transparent sheet of paper over a darker, regular sheet) to the immediate left of the Effects button on the Media Selector pane's toolbar. VideoWave opens the Media Selector - Overlays pane displaying the thumbnails for the first two rows of all the overlays you can choose from. To narrow the display to certain subcategories of overlays, click the drop-down button to the right of the drop-down list box that currently contains All and then click the subcategory to display (Edges, Frames, Motion, News Banners, Textures, or My Overlays) on this list.

You can add a particular effect or overlay to an individual scene panel or to all the panels in the entire production. To add an effect or overlay to an individual scene panel, you drag the effect or overlay's thumbnail from the Media Selector - Effects or Media Selector - Overlays pane to the Production Editor pane. Then drop it on the particular scene panel to which you want it to apply. After applying an effect to a particular scene panel, the Effects icon (the starburst) appears in the lower-left corner of that panel's thumbnail. So too, after applying an overlay, the Overlays icon (a transparent sheet of paper over a darker, regular sheet) appears in the lower-left corner of the panel's thumbnail.

To apply a particular effect or overlay to all the panels in the entire video production, you drag the effect or overlay thumbnail from the Media Selector pane and drop it on the Production Editor Background (that is, in the blank space in the area surrounding specific scene or transition panels). Note that when you add an effect and/or overlay to the entire video production, the Production Editor pane gives you no visual clue as to its existence. The only way to tell that a production is using a special effect or overlay is by recognizing that fact when you review the movie in the Production Preview pane.

You can sometimes effectively combine an effect with an overlay to lend a definite mood to your production. For example, to give your movie a really old feel, try combining the Low Sepia or Medium Sepia special effect with the Old Photo overlay. Together, your movie seems more like something produced around the turn of the last century (that is, the early 1900s) than something produced with twenty-first century computer software.

Removing special effects and overlays

Sometimes after reviewing the footage with a special effect or overlay that you've added to a scene in the Production Preview pane, you'll decide that you definitely don't want to keep it. To remove an effect from a scene panel, right-click the panel and then click Remove⇨Effects on the shortcut menu. To remove an overlay, you follow the same procedure except that you click Remove⇨Overlays on the panel's shortcut menu.

If you've added an effect or overlay to an entire video production and then decide that you need to lose it fast, you need to right-click somewhere in the Production Editor Background (that is, in the space in between the scene and transition panels) and then click the Remove⇨Effects or the Remove⇨ Overlays options on the shortcut menu.

Customizing special effects and overlays

You don't have to use a particular special effect or overlay exactly as it comes out of the box. VideoWave enables you to customize the look and feel of an effect or overlay that you apply to a particular scene panel or the entire video production. What controls are available for customizing an effect or overlay and how exactly you're able to use them to customize it depend entirely upon the particular effect or overlay you're customizing. When customizing filtering effects, most of them enable you to adjust their color and tint settings. When customizing cutout overlays, most of them enable you to adjust the size and positioning of the cutout through which the video plays or the sill image is displayed.

To customize an effect that you've added to a scene panel, you right-click the panel and then choose Edit⇨Effects on its shortcut menu. To customize an effect added to the entire production, right-click somewhere in the Production Editor Background and then choose Edit⇨Effects on the background's shortcut menu. VideoWave then opens to the Effects Editor dialog box for that particular effect, and you use its controls to modify the effect's settings.

To customize an overlay that you've added to a scene panel, right-click the panel and then choose Edit⇨Overlays on the panel's shortcut menu. To customize an overlay added to the entire production, right-click somewhere in the Production Editor Background and then choose Edit⇨Overlays on the background's shortcut menu. VideoWave opens the Overlay Editor dialog box for the particular overlay, and you can use its controls to modify the overlay's settings.

Figure 10-17 shows you the Overlay Editor dialog box that opens when you choose the Edit⇨Overlay command on the shortcut menu for a panel to which the Old Photo overlay has been applied. As you can see in this figure, above the Preview display, you find the Save Custom Overlay and Turn on the Ability to Position the Overlay on the Screen buttons.

To modify the thickness of the old photo frame in the Preview display, you can drag the Zoom slider control on the right side slightly to the right. To be able to move the old frame in relation to the video background, you can click the Turn on the Ability to Position the Overlay on the Screen button and then drag the frame with the mouse.

Save custom overlay

Turn on ability to position overlay on screen

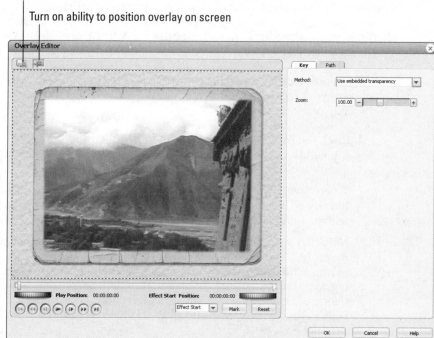

Figure 10-17:
Customizing
the Old
Photo
overlay
applied to a
particular
scene panel
in the
Overlay
Editor.

You can save the modifications you make to the Old Photo overlay by click-ing the Save Custom Overlay button and then entering a new name for the overlay (such Narrow Old Photo) in the Save dialog box before you click the OK button. After that, the name of your customized overlay (Narrow Old Photo in this example) is listed as part of the My Overlays subcategory. You can then apply the customized overlay to your current and future video pro-ductions by selecting its name in the Media Selector - Overlays pane.

Adding audio clips to your video production

VideoWave makes it easy to add background audio to your video productions. When adding audio, you have a choice between adding a prerecorded audio file and recording your own narration sound track for your video production. You can even add both types of audio tracks to the same video production if you so desire (although you have to be careful that the different audio tracks don't start competing with each other for the poor audience's limited listening attention span).

Keep in mind when adding either or both types of audio tracks to your video production that this audio plays in the background of the movie without in anyway canceling the audio that's been recorded as part of the video clips added to the production. In some cases, this will mean that your background audio tracks will compete with the sound recorded as part of each individual video clip. As a result, you may end up having either to turn down the volume on the background audio tracks or on the audio that's part of each video clip (I give you instructions on how to adjust the volume of each kind of audio clip later in this chapter).

Often, a prerecorded audio file can serve as a background track that sets the mood of your movie. To add a prerecorded audio file to your entire video production, follow these steps:

1. **Click the Add Background Audio to Production button (the one with the eighth note and the plus sign) in the middle of Production Editor pane's toolbar.**

   VideoWave opens the Select Background Audio dialog box where you locate and select the audio file that you want played as the background music or narration for your movie.

   Note that you can only add audio files in the Select Background Audio dialog box for which you have the Digital Management Rights. If you try to add a file whose thumbnail has a small padlock in the lower-right corner, when you click the Open button, VideoWave will display an alert dialog box indicating that you don't have the rights to the audio you selected and VideoWave will fail to add the selected track to your video production.

2. **Select the audio file in the folder or media collection that you want to add as the background audio in the Select Background Audio list box and then click the Open button.**

   VideoWave closes the Select Background Audio dialog box and adds your selected audio file to the production. Depending upon the length of the audio file that you select and the length of your video production, the Fit to Audio button may become active (if it remains grayed out, it means that there's just too much of a difference between the length of the movie and the audio file to fit the video production to the background audio).

   If the Fit to Audio button becomes active and you want VideoWave to adjust the length of your video production so that it matches that of the total background audio, you can click this button. When you do, VideoWave displays a Fit to Audio dialog box that indicates the discrepancy between the duration of the video and still images in your movie and the background audio and that informs of what types of changes will be made to the duration of your video and image panels to obtain the desired length. (This feature works best, by the way, when your video contains color panels and scene panels with still images whose duration can be modified as needed to get the overall length of the movie to match that of the audio.) When you click the OK button in the Fit to Audio dialog box, VideoWave modifies the length of the video production so that it exactly meshes with that of the background audio.

3. **(Optional) Click the Fit to Audio button on the Production Editor pane's toolbar and then click the OK button in the Fit to Audio dialog box to adjust the length of the video production so that it fits exactly that of the background audio.**

Recording a narration for your video production

To record you own narration for the video production, you click the Add Narration to Your Production button (the one with the old-fashioned microphone) on the Production Editor pane's toolbar. VideoWave then temporarily puts the program into Timeline view and replaces the Media Selector pane with a Narration pane (like the one shown in Figure 10-18).

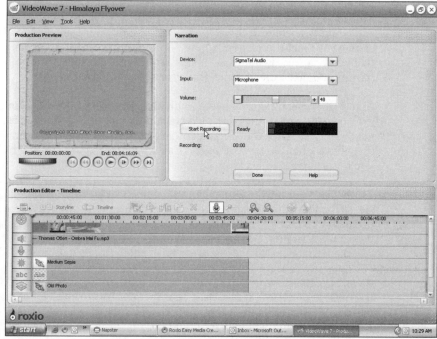

Figure 10-18: Recording a narration track for the video production you're creating.

The great thing about recording the narration track for your video is that you get to watch the video footage in the Production Preview pane as you actually record the accompanying narration. This enables you to describe in words what the audience is seeing as you watch the video footage (which is helpful even if you're reading from a prepared script, which is always recommended).

Before you begin recording your narration, you may need to select the Input device (which is most often the microphone that's built into your computer or that you've connected to your computer) and fiddle with the Volume slider (which usually should be somewhere in the center). Unless you intend to narrate the movie from the very beginning, you will also need to use the Scrubber button or the Jog Wheel in the playback controls at the bottom of the Production Preview pane to cue up the frame at which you want the narration to start.

To begin recording, click the Start Recording button and begin speaking directly into the microphone (in a normal tone). As you speak, VideoWave will automatically begin playing the movie from the current frame in the Production Preview pane. You can then tailor your comments to the actual footage that's being shown (I often remember details when watching the footage that I'm able to capture as part of the narration).

As soon as you finish making your narrative comments, click the Stop Recording button (which replaces the Start Recording button the moment you click it). As soon as you click the Stop Recording button, VideoWave saves your recorded audio as a WAV file with the filename Nar (standing for Narration) followed by the next available sequential number as in Nar1.wav for the first narration track that you've saved. In addition, a blue bar with this filename now appears in the Narration track in the Production Editor - Timeline pane.

Note that you can record several individual narrations for different scenes in the movie as part of the Narration track. Just cue up the starting frame for the next narration, click the Start Recording button, record your comments for the next segment in the video, and then click the Stop Recording button when you're through.

To preview your movie with its new narration track, drag the Timeline Playback Head (the vertical line extending down from an upside down triangle in the Production Editor - Timeline pane) until it's right at the beginning of the narration in the Narration track (the one with the old fashioned microphone icon) and then click the Play button in the Production Preview pane.

If you're satisfied with what you now see and hear, click the Done button at the bottom of the Narration pane to return to the normal VideoWave window where the Production Editor is in its default Storyline mode. If you don't like what you hear and would like to rerecord one or more of your narrations, click the WAV file in the Narration track and then press the Delete button to first remove the narration and then use the Start Recording and Stop Recording buttons to rerecord your comments.

Adding audio clips to individual panels in the video production

Instead of, or in addition to, a background audio file that plays through the entire video, you can also add audio files to the individual items (color panels, video clips and still images). These audio clips then play only as long these particular panels play in the video production. These audio clips can contain prerecorded sound effects, narration, or music that you want should just play as part of the panel.

To add an audio clip to a particular panel, select its audio file in the Media Selector pane, drag its thumbnail to the Production Editor pane and then drop it on the particular scene panel to which it is to be associated. VideoWave lets you know that you've added an audio file to that panel by displaying a speaker icon in the lower-left corner of the panel.

The program automatically trims any clip that runs longer than the duration of the panel to which it is affixed (if the audio clip is shorter than the panel's duration, you can loop it so that it repeats until the panel finishes playing — see "Editing audio clips in Timeline mode" later in this chapter for details).

Working in Timeline mode

Recording a narration track for your video production gives a taste for working with your video production in Timeline rather than the default Storyline mode. Figure 10-19 shows you the VideoWave window after switching from Storyline to Timeline mode by clicking the Timeline button near the beginning of Production Editor pane's toolbar. The Production Editor pane in this figure shows the information that I've added to the entire video production in the Video, Background Audio, Narration, Effect, and Text tracks (there's also an Overlay track with the name of the overlay that's been applied to the entire video production that isn't visible in this figure).

When you switch to Timeline mode, the Production Editor pane presents all the information in your current video production in individual tracks rather than by sequential panels. By default, Timeline mode displays the information for the entire video production in the Background Audio, Narration, Effect, Text, and Overlay tracks beneath the Video track in the Production Editor pane.

Hide and seek Track style

If you haven't added an effect, text, or overlay to the entire video production and aren't likely to, you can make more room for yourself in the Production Editor pane by hiding the Effect, Text, and Overlay tracks. If you want to be able to edit the audio that's recorded as part of the video clips added to the Video track (referred to as native audio), you can display the Native Audio track. Also, if you want to add an audio clip to the video production as a sound effect or have already done so, you need to display the Sound Effects track in order to add the audio clip to it (by dragging its audio file from the Media Selector and dropping it onto this track in Production Editor pane) and to later be able to edit the audio clip.

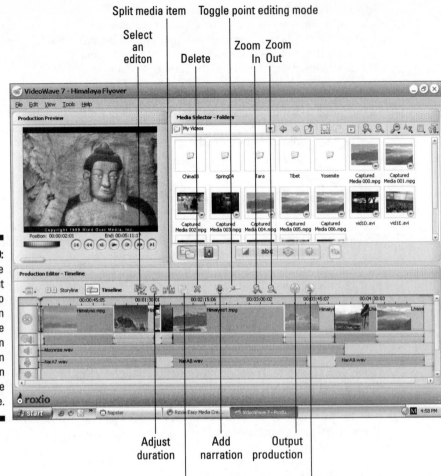

Split media item   Toggle point editing mode

Select
an
editon   Delete   Zoom Zoom
                                  In   Out

Figure 10-19:
Editing the
current
video
production
in the
Production
Editor when
it's in
Timeline
mode.

Adjust   Add   Output
duration   narration   production

Rotate selected photos 90 degrees   Burn production to disc

To hide certain tracks that you don't need in the Production Editor pane or to
display tracks that are now temporarily hidden click the Show/Hide Tracks
button at the very beginning of the Production Editor - Timeline pane's toolbar. VideoWave opens the Show/Hide Tracks dialog box that has check boxes
in front of the names of all the tracks you can view in the Production Editor -
Timeline pane (Native Audio, Background Audio, Narration, Sound Effects,
Effect, Text, and Overlay). To display a particular track in the Show/Hide
Tracks dialog box, click the track's check box until it contains a checkmark.
To hide a particular track, click its check box until the checkmark is cleared.

Marking time with the Timeline ruler

At the top of the tracks in the Production Editor - Timeline pane, you find the Timeline ruler. This ruler enables you to estimate the relative length of the individual items in the tracks below. You can zoom in and expand the level of detail in the tracks at the place in the Timeline ruler that you click with the Hand mouse pointer and then drag to the right. So too, you can return to your previous level of detail by dragging the ruler to the left.

Keep in mind that the zooming in and out that you do by dragging the Timeline ruler (one of the coolest features of VideoWave in my humble opinion) is more generalized than zooming in and out by clicking the Zoom In and Zoom Out buttons on the Timeline toolbar. Use these buttons to zoom in and out on the particular part of the Video track displayed in the Production Editor pane after using the ruler-dragging method to bring that part into view in Production Editor.

The benefits of editing your video production in Timeline mode

At first blush, the benefits of editing your video production in Timeline mode may not be apparent. Actually, there are two main benefits to editing your video production in Timeline mode:

✔ In the tracks in Timeline mode you can add multiple items including audio clips, narration, text, special effects and overlays to the entire video production or to a single still image or video clips the production contains

✔ By comparing information in different tracks In Timeline mode you can see clearly how the different elements of the video production overlap and relate to one another

The first benefit point is by far the most important. If you try, for example, to add two different audio files that you want to play one after the other as the background audio for your video production in Storyline mode, VideoWave will ask you if you want to replace the first audio file as soon as you try to add the second one. If, however, you switch to Timeline, you add the second audio file right after the first one in the Background Audio track simply by dragging it into position on this track.

When editing in Timeline mode, you need to be aware that there are two views that you can switch between:

✔ **Production level** (the default) in which the tracks in the Production Editor - Timeline pane show only the elements applied to the entire video production

✔ **Internal tracks** in which the tracks in the Production Editor - Timeline pane show only the elements applied to the particular still image or video clip in the production that you have selected

To switch from the Production-level view to the Internal tracks view, you simply locate the still image or video clip in the Video track whose internal tracks you want displayed and then double-click somewhere within that image or clip. The Production Editor - Internal Tracks pane then appears at the bottom of the VideoWave window. This pane contains the tracks for just the still image or video you double-clicked. You can then edit the audio, text, effects, and overlays applied only to this element in the appropriate tracks in this view. When you're finished editing in the localized Internal Tracks view, you can return to the more general Production-level view by clicking the Done button (the one with the green bent arrow) that's added to the left side of the Internal Tracks toolbar.

When editing elements in the tracks of the Production Editor (either in the Production-level or the Internal tracks view), you can drag the bars representing the different types of media items (audio, effects, text, overlays, and what not) to resize or reposition them on its particular track. To resize an item (such as an effect or an overlay, position the mouse pointer at the end of the item in its track and then when the mouse pointer turns into a double-pointed arrow, drag its blue bar to the left (to make it shorter) or to the right (to make it longer).

When editing certain items such audio clips, effects, text, and overlays at the Production-level view, you can split the items in two at the position of Timeline Playback Head in the Production Editor by clicking its track and then clicking the Split Media Item at the Current Position button. After splitting an item, you can then resize and drag its now separate parts to different positions on the timeline so that they each affect only a certain part of the video production.

Editing audio clips in Timeline mode

Although you can edit the length and the position (how long and where they play) of the audio clips in your video production by directly manipulating their bars in their respective tracks (Native Audio, Background Audio, Narration, and Sound Effects) in Production Editor, if you want to the trim the audio or modulate its volume or adjusting some other aspect of its sound, you need to open the clip in the Audio Editor.

To do this, locate the audio clip in its track in the Production Editor - Timeline pane and then double-click -click somewhere on it or right-click and then click the Edit option on its shortcut menu. VideoWave then generates a preview of the selected audio clip and opens it in the Audio Editor window similar to the one shown in Figure 10-20.

Reset all points

Remove selected point
from envelope

Zoom
in

Zoom
out

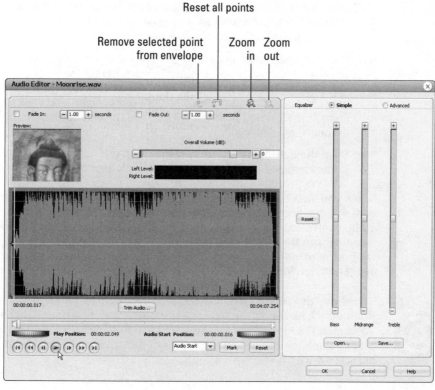

Figure 10-20:
You can edit
the sound
quality and
volume of
audio clip
and trim or
loop it in the
Audio Editor
window.

In the Audio Editor, you can make any of the following edits to the selected audio clip:

- ✔ **Adjust the overall volume of the audio clip** by dragging the Overall Volume (dB) slider to the right (to increase the volume) or the left (to diminish the volume)

- ✔ **Adjust the volume throughout the audio clip** by clicking different places in the waveform envelope to add edit points that you can then drag up above the centerline to increase the volume or down below the centerline to diminish the volume

- ✔ **Fade the volume in at the start and out at the end of the audio clip** by clicking the Fade In and Fade Out check boxes and then enter the fade-in and fade-out times in the associated text boxes (in seconds) or select them by clicking the Plus (+) or Minus (–) buttons

- ✔ **Equalize the sound in the audio clip** by dragging the Bass, Midrange, and/or Treble sliders in the Equalizer area to the right (to modulate the sound using a 10-band equalizer, click the Advanced option button at the top of Equalizer area; to select a predefined equalization, click the Open button and click its name in the Media Selector; to save your customized settings, click the Save button and enter a name for the audio settings in the Save dialog box)

✔ **Trim the audio clip** by clicking the Trim Audio button to open the Audio Trimmer. There, you drag the Audio Start marker to the new start position and click the Set Start Point at the Current Position button before you drag the Audio End marker to the new end position and click the Set End Point at the Current Position button. You then complete the trimming sequence by clicking OK.

✔ **Loop the audio clip** by clicking the Loop check box in the Audio Trimmer dialog box before clicking its OK button

When you finish making some or all of these editing changes to your audio clip, you can preview the modifications by clicking the Play button in the audio controls at the bottom-left of the Audio Editor window. When you're satisfied with the tweaks and edits you've made to your sound clip, click the OK button to close the Audio Editor and put the new audio settings into effect in VideoWave window.

To remove the audio portion that's been recorded as part of a video clip, double-click its clip in the Native Audio track and then drag the Overall Volume (dB) slider all the way to the left so that in the future the video clip plays completely silently in the movie as though it no longer had any audio associated with it.

Outputting the Video Production

When you finish having fun with the hundreds of VideoWave editing features and finally have your video production just the way you want it and all the last-minute changes are saved with the File⇨Save command (in the native VideoWave 7 DMSM file format), you're ready to output your finished production as a movie that you can share it with the rest of the world (Sundance look out!).

VideoWave attempts to make outputting your finished production as easy as possible. All you have to decide during this process is where you want the finished movie shown (on what device) and in what quality (which determines how much compression is used in the final video file and how large the file is).

To output your finished and saved video production, click the Output Your Production to in Different Formats button near the end of the Production Editor pane's toolbar or choose File⇨Output Production To on the Video-Wave menu bar. VideoWave displays the VideoWave window similar to the one shown in Figure 10-21 that contains the program's Output To wizard.

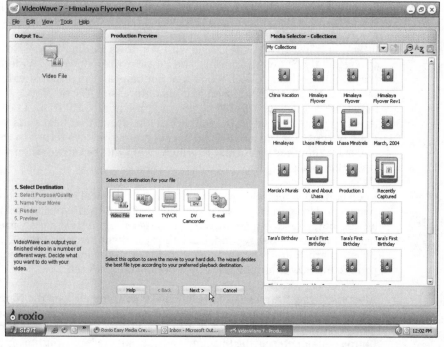

Figure 10-21:
Outputting
your
finished
video
production
with the
Output To
wizard in the
VideoWave
window.

Here, you must select from the following destinations for your movie before
you click the Next > button:

- **Video File** to make a movie that you can play on your computer using a
  program such as Windows Media Player

- **Internet** to make a movie that you can upload to a Web site on the Internet

- **TV/VCR** to make a movie that you can output to a video cassette tape
  and then show on TV

- **DV Camcorder** to make a movie that you can output to digital tape on
  your DV camcorder

- **E-mail** to make a movie that you can send as an attachment to an e-mail
  message

As soon as you click the Next> button the next window in the Output To
wizard appears. The options that this window contains depend upon which
destination you selected in the initial window. In general, in this window, you
need to specify the quality of the movie that you're making. In selecting the
quality of the final video file, you are necessarily selecting the amount of
compression to be used and how large the resulting file will be (the higher
the quality, the less the compression and the bigger the final video file).

Note that when you select Video File as the destination, you must also select the purpose of the video file in the Purpose drop-down list box (you select the Playback on This Computer option on the drop-down list when your intention is just to play the movie with Windows Media Player). Note too, if you select the Show All option in the Purpose drop-down list, VideoWave displays another drop-down list box that contains all the possible video formats (MPEG-1, MPEG-2, compressed and uncompressed AVI, or WMV), the physical movie sizes (such as 320x240 pixels), and the number of frames per second (fps). You can then select the individual file format that best suits your immediate purpose for the movie (you can, of course, always return to this wizard and select another file format to which to output the movie when your purpose changes).

Keep in mind when selecting a video format, physical movie size, and frames per second from the Purpose drop-down list that each aspect affects the overall size of the resulting movie file. The larger the physical movie size and the higher the frames per second, the larger the resulting movie file. Large movie file sizes are not only more difficult to share on the Internet but require more processing power for playback on a personal computer.

After specifying the quality of the finished movie and clicking the Next > button, the wizard prompts you to enter a filename for the finished movie (you can also change the location on your hard disk by selecting a new folder with the Browse button). After entering the filename and clicking the Next> button again, the wizard normally presents you with a window that contains a Render File button.

Click the Render File button to have the VideoWave Output To wizard create the finished movie file by rendering it frame-by-frame in the video file format that conforms to the destination and purpose you designated for the final movie file. If, for example, you select the Internet or E-mail as your destination, VideoWave renders the video production into a WMV file ready to upload to the Internet or send as an e-mail attachment. If, however, you select Video File (with Playback On This Computer) or TV/VCR as your destination, the program renders your production into an MPEG video file. And when you select DV Camcorder as your destination, the program renders your production into an AVI video file.

After the wizard finishes rendering the video file, you can then click the Preview button to preview the finished product. For all destinations except for Video File, the Output To wizard then presents you with a button that you click to output the finished file to its target destination:

  ✔ **Upload to Internet** when you've selected Internet as the destination and you want to upload the file to a particular URL on the Internet

  ✔ **Send E-mail** when you've selected E-mail as the destination and you want to open a new message in your E-mail program with the movie attached to it

✔ **Output My Video** when you've selected TV/VCR or DV Camcorder as the destination and you want to open transfer the movie file to video cassette tape on a VCR or a digital video tape on your Camcorder attached to the computer

After you finish transferring the final movie file to its desired destination, click the Done button in the VideoWave window to close the Output To wizard and return to the normal VideoWave window.

Burning the Video Production to Disc

Instead of outputting your finished video production to video file, you can just send it to a DVD disc instead. To burn your finished and saved video production to a DVD disc, click the Burn Production to Disc button at the very end of the Production Editor pane's toolbar or choose File➪Burn Production to Disc on the VideoWave menu bar.

As soon as you choose this command, the VideoWave application closes, the DVD Builder application launches, and the Project Type dialog box appears. Here, you must select the type of DVD project you want to build (DVD, Video CD, Super Video CD, or DVD on CD) and then click OK. You must then click the Burn button on the far right of the Menu Editor pane's toolbar or choose File➪Plug & Burn on the DVD Builder menu bar and follow the prompts in the Burn Setup and Burn Progress dialog boxes to actually copy your movie onto a DVD disc (see Chapter 11 for details on this burning process and how to make your finished video file into a movie title in a larger DVD project).

Chapter 11

Building and Burning DVDs

. . . .

. . . .

*D*VD Builder is the place to go to when you want to build and burn your DVD projects. With DVD Builder, you can construct projects that play on standalone DVD players (including the latest machines using the newer VCD and SVCD formats) as well as your computer's DVD drive. As with all the other applications in the Roxio Easy Media Creator 7 suite, DVD Builder makes it as easy as possible to build and burn sophisticated DVD discs.

This chapter acquaints you with all the aspects of using DVD Builder to create your DVD projects and burn them to disc. It starts by familiarizing you with the different DVD projects supported by DVD Builder. The chapter then goes on to introduce you to the DVD Builder window and its features (which will be very familiar to those of you who have used the information in Chapter 11 to design and build video productions in the VideoWave application). As part of this introduction, you find out how to use and customize DVD Builder's built-in themes, add new DVD titles to your project, as well as how to create a menu system for selecting titles you add to your DVD.

The chapter ends by giving you pointers on how to preview and test out your DVD project before burning it to disc and then giving you the ins and outs of burning your finished project to disc.

Launching DVD Builder and Selecting Your DVD Project

You can launch DVD Builder from the Easy Media Creator Home window by clicking the Create New DVD link in the DVD column or the DVD Builder link in the Applications column. If the Easy Media Creator Home window is not open, you can launch DVD Builder from the Windows XP taskbar by clicking the Start button, then highlighting All Programs on the Start menu and Roxio on the All Programs submenu before clicking DVD Builder on the Roxio submenu.

When you first launch DVD Builder, the Project Type dialog box appears, giving you a chance to select the type of DVD project you want to build (see Figure 11-1). DVD Builder automatically selects the DVD option button in the Project Type dialog box as the default project type. If you know that you will mainly be building one of the other types (Video CD, Super Video CD, or DVD on CD) instead, after clicking that other type's option button, be sure that you click the Set as Default for New Projects check box before you click the OK button.

Figure 11-1:
The first thing you must do after launching DVD Builder is to select the type of DVD project you want to build.

When selecting a type for your new DVD project, you have a choice in creating the following types:

- ✔ **DVD** to create a project for a DVD-Recordable disc that can hold up to two hours of high-quality video in the DVD-Video or DVD+RW format for playback on most standalone DVD players and computer DVD drives

- ✔ **Video CD** (also known as VCD) to create a project for a CD-Recordable disc that can hold up to 74 minutes of video on a 650MB CD or up to 80 minutes on a 700MB CD in the Video CD (VCD) format for playback in some of the newer standalone DVD players and computer DVD drives

✔ **Super Video CD** (also known as SVCD) to create a project for a CD-Recordable disc that can hold between 35 and 60 minutes of high quality video on 650/700MB CDs in the Super Video CD format for playback on some of the new standalone DVD players and computer DVD drives

✔ **DVD on CD** to create a project for a CD-Recordable disc that can hold between 15 and 20 minutes of video in the mini DVD format for playback only on computer DVD drives

After selecting the type of DVD project you want to create, click the OK button to close the Project Type dialog box and begin building your new DVD project.

Getting Cozy with the DVD Builder Window

As soon as you close the Project Type dialog box, the empty DVD Builder window similar to the one shown in Figure 11-2 appears. As you can see in Figure 11-2 the DVD Builder window is divided into three panes: the Edit Task pane on the left side, the Menu Editor pane at the top right, and the Production Editor pane right below it.

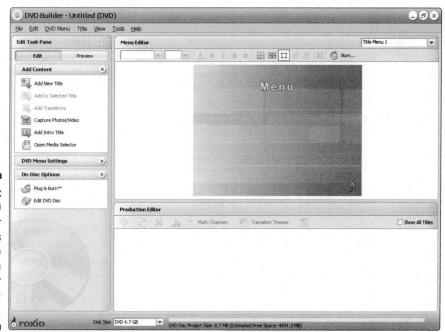

Figure 11-2:
The DVD Builder window is the place where you build your new DVD project.

The big difference between the titles of a DVD project and the titles in a DVD project

Please don't get confused between the titles that you add to DVD project and the titles that you place in your DVD project. The former, the titles of the DVD project, refer to the textual labels that assign to the menu screen and navigation buttons that describe their function in the project. The latter, the titles in the DVD project, refer to the video productions that you add to the project and the menu buttons you assign to them. The video productions in your DVD titles (often prepared in VideoWave, although you can create them in DVD Builder as well) can consist of a sequence of video clips or still graphic images or a combination of the two.

To avoid confusion between the titles of the DVD project and the titles in it, in this chapter I will refer to the titles that you assign to the menu or the menu buttons in the project as names or labels. That way, when you see the term titles in the text, you know to think of the video productions and associated menu buttons that you add to your DVD project.

To any of you who are the least little bit familiar with any of the other applications in the Easy Media Creator suite, the pane layout in this window should seem very familiar. As with the VideoWave application, DVD Builder places the links to the different types of tasks you create in the pane on the left side of the window, while dividing the right side into upper and lower panes where you do the work.

The main difference between the VideoWave and DVD Builder windows is that the upper-right pane in DVD Builder (the Menu Editor pane) holds not the source of the elements that you add to the Production Editor pane below (as in VideoWave) but rather the layout of the main screen of your DVD project. What this means in practical terms is that you work with the upper Menu Editor pane in DVD project almost as much, if not more, as you do the Production Editor pane.

The Edit Task pane

The Edit Task pane shown in Figure 11-3 holds the links to the common tasks that you perform in building your DVD project. At the top of this pane, you find the Edit and Preview buttons (with the Edit button pressed by default). Beneath these buttons, the Edit Task pane is divided into three smaller panes (from top to bottom):

✔ **Add Content** with the links for adding new DVD titles to the DVD project and links for adding content and transitions to the title you're currently editing and capturing photos or video for it

✔ **DVD Menu Settings** with the links for selecting a theme for your DVD project, selecting a background graphic or audio

✔ **On-Disc Options** with the links for using the Plug & Burn link to record videotape from a device connected to your computer directly to a CD or DVD disc and editing the content on a rewritable DVD disc

Note that you can hide the options in any of the smaller panes that you're currently not using (Add Content, DVD Menu Settings, and On-Disc Options) in the Edit Task pane by clicking its collapse button (the one on the right of the pane's title bar with the two upward-pointing arrowheads). To redisplay the options in a particular sub-pane, click its Expand button (that replaces the Expand button as soon as you click it marked with the two downward-pointing arrowheads).

You click the Preview button at the top of the Edit Task pane to put DVD Builder into preview mode, wherein you can not only review the titles you've added to the DVD project but also simulate using your onscreen menus to navigate these titles and play them (see "Previewing the finished DVD project" later in this chapter for details).

Figure 11-3:
The Edit Task pane contains the most common editing commands that you use in building your DVD project.

The Menu Editor pane

The Menu Editor pane shown in Figure 11-4 is the place where you design the look and feel and layout of your DVD project. The display screen in the center of this pane contains the name of the DVD project's menu, the menu buttons that your users click to play the titles (that contain the video and still images you want played — see the following sidebar) in the DVD, and the labels that identify these menu buttons as well as the background graphic on which these buttons and labels are placed. (Note that the arrangement of these menu buttons and their labels form the main menu system for your DVD project.)

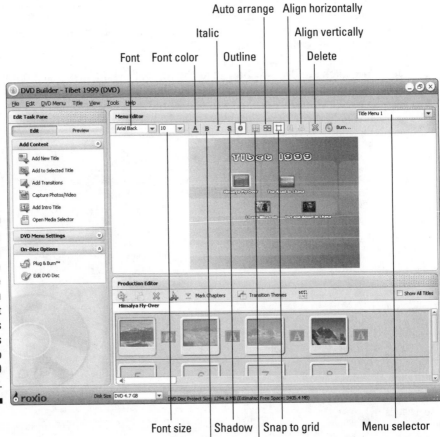

Figure 11-4:
The Menu Editor pane is the place where you add and edit the menus for the titles you add to your DVD project.

The Production Editor pane

The Production Editor pane shown in Figure 11-5 should be old hat to any of you who have experience using the almost identical Production Editor pane in the VideoWave application in its default Storyline mode. The Production Editor pane in the DVD Builder window is a little different in that it displays only the contents of the title whose navigation button is currently selected in the Menu Editor pane above (although you can display all the titles in your DVD project in this pane by clicking the Show All Titles link to put a check-mark in its check box).

The Production Editor pane displays the video clip and/or still image contents in the current title in a series of scene panels separated by transition panels which contain the particular scene transitions that you take you from one panel to the next (see Chapter 10 for details on adding video clips and still images to the Production Editor pane in Storyline mode).

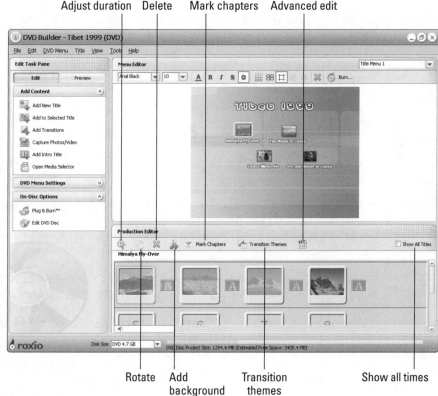

Adjust duration   Delete   Mark chapters   Advanced edit

Figure 11-5:
The Production Editor pane is the place where you edit the titles that you add to your DVD project.

Rotate   Add background audio   Transition themes   Show all times

The Production Editor pane toolbar contains the basic tools you need to edit the contents of a DVD title, including adjusting the duration of the video clip or still image in the current panel, rotating the orientation of a still image in the current panel, removing a panel from the title, adding background audio for the title, and adding transitions between specific title panels. In addition, this toolbar contains a Mark Chapters button that you can use to mark specific jump points in the title — that is, pauses in the video sequence or photos where your users can directly jump to by clicking the Next Chapter button (> |) with their DVD remote controls.

The last tool on the Production Editor pane toolbar is the Advanced Edit button that you can use to launch the VideoWave application and open the title in its window as a Storyboard production in Storyline mode (see Chapter 10 for details).

Building Your DVD Project

After you launch DVD Builder and select the type of DVD project you want to build, you're ready to begin designing the project's menus and adding the titles you wan it to contain. The following sections take you through the general steps from selecting the theme for your new DVD project all the way to previewing the finished project prior to burning it to CD or DVD disc.

Selecting the project theme

The first thing you want to do in a new DVD project is select its theme. DVD Builder offers a whole bunch of prefab themes that include the graphics for the menu background, the look of the menu, chapter, and navigation buttons, the fonts used in displaying the main menu and chapter menu names and the button labels, and even the background music that plays whenever the main menu screen is displayed (indicated in the Menu Editor pane by the presence of an eighth note in the lower-right corner of main menu screen).

To select a theme for your new DVD project, click the Theme link in the DVD Menu Settings portion of the Edit Task pane or choose DVD Menu⇨Change Menu Theme on the DVD Builder menu bar. DVD Builder opens the Menu Theme dialog box shown in Figure 11-6. This dialog box contains two tabs on the left side: the Predefined Themes tab, which contains 17 prefab themes to choose from, and the Custom Themes tab, which contains any customized themes that you've designed and saved. On the right side, this dialog box contains two more tabs: the Main Themes that displays the background, menu buttons, and the font used by the main menu screen for the theme selected on the Predefined Themes or Custom Themes tab and Chapter Menus that shows the background graphic, the chapter and navigation buttons, as well as the font used on the chapter menu screen (chapter menus are created only when you add chapters to a title *and* you elect to have menus created for the chapters — see "Adding chapters to a title" later in this chapter for details).

Figure 11-6:
You can select a predefined or customized theme for your new DVD project in the Menu Theme dialog box.

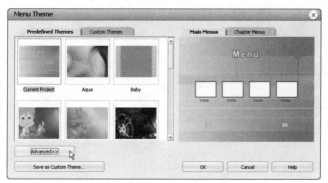

To preview the type of background graphic, menu, chapter, and navigation buttons, and the font that a particular predefined theme uses, click its thumbnail on the Predefined Themes tab and then view the preview on both the Main Menus and Chapter Menus tabs.

To customize the look of a predefined theme that you've selected on the Predefined Themes tab, click its thumbnail. Then click the Advanced >> button at the bottom of the Menu Theme dialog box to expand this dialog box to the Advanced Theme dialog box similar to the one shown in Figure 11-7. You can then use the controls in the lower half of the Advanced Menu Theme dialog box.

You can then use the controls in the lower half of the Advanced Menu Theme dialog box to customize the look and feel and layout of the basic theme. For example, you can change the background graphic used in the theme by clicking the Browse button to the right of the Photo/Video drop-down list and then selecting one of your own photos in the Browse Folder dialog box. Likewise, you can select a new audio file to use as the main menu screen background music by clicking the Browse button to the right of the Audio drop-down list and then selecting a new audio file in its Browse File dialog box.

If you don't want any audio playing when your users are viewing the main menu screen (this can be obnoxiously repetitive because even when it fades out, it always starts right up again), click the drop-down button attached to the Audio drop-down list and then click None at the very bottom of this list.

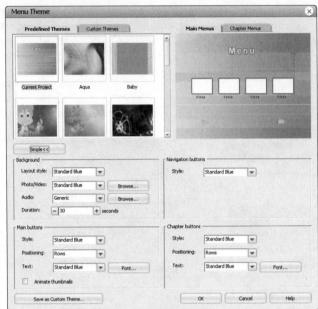

Figure 11-7:
You can customize a predefined theme for your new DVD project in the Advanced Menu Theme dialog box.

After you finish customizing the layout and look and feel of the predefined theme to your satisfaction, you can save your changes as a custom theme. Click the Save as Custom Theme button at the bottom of the Advanced Main Theme dialog box and then enter a name for your custom theme in the Save Theme dialog box. Then click the OK button. To apply the custom theme you've saved, you then click the OK button in the Advanced Main Theme dialog box.

Modifying the name of the first main menu screen

After you select the theme you want to use in your new DVD project, you probably want to change the generic name of the main menu from the completely uninspiring names such as **Menu**, **Wedding**, and **Baby** to something more descriptive such as **The French Riviera**, **Wedding Bells**, and **Baby's First Year**.

To modify the name of the main menu, click the I-beam mouse pointer somewhere in its generic name in the preview in the Menu Editor pane to display its bounding box and then edit the text. To change the font, font size, or the attributes used by main menu name, right-click the name and then click the Change Font option at the top of its shortcut menu.

The Font dialog box opens where you can select a new font, font size, change the text enhancements (Bold, Italic, Outline, and Shadow), as well as select new colors for the text, text outline, or shadow.

To reposition the main menu name on the main menu screen, click the name to display its bounding box and then position the mouse pointer on one of the edges of the bounding box. When the pointer changes to a four-headed arrow, you can drag the name to a new place on the screen. To nudge the name just a little after dropping it in its new position, press the appropriate arrow keys on your keyboard (left-arrow to nudge to the left, right-arrow key to nudge to the right, and so on).

Keep in mind that the main menu name is restricted to a single line (there's no way to add a second line). If the text of your modified name extends beyond the edges of the screen, you will have to reduce the font size of the text until it all fits on the screen. Keep in mind as well that any text that extends beyond the safe areas on the left or right side of the main menu screen may be cut off when the DVD project is played on some televisions. Click the Show/Hide Safe Area for Televisions button on the Menu Editor pane's toolbar to display the safe area and check if any text is in danger of being cut off (indicated by characters in the unsafe, checkerboard area).

Adding titles to your DVD project

After you have the theme and the main menu name settled, you're ready to start adding the titles with the content you want to play to your DVD project. Most of the time, these titles will be in the form of video productions that you've created ahead of time in the Easy Media Creator's VideoWave application (see Chapter 11 for details). If you haven't created a video production ahead of time, you can also create a title for your new DVD project by adding the media content and creating it as you go.

Adding existing video productions as titles

To add a new title from an existing VideoWave production, click the Add New Title link at the top of the Add Content area in the Edit Task pane or choose DVD Menu⇨Add New Title and then click the name of the DMSM file (the file-name extension given to Roxio Media Production files) in the Add Media to Project dialog box before you click the Add button.

DVD Builder then adds a menu button with the name of the video production's filename in the Menu Editor pane while at the same time adding the contents of the video production to Production Editor pane below (see Figure 11-8).

Figure 11-8:
Adding an
existing
VideoWave
video
production
as the first
title in a
new DVD
project.

I encourage you to create the different titles for your DVD project in the
VideoWave application beforehand and then assemble them in your project
by adding them as individual titles. That way, you'll have each title laid out
and working exactly the way you want it before you launch DVD Builder.
Having your titles completed beforehand makes assembling them and burning them with DVD Builder a snap.

Creating new titles as you add their content

Sometimes, you need to add a title to your new DVD project that you haven't
already assembled beforehand as a VideoWave production. To create a new
title as you add its content, click the Add New Title link at the top of the Add
Content area in the Edit Task pane or choose DVD Menu⇨Add New Title and
then select the name of the video or graphic file that you want to add to appear
at the beginning of the new title in the Add Media to Project dialog box.

DVD Builder then adds a menu button for the new title in the Menu Editor
pane. This button uses the first frame or the graphic in the file you selected
as its image and the name of the file you selected as its label. The program
also inserts the video clip or still image in the first scene panel in the
Production Editor pane below.

To add other video clips and/or still graphic images (and photos) to the new title, click the Add to Selected Title link in the Add Content area of the Edit Task pane. Then select the name of the video or graphic file that you want to appear in the next panel in the Add Media to Project and click the Add button.

DVD Builder then adds the video clip or photo you next selected to the next panel in the Production Editor pane. You can continue in this manner, adding video clips or still images until your new title contains all the video clips and/or still images you want for that title in the sequence you want them to play back.

After adding all the video clips and/or still images, you can click the Transitions Themes link on the Production Editor pane's toolbar to add similar transitions in between all the panels in your new title. You can click the Advanced Edit button at the end of this toolbar to open the new title in the VideoWave window where you can do all sorts of edits including adding individual transitions between the panels and annotating them with text (see Chapter 10 for detailed information on all the types of editing that you can do with VideoWave).

Renaming, repositioning, and resizing menu buttons

Many times after adding a number of different titles to a menu screen, you find that you need to rename, reposition, and even resize their menu buttons. To rename a menu button, click the insertion point in its label (beneath the thumbnail image) and then edit the name as you would any other text. When you finish editing the menu button's name, click the mouse button somewhere on the screen background outside of its text box.

To reposition a menu button on its menu screen, click the button's thumbnail and then position the mouse pointer somewhere within the thumbnail image. When the pointer changes into a four-headed arrow, drag the button to its desired position. Note that, by default, the Snap to Grid button on the Menu Editor pane's toolbar is selected so that the button automatically goes to the nearest gridline on an invisible grid when you drop the button into place by releasing the mouse button. If you want to be able to position in between the invisible gridlines, click the Snap to Grid button to deselect it and then drag the button to the desired position or nudge it into place with the appropriate arrow keys on your keyboard.

To reposition more than one button at a time, Ctrl+click the buttons and then drag their images to the desired position. If you want DVD Builder to automatically align the selected buttons for you on a horizontal line, click the Align Horizontally button on the Menu Editor toolbar. To automatically align the selected buttons vertically, click the Align Vertically button on this toolbar instead.

Click the Auto Arrange button on the Menu Editor pane's toolbar to have DVD Builder automatically rearrange all the menu buttons at one time according the layout for the theme that your DVD project uses. Note that if you later want to manually reposition one or more of the buttons individually, you first need to click the Auto Arrange button on the Menu Editor toolbar. To align buttons in a row, Ctrl+click all the buttons that should line up in a single row to select their images and then click the Align Horizontally button. To then align buttons a single column, Ctrl+click all the buttons that should line up in that column and then click the Align Vertically button.

Many times the menu buttons that you add to a menu screen are larger than you want them to be. To avoid overcrowding on the menu screen and over-lapping the text of the button labels, you may want to make the buttons smaller (DVD Builder automatically reduces the size of a button's label when you make its button image smaller).

To resize a menu button, click its image to select it (indicated by the white border around the image with teeny-tiny sizing handles in each corner). Then position the mouse pointer in one of the corners on a sizing handle. When the mouse pointer changes into a double-headed arrow, drag the pointer toward the center of the image to make the button smaller or away from the center to make the button larger.

Inserting a new title menu screen into the DVD project

Many of your DVD projects, especially those of the DVD project type that you burn to DVD discs, will require too many titles for just the one main menu screen. To add new a title menu screen to your DVD project after you fill up the main menu screen, choose DVD Menu⇨New Menu on the DVD Builder menu bar. DVD Builder then adds a new blank title menu screen using the same background graphic and generic menu name as the main menu screen.

The program also adds a Previous navigation button (in the style of the theme you selected for the project) that the user can click to return to the main menu screen, while at the same time adding a Next navigation button to the main menu screen that the user can click to display this second title menu screen and have access to its menu buttons.

You can then rename this second title menu screen and add new titles to it just as you did in the main menu screen. To jump between the menu screens, you click the Menu Selector drop-down list button and then click the numeric name of the title menu screen to which you want to jump (Title Menu 1 is the name given to the main menu screen of your DVD project).

You can add as many title menu screens as you need to accommodate all the titles you want to add to your DVD project. Just watch the DVD Disc Project Size indicator at the bottom of DVD Builder window as you add your titles to see how close you're coming to filling up the disc.

Adding an Intro Title to your DVD project

An Intro Title is one that automatically plays at the beginning of your CD or DVD disc when the user puts the disc into his or her DVD player. When the Intro Title finishes playing, the main menu screen appears and stays on screen, from which you can select the next title that you want to watch.

To add an Intro Title to your DVD project, click the Add Intro Title link in the Add Content area of the Edit Task pane or choose DVD Menu⇨Add Intro Title on the DVD Builder menu bar. DVD Builder then opens the Add Media to Project dialog box where you can select the video production, video clip, or still image that you want to use as the Intro Title for your DVD project.

When you click the Add button to close the Add Media to Project dialog box after selecting the media file, DVD Builder displays the Intro DVD Builder window similar to the one shown in Figure 11-9. This window shows the photo or the first frame of the video clip you selected in the Add Media to Project dialog box in the Menu Editor pane and panels and transitions in the file in the Production Editor pane below. The Edit Task pane at the left side of this window, however, contains only the Add Contents options. Also, the name, Intro, appears in the text box of the Media Selector drop-down list in the upper-right corner of the Menu Editor pane.

Figure 11-9:
Adding an Intro Title containing a still photo annotated with explanatory text to the DVD project.

For your Intro Title, you may want to add a color panel or still photo on which you place some introductory text with an overview of the disc's contents or the credits for your production, including yourself, of course, as the director, best boy, key grip, and who knows what else!

Dividing a title into chapters

Sometimes, you'll want to break up a long video sequence in a title or provide certain jump points in a title composed of a long sequence of photographic images. You do this by adding chapters to the title. When you add chapters to a title, your users can jump back and forth to these jump points by clicking the Previous (|<) and Next (>|) buttons on their DVD player's remote control. When creating chapters for a title, you also have the option of creating chapter menus whose buttons your users can click to jump back and forth between the title's chapters.

To mark the chapters in one of the titles in your DVD project, follow these steps:

1. **Select the title menu in the Menu Selector drop-down list box that contains the title for which you want to add chapters and then click its button to select it.**

2. **Click the Mark Chapters buttons on the Production Editor pane's toolbar or choose Title➪Mark Chapters on the DVD Builder menu bar.**

   DVD Builder opens the Mark Chapters dialog box similar to the one shown in Figure 11-10. Here, you can add, change, or delete chapter makers in the current title. When adding chapter markers, you can have DVD Builder automatically detect chapters by looking for changes in brightness and color between successive frames and the pauses in the title and add chapter markers at each pause. Or you can add them manually by scanning the frames or photos in the title.

   To use DVD Builder's Auto Detect feature to detect the changes or pauses and add the chapter markers for you, click the Auto Detect button. To increase the program's sensitivity in differentiating chapters by changes in the brightness and color of frames, you drag the Sensitivity slider to the right or click the Plus (+) button. To control how long a pause must be before the Auto Detect feature will insert a new chapter marker, enter the number of seconds in the Minimum Seconds Between Chapters text box or select a new value by clicking its Plus (+) or Minus (–) buttons.

   To add the chapter markers manually, you use the playback controls (Previous Frame, Play, and Next Frame or the Plus (+), Minus (–), and scroll button) found under the title's preview on the left side of the dialog box to find the frame or photo where you want to start a new chapter. When you come upon this frame or photo, you then click the Add button to add a new chapter marker (whose thumbnail with its time code then appears in the list box on the right side of the dialog box).

3. **To have DVD Builder detect and add the chapter markers for you, click the Auto Detect button. To add the markers yourself, use the playback controls to display the frame (or photo in a slideshow title) where the marker is to occur and then click the Add button.**

Sometimes DVD Builder's Auto Detect feature adds chapter markers that you decide you really don't need to retain. In that case, you can follow Step 4 to remove the unwanted chapter marker

4. **(Optional) To remove any chapter marker that you don't want to use, click its thumbnail in the list box on the right and then click the Remove button.**

If your project is a DVD or DVD or CD, you can have DVD Builder create chapter menus that act as submenus for selecting and playing particular chapters in the title.

5. **(Optional) To have DVD Builder create chapter menus for the chapter markers displayed in the list box on the right side of the Mark Chapters dialog box, click the Create Chapter Menus check box to put a checkmark in it.**

When you have chapters you want in your title, you're ready to have DVD Builder create them.

6. **Click the OK button to close the Mark Chapters dialog box and add the chapter markers to your project.**

Figure 11-10: You use the controls in the Mark Chapters dialog box to add, change, or delete chapter markers in the current title.

If you added chapter menus to your title, you can see check them out when you preview the finished DVD project as described in the section immediately following. For the Chapter menu screen, DVD Builder automatically assigns the name of the title as the screen label and sequentially numbers and arranges the chapters (with their thumbnails) on this screen. Unfortunately, DVD Builder provides no way for you to rename the Chapter menu screen or the chapters themselves (I prefer something a little more descriptive than 1, 2, 3, and the like for my chapters).

Previewing the finished DVD project

After you've got all the media you need in your DVD project, it's time to pre-view the final production before you burn it to DVD or CD disc. To preview the DVD project you're working on, you simply click the Preview button at the top Edit Task pane to the immediate right of the Edit button.

As soon as you click the Preview button, a DVD Builder window similar to the one shown in Figure 11-11 appears. This window contains two panes: the Playback Controls pane on the left, which contains a virtual DVD remote control, and the Preview pane on the right, which contains a preview of your project's Main menu screen.

If your project contains an Intro Title (see "Adding an Intro Title to your DVD project" earlier in the chapter for details), the Intro button at the top of the DVD Controls will be available (otherwise it's grayed out) as well as the Menu button. To preview the Intro Title in your DVD project, click the Intro button in the virtual DVD remote (remember that the Intro Title plays automatically on the disc you create from this project as soon as the user puts the disc in the player).

To preview the other titles on the Main menu, click the Left, Right, Up, and Down controls on the virtual remote until the title you want to view is selected (indicated by a highlighted outline around its thumbnail) and then click the OK button on the virtual remote. When the title begins playing, you can then use the other playback controls such as Pause and Fast Forward to preview its contents. If you added chapter markers to your title, you can use the Next Chapter and Previous Chapter buttons to jump to and from different chapters in the title.

When you finish previewing a certain title, you can return to the Main menu screen by clicking the Stop button. If your DVD project contains more than one menu screen, you can advance to the next menu screen by highlighting the Next button (an arrow in the project's selected theme pointing to the right) near the bottom of the Main menu screen and then clicking the OK button on the virtual remote. You can then return to the Main menu screen by highlighting this new menu screen's Back button (an arrow in the style of the selected theme pointing to the left) and clicking the remote's OK button.

If a title that you select for previewing contains Chapter menus, its Chapter menu screen appears when you highlight its title thumbnail and click the OK button in the virtual remote. You can then play a particular chapter by highlighting its chapter thumbnail and then clicking the OK button on the virtual remote. You can also advance to the next chapter in the title by clicking the Next Chapter button or to an earlier chapter by clicking the Previous Chapter button.

When you click the Stop button after previewing a particular chapter, DVD Builder returns you to the Chapter menu screen. To return to the menu screen from which you selected the title containing the chapters you just previewed, you highlight the Up button (the one with the arrow in the style of your project theme that points upward) and then click the OK button on the virtual remote control.

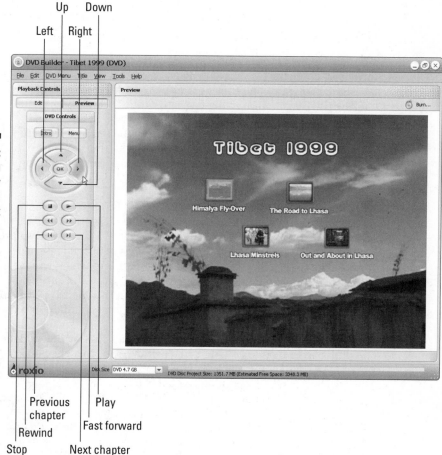

Figure 11-11:
You can preview your final DVD project in the Preview pane by using the DVD Controls in the Playback Controls pane.

When you finish previewing the titles on your DVD project, click the Edit button above the DVD Controls to return to the original DVD Builder window divided into the Edit Task Pane, Menu Editor, and Production Editor. From there, you can make any necessary changes that you noted when previewing the titles in the project, or, if everything looks good, you can burn the DVD project to CD or DVD disc.

Burning DVD Projects to Disc

After you preview your DVD project and make any necessary last-minute changes to it, you're ready to burn it to disc. The procedure for burning your DVD projects to CD or DVD disc (depending upon the project type — see "Launching DVD Builder and Selecting Your DVD Project" earlier in this chapter for details) with DVD Builder is very much like burning a data disc project (see Chapter 3) or audio CD or MP3 project (see Chapter 7) with Creator Classic.

After saving the finalized DVD project in the program's native DMSD file format by choosing File⇨Save or File⇨Save As and putting a blank CD-R or DVD-R disc in your computer's CD or DVD drive, you begin the process by clicking the Burn button at the far right of the Menu Editor Pane's toolbar.

DVD Builder then opens the condensed version of the Burn Setup dialog box. To expand this dialog box and display all the settings for this dialog box (as shown in Figure 11-12), click the Show Advanced Settings button near the bottom of the original Burn Setup dialog box.

As you can see in Figure 11-12, by default, the Burn to Disc check box is selected so that DVD Builder burns your DVD project to the type of disc called for by the project's type. If you also want to save the DVD project as an image file on your hard disk, click the Save Image File check box and then use its Browse button to select the folder into which to save this file in the Save Image dialog box. An image file contains the entire contents of your DVD project and you can burn discs from this file later by using the Easy Media Creator's Creator Classic application (see Chapter 3).

DVD Builder also selects the Finalize Disc check box by default when burning the project to a DVD-R, DVD+R, or DVD-RAM disc (this check box option is grayed out when you're recording to a DVD-RW or DVD+RW disc). When the Finalize Disc check box contains a checkmark, you cannot later add more files after you burn your DVD project to disc. Note that you can safely de-select the Finalize Disc check box option when you intend only to view the disc in your computer's drive and want to be able to later add more files to it. If, however, your intention is to burn a DVD disc for viewing in a standalone DVD player, you must finalize the DVD-R, DVD+R, or DVD-RAM disc in order to be able to play it in these types of players.

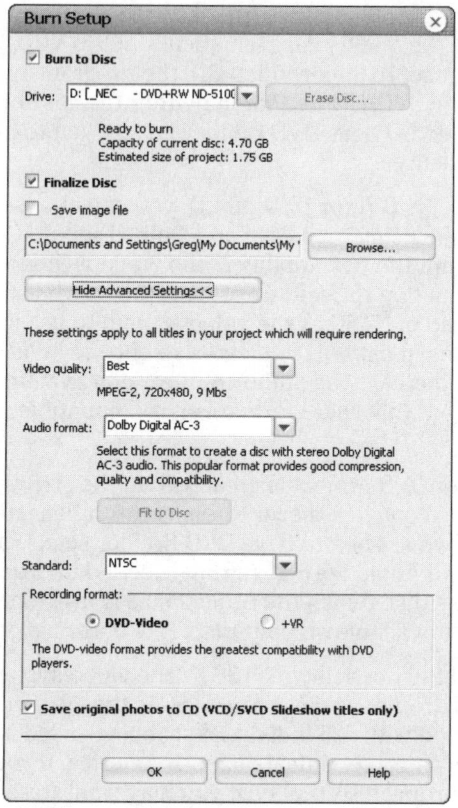

Figure 11-12:
You select
the settings
for burning
your
finalized
DVD project
to disc in
the Burn
Setup
dialog box.

The steps for selecting the other burn settings and then burning your project to disc are as follows:

1. **(Optional) If you've inserted a rewritable disc that already contains files into computer's drive, click the Erase Disc button to remove these files.**

   The Erase Disc button is only available when you're not using a blank disc and the disc is rewritable. If you're using a blank disc, you may skip to Step 2 if you want to review and possibly change any of the settings for disc's video quality, audio format, video system, or recording format. If you don't want to make any changes to these settings, skip to Step 3.

   When making changes to these settings, keep the following things in mind:

   • If the DVD project is DVD or DVD on CD, you can change the Video Quality settings from the default of Best to Good, Medium, or Low in order to increase the amount of data compression applied to the files in your project (while at the same time lowering the visual

quality of the video and still images). Note that if your project is
set to Video CD, the quality is automatically set to VCD, just as
when the project set to Super Video CD, the program automatically
sets the quality to SVCD. Note that in neither the case of a Video
CD or Super Video CD does DVD Builder enable you to modify its
default Video Quality.

- If the DVD project is DVD or DVD on CD, you can choose between
compressed audio using the LPCM and Dolby Digital AC-3 default
format. If you want the best-quality audio, you can choose the
LPCM audio format on the Audio Format drop-down list. If you
select PAL instead of NTSC as the video system to use in the
Standard drop-down list box, you can also choose MPEG as the
audio format to increase the audio compression even further
(just be aware that this audio format is not compatible with all
DVD players).

- If the size of your DVD project is greater than the size of the disc
you're using, you can click the Fit to Disc button beneath the Audio
Format drop-down list box to have DVD Builder select both the
Video Quality and Audio Format settings needed in order to fit all
your titles on the disc (when the project size is less than the total
amount of space available on your disc, this button is grayed out).

- By default, DVD Builder selects NTSC as the video system to use
in the Standard drop-down list box (NTSC is the system of 29.97
frames per second with 525 individual scan lines used in North
America, Japan, and a good deal of South America. If you're making
the disc for a European DVD player, you may want to select PAL in
the Standard drop-down list (the standard system of 25 frames per
second with 625 individual scan lines favored in Europe).

- By default, DVD Builder selects the DVD-Video option button as the
default Recording Format setting (which is the standard recording
format for commercial DVDs and is compatible with all types of
DVD players). Select the +VR option button to select the DVD+RW
Video Recording Format to create a disc that can be edited by a
DVD+RW video recorder (just note that +VR playback is not compatible with all types of DVD players).

- By default, DVD Builder selects the Save Original Photos to CD
(VCD/SVCD Slideshow Titles Only) check box at the bottom of the
Burn Setup dialog box to copy the still images used in the DVD pro-
ject to a directory on the CD when you burn the project to a disc.
Deselect this check box only if you don't want the still images
copied in your VCD or SVCD slideshow.

2. **Click the Show Advanced Settings button to display the options in
the Advanced Burn Setup dialog box and then make any necessary
changes to the video quality, audio format, video system, and recording format settings with the associated drop-down list boxes.**

Now you're ready to close the Burn Setup dialog box and proceed to the Burn Progress dialog box which keeps you informed of the program's progress in encoding and then writing and finalizing all the titles and the menus in your DVD project to CD or DVD disc.

3. **Click the OK button at the bottom of the Burn Setup dialog box to close it and then open the Burn Progress dialog box which keeps you informed of its progress in burning the individual titles and menus in your DVD project to CD or DVD disc.**

After DVD Builder finishes burning your DVD project to disc, a DVDBUILDER dialog box appears that enables you to play your disc using any of the DVD video and movie playing software programs on your computer (including, of course, the Windows Media Player). To play the disc, click the program you want to use to play your disc and then click the OK button. To close this dialog box without playing the disc, click the Cancel button instead.

After closing the DVDBUILDER dialog box (and the software such as Windows Media Player, if you chose to play the disc), you are returned to the Burn Status dialog box (which now shows the Overall Status and Current Operation as complete). Close this dialog box by clicking its OK button to return to the DVD Builder window from which you initiated the burn operation.

Regardless of whether you play a newly burned DVD disc in your computer's DVD drive using software such as Windows Media Player, you will definitely want to try playing the new DVD disc in your standalone DVD Player using its remote control to test out and select the various titles on the disc's menus. Note that you can also prepare an adhesive label for your DVD disc and inserts for its jewel case using Roxio's Label Creator (as described in Chapter 8). If you don't want to take the risk of applying an adhesive label to the disc (see the end of Chapter 2 for my warning on using adhesive labels on discs), identify the disc by writing its name with a non-solvent based marker on the label (what is commonly called the top) side of the disc. Of course, you never, never write on the bottom, shiny side of the disc, as this is the side the laser reads.

Plug & Burn: From tape to disc in one step

DVD Builder's Plug & Burn feature enables you to burn your raw, unedited digital video directly from your camcorder or your TV or VCR connected to your computer directly to a DVD disc in your computer's DVD drive. This is a great feature for transferring video such as lectures or live entertainment events (when video recording is not prohibited) where editing is not really required for the DVD disc.

To use the Plug & Burn feature, connect your camera, TV, or VCR to the computer using the appropriate cable and then insert a blank DVD disc in your computer's DVD drive. Then follow these steps:

1. **Launch DVD Builder and then click the Plug & Burn link in the On-Disc Options area of the Edit Task Pane.**

   DVD Builder opens a Plug & Burn dialog box similar to the one shown in Figure 11-13. This dialog box contains a preview area with playback controls below it where you can cue up the frame when recording from a video or cassette tape from which you want to begin recording.

   By default, DVD Builder captures your video at the best quality using the Dolby Digital AC-3 compressed audio file format in the NTSC standard recording format. To modify these settings or the audio recording level or balance, you open the Capture Settings dialog box by clicking the Capture Settings button in the Plug & Burn dialog box.

   By default, the program burns the video using the DVD-Video recording format rather than the +VR format, the so-called DVD+RW Video Recording Format that can be edited by a DVD+RW video recorder. To change the recording format, open the Burn Settings dialog box and then click the +VR option button in the Capture Burn Settings dialog box.

2. **(Optional) Make any necessary changes in the Capture Settings dialog box and/or Burn Settings dialog box (opened by clicking the Capture Settings and Burn Settings buttons, respectively).**

   Next you need to enter a new name for your DVD disc in the New Title Name text box.

3. **Click the Insertion point in the Next Title Name text box and drag through the temporary disc name before you begin typing to replace this text with the name you want the DVD disc to have.**

   If you're recording a video or cassette tape and you want to record the entire tape, you first need to rewind the tape before you click Capture Entire Tape. If you're recording from tape and you want to begin recording from a particular frame in the video, you need to use the playback controls to display this starting frame in the preview area before you click the Start Capturing button. If you're recording from your TV tuner, you need to select the right channel before you click the Start Capturing button.

4. **If recording a video or cassette tape, find the frame in the tape where you want to start recording (this is the first frame if you want to record the whole tape) and then click the Start Capturing or Capture Entire Tape button. If recording from your TV tuner, select the right channel and then click the Start Capturing button.**

   As soon as you click the Start Capturing button, it becomes a Stop Capturing button. If you want to pause the video capture (either to miss a commercial break or find a new place in the tape), click the Stop Capture button. Then, when you want to restart the recording (after the break or when you've cued the tape), click the Capture Again button (which replaces the Stop Capture button as soon as you click it). Note that each time you click Start Capture after stopping it, DVD Builder creates a new title for the disc.

5. **As soon as you finish recording your video, click the Close button at the bottom of the Plug & Burn dialog box.**

As soon as you click the Close button to close the Plug & Burn dialog box, DVD Builder displays the Burn Status dialog box which keeps you informed of the program's progress as it begins burning your captured video to the DVD disc in your computer's drive. As soon as the program finishes burning all the titles, the DVDBUILDER dialog box appears where you can select a software program such as Windows Media Player to play your disc.

After you close the playback software program or click the Cancel button in the DVD BUILDER dialog box, you still need to click the OK button in the Burn Status dialog box to close it. The program returns you to the DVD Builder window where the title saved on disc appears in the Production Editor pane. You can then close the DVD Builder window or start a new DVD project by choosing File➪New on the menu bar or open an existing project for further editing by choosing File➪Open or File➪Open Recent and then selecting the DMSD file to open.

Figure 11-13: You use the settings in the Plug & Burn dialog box to burn raw digital video directly from camcorder to DVD disc.

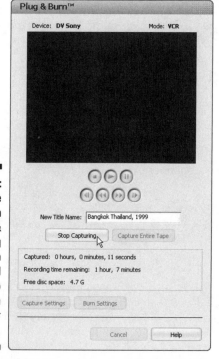

Editing a rewritable DVD disc

DVD Builder enables you to edit the contents of a DVD project on a DVD-R, DVD+R, or DVD-RAM disc that has *not* been finalized or on any DVD-RW or DVD+RW (you can always edit the titles on these types of rewritable discs provided that they are not already full of data). To edit a DVD project, you insert the DVD disc in your computer's DVD drive, launch DVD Builder, and then click the Edit DVD Disc link at the bottom of the On-Disc Options in the Edit Task Pane. Select the drive with the DVD disc in the Disc to Record To drop-down list box in the Edit DVD Disc dialog box and then click the OK button.

DVD Builder then opens the DVD project in the DVD Builder window where you can use any of its editing features to create additional titles (provided that there's sufficient free disc space) or edit the contents of the existing titles. When you finish editing the DVD project, save the changes to the project by choosing File⇨Save or File⇨Save As (if you want to retain the original unedited DVD project on your hard disk) on the DVD Builder menu bar and then click the Burn button at the far right of the Menu Editor pane's toolbar or choose File⇨Burn on the menu bar.

The Burn Status dialog box opens, showing you the progress while the edited DVD project is burned to the DVD disc. When the program finishes burning the updated project, click the OK button to close the Burn Status dialog box and return to the DVD Builder window.

Part V

The Part of Tens

The 5th Wave   By Rich Tennant

DAD ADDS MULTIMEDIA SOUND AND GRAPHICS TO THE TRADITIONAL CAMPFIRE GHOST STORY.

In this part . . .

Part V, the delightful Part of Tens, is the place to go to get some quick, concise information about the versatile components and features offered in Roxio's Easy Media Creator 7. Chapter 12 briefs you on each of the major components in the suite with valuable information on what in the world it's good for. Chapter 13 gives you my take on the ten coolest features (many of them new) offered by the Easy Media Creator.

Chapter 12

Top Ten Components of Easy Media Creator 7

As you soon discover when you start using Easy Media Creator 7, it's more like a combo of different mini-programs than a single software program. This chapter looks at each of the top ten modules in the Easy Media Creator suite, with an eye toward its basic functions and features. Use this list to get the lowdown on each of the major applications and tools that you use to collect, organize, and create cool projects using all the different forms of digital media: audio, still image, and video.

Roxio Disc Copier

Roxio Disc Copier is the application to use when you need to duplicate the CD and DVDs that you create and burn with the other Easy Media Creator components including Creator Classic and DVD Builder. In addition, you can use this nifty program to make backup copies of non-protected the commercially produced CDs and DVDs.

The greatest thing about this program is that you don't need to have two CD or DVD drives on your computer in order to make your copies: Disc Copier can make backups using one CD or DVD drive by temporarily copying the disc files from the original CD or DVD disc to your hard disk and then copying these files from the hard disk onto a new CD or DVD disc that you put in the same drive.

You can access this program from the Easy Media Creator Home by clicking any of the four following links:

- ✔ **Copy Audio CD** in the Music column
- ✔ **Copy Data Disc** in Data column
- ✔ **Copy DVD** in the DVD column
- ✔ **Disc Copier**

See Chapters 3 and 8 for details on using Disc Copier to make backup copies of data and audio CDs.

Audio and Data Discs Thanks to Creator Classic

Creator Classic is the place to go when you need to compile diverse data or music files into a single project. You can then use Creator Classic to burn CD or DVD discs from the data or audio media files you add to your particular projects.

Creator Classic supports the creation of data backup discs from Data Disc projects as well as standard Audio CDs from Audio CD projects and the more-and-more popular MP3 discs from MP3 Disc Projects. In addition, you can use Creator Classic to create two different kinds of special projects that mix data and audio. You can burn Enhanced CDs that combine data and audio in separate sessions that can be played in any CD player or CD-ROM drive (CD players play only the music tracks in the later sessions, while CD-ROM can read both the data in the first session and the audio files in the later sessions) from Enhanced CD Projects. You can also burn Mixed-CDs that combine data and audio in a single session that can only be played in your computer's CD-ROM or DVD drive with software programs like Windows Media Player from Mixed Mode CD Projects.

When creating audio CDs, Creator Classic makes it easy to obtain track, artist, and album information from the Gracenote CD online database. You can also use Creator Classic's features to edit the tracks that you add to your audio project, including merging different tracks into one as well as adding transitions between them.

From the Easy Media Creator, you can launch Creator Classic by using any of the following links:

✔ **Create New Audio CD** to launch Creator Classic and start a new Audio CD Project

✔ **Create New MP3 Disc** to launch Creator Classic and start a new MP3 Disc Project

✔ **Copy Files to Disc** to launch Creator Classic and start a new Data Disc Project

✔ **Create Backup Disc** to launch Creator Classic and access the Backup Projects pane

✔ **Creator Classic** to simply launch the Creator Classic program where you can start any of the projects listed above as well as an Enhanced CD Project and a Mixed-CD project.

See Chapter 3 for specific information on creating Data Disc projects and data backup discs. See Chapter 7 for detailed information on creating Audio CD, MP3 Disc, Enhanced CD, and Mixed-CD Projects.

Getting the Media You Need with Capture

The Capture utility enables you to acquire digital media files from both digital and analog sources connected to your computer. You can use Capture to acquire still images from scanners and digital cameras connected to your computer. You can also use Capture to acquire digital video directly from your digital camcorder or from an analog device such as your VCR connected to your computer. And if that's not enough for you, you can use Capture to acquire audio files from audio CDs in your computer's CD-ROM or DVD drive, as live audio using a microphone, or from other some other analog playback device such as a record player or audio cassette player connected to your computer. And finally, you can use Capture to acquire individual movie titles from unencrypted DVD discs (usually the ones you create with DVD Builder) that you put in your computer's DVD drive.

To launch Capture from the Easy Media Creator Home, you can click any of the following links:

✔ **Import Photos** in the Photo column

✔ **Capture Video** in the Video column

✔ **Capture** in the Tools column

To get detailed information on using Capture to acquire any of the previously mentioned types of digital media, see Chapter 9.

Audio Recording and Editing with Sound Editor

The Sound Editor tool enables you to record audio from various digital and analog audio devices connected to your computer and to edit audio files that you've already acquired. In addition, you can use Sound Editor to convert one type of audio file into another (for example, if you have an audio file saved in the uncompressed WAV audio file format that you want to add to an MP3 Disc Project that you're preparing with Creator Classic). You can open it in Sound Editor and then convert it to a compressed MP3 file (after selecting the audio quality and the amount of compression).

When it comes to editing audio files, Sound Editor not only enables you to trim the audio file, add fade-in and fade-out effects at the beginning and end, and adjust the overall volume, but it also enables you to insert or remove silences in a recording, add track breaks, as well as enhance the audio using any of a number of useful and some not so useful but zany and fun special effects.

To launch the Sound Editor from the Easy Media Creator Home, click the Sound Editor link in the Tool column. For detailed information about using Sound Editor to both record and edit audio files, see Chapter 5.

Disc Labeling with Label Creator

Label Creator is a really fun and surprisingly efficient utility for designing and printing labels and jewel case inserts for the CD and DVD discs you create with its Creator Classic and DVD Builder applications. Label Creator makes short work of the design end of the process by offering you a wide variety of disc label and jewel case inserts to choose from. In addition, its Auto-Fill feature enables you to automatically obtain the track, artist, and album information for audio CDs and volume information for data discs.

After designing your disc labels and jewel case inserts, you can use Label Creator to print out labels either on plain paper, specially prepared adhesive disc label, or even directly on your disc as well as on perforated case insert paper. The utility also makes it easy to make any necessary printing adjustments to get the label and case inserts to print just where you want them on the page.

To launch Label Creator from the Easy Media Creator Home, click the Label Creator link in the Tools column. You can also launch this utility from the Burn Progress dialog box when burning a CD or DVD disc with Creator Classic by clicking the Start Label Creator button. For complete information on using the Label Creator, see Chapter 8.

Getting Your Media Organized with Media Manager

Media Manager is a godsend when it comes to managing all the different files of different media types that you end up using with the projects you create with the various Easy Media Creator applications. Among the most useful of its features are its media collections. Collections are special files that gather together whatever media files you add to them without requiring you to physically locate the files together in the same file folder on your hard disk. Because collections don't require you to physically relocate the media files they contain, you can make the same media file (such as a company logo or often-used audio track) a part of as many different collections as you want. Whenever you open a particular collection in the Media Manager window, all of its files are available to you without your having to pay any attention to where in the world they're actually located on computer system.

In addition to organizing your media files into collections, Media Manager also makes it easy to find specific media files by tagging them with keywords, textual comments, and sound tags. You can then later use Media Manager's Search feature to quickly and easily find media files that contain the same keyword or commentary text. Media Manager also makes it easy to back up your media files on disc using the same burn engine as Creator Classic.

You can launch Media Manager from the Easy Media Creator Home by clicking the Media Manager link at the top of the Tools column. To get detailed information on using Media Manager's cool features for organizing your media files, see Chapter 4.

Enhancing and Organizing Digital Photos with PhotoSuite

PhotoSuite provides multipurpose editing for your digital photos. In addition to being able to make enhancements that fix flaws such as redeye, over- and under-exposure, and blurriness, you can also do standard editing such as rotating, cropping, and resizing images. PhotoSuite also has tools that enable you to annotate your photos by adding text and to retouch them by painting and drawing on them.

Beyond these very useful but very typical photo editing features, PhotoSuite offers some really exciting and unusual ones. The program makes it easy to superimpose multiple photos on top of one another to create photo montages. The program also offers several different project templates for placing your photos in projects such as photo collages, greeting cards, gift tags, postcards, and calendars. Last but not least, PhotoSuite contains a Photo Stitch feature that enables you to create sweeping panoramas from multiple individual photos that pan a landscape and overlap one another.

Of course, the program makes short work of printing photos, either individually, in groups, or even as contact sheets. PhotoSuite also makes it easy to share your edited photos with friends and family by sending them as e-mail attachments or by uploading them to the Roxio Photo Center.

To launch PhotoSuite from the Easy Media Creator Home, you can click any of the following links:

- ✔ **Edit and Fix Photos** in the Photo column to launch PhotoSuite and display the Open dialog box where you can select the photo file to edit

- ✔ **E-mail Photos** in the Photo column to launch PhotoSuite and open the E-mail pane in its program window

- ✔ **Create Greeting Card** in the Photo column to launch PhotoSuite and open the Create a Project pane in its program window

- ✔ **PhotoSuite** in the Applications column to simply open the PhotoSuite program

For complete information on using PhotoSuite to enhance your photos or in any of its photo editing projects, see Chapter 6.

Easy Video Editing with VideoWave

VideoWave is one of the most amazing digital editing programs available for personal computers. It combines an easy-to-use interface and a couple of step-by-step wizards with sophisticated video editing features and the option between editing the production in its default Storyline or new Timeline mode.

VideoWave enables you to add background audio or actually narrate your production in real time. The program also offers you a choice among a wide variety of scene transitions along with a good assortment of text, overlay, and filter effects. In addition, VideoWave contains a powerful Motions Pictures effect that enables you to pan and zoom around still images (giving them the illusion of motion) and video clips (enabling you to focus on the action within the frames).

When you complete the editing of your video production, VideoWave makes it easy to output your finished movie to whatever format suits your needs, be that showing the movie on your computer with the Windows Media Player, uploading it to the Internet for viewing on the Web, sending it to an external device such as your VCR or digital video camera, or even sending it as an e-mail attachment.

To launch VideoWave from the Easy Media Creator Home, you can click any of the following links:

- ✔ **Edit Video** in the Video column to launch VideoWave and open a new production in Storyline mode

- ✔ **Create Slideshow** in the Photo column to launch VideoWave and start a Storyboard production

- ✔ **Auto Edit with CineMagic** in the Video column to launch VideoWave and start the CineMagic wizard

- ✔ **Guided Edit with StoryBuilder** in the Video column to launch VideoWave and start the StoryBuilder wizard

- ✔ **VideoWave** in the Applications column to launch VideoWave and open a new production in Storyline mode

For details on using VideoWave, refer to Chapter 10.

Creating and Burning DVD Projects with DVD Builder

The DVD Builder application enables you to assemble your digital video and still images into DVD projects that you can then burn to CD or DVD disc complete with menus for viewing in standalone DVD players or in your computer's DVD drive. DVD Builder makes it easy to assemble your media in finished productions using readymade themes that you can easily customize.

When you're finished assembling, editing, and previewing your DVD project, you can then use the program to burn the finished production to disc using the standard DVD, VCD (Video CD), or SVCD (Super Video CD) formats. In addition to its powerful tools for assembling DVD projects, DVD Builder also includes its new Plug & Burn and Edit DVD Disc features. Plug & Burn enables you to burn your video direct from camcorder or video cassette player to DVD disc. The Edit DVD disc player enables you to edit the titles on an existing

DVD disc (which has been neither encrypted nor finalized) and then burn the changes you make using the DVD Builder editing tools onto the disc.

To launch DVD Builder from the Easy Media Creator Home, you can click any of the following links:

- ✔ **Create New DVD** in the DVD column to launch DVD Builder and open the Project Type dialog box where you select the type of DVD project to create

- ✔ **Plug & Burn** in the DVD column to launch DVD Builder and open the Plug & Burn dialog box for burning video tape directly to DVD disc

- ✔ **DVD Builder** in the Applications column to launch DVD Builder and open the Project Type dialog box where you select the type of DVD project to create

For complete details on using DVD Builder, see Chapter 11.

Copying Files on the Fly with Drag-to-Disc

Last but certainly not least is Drag-and-Drop, the program that makes it a snap to backup media files of any type on disc. All you have to do to start a backup is put a CD or DVD disc in your computer's CD-ROM or DVD drive, drag the icons for the folder or file to backup from the Windows Explorer, and then drop them on the Drag-to-Disc program icon which you keep on your Windows desktop at all times when using the computer. The Drag-to-Disc program formats the CD or DVD disc if the disc requires it and then proceeds to copy the files. You can continue to copy files to the disc if there's still additional space.

In addition to copying media files to disc on the fly, Drag-and-Drop offers a nifty little ScanDisc utility that can check your disc for errors and attempt to repair discs whose files have become unreadable or otherwise corrupted.

To launch Drag-to-Disc (when its program icon doesn't automatically appear when you start up Windows) from the Easy Media Creator Home, click the Drag-to-Disc link in the Applications column. To get more information on using Drag-to-Disc to backup files, see Chapter 3.

Chapter 13

Ten Coolest Features in Easy Media Creator 7

. . . .

In This Chapter

▶ Easy Media Creator 7's Home

▶ Napster access from the Easy Media Creator Home

▶ CineMagic and Storyboard wizards in VideoWave

▶ Timeline video editing in VideoWave

▶ Impromptu movies, slideshows, and playlists with QuickShow

▶ Panoramas with PhotoSuite's Photo Stitch feature

▶ SmartScan in VideoWave

▶ Plug & Burn in DVD Builder

▶ DVD video copies with Disc Copier

▶ Edit DVD Disc in DVD Builder

. . . .

*R*oxio Easy Media Creator 7 sports some very remarkable and definitely cool features for working with all types of media. This chapter highlights the ten coolest of the cool with an eye toward how they can help you get your work done in crack time or, at the very least, have yourself a rocking good time! As I note, some of these features are brand spanking new to version 7 of this suite, but whether new or old, they are all just plain great to use.

Home Is Where Access to Every Easy Media Creator Component Is

In Easy Media Creator 7, the new Home module is the be-all and end-all of the various applications, tools, and utilities. This new module gives you instant access to all these Easy Media Creator components with its single-click hyperlinks arranged into the categories of Applications and Tools. In addition, the Easy Media Creator Home enables you to launch just the module you need to use by selecting links to common tasks, these task links being arranged into media categories (Music, Data, Photo, Video, and DVD) along the top of the Home window.

The Easy Media Creator Home even makes it easy to open projects that you've created (while at the same time launching its associated application or tool) for further editing by listing all the various types of productions and projects you've worked on in the Recent Projects pane along the bottom of the Home window.

I guess the best thing about Home is the way that it interconnects Easy Media Creator's diverse components. By launching different applications and tools using its links, you're assured that you'll return Home the moment you exit the program or utility that you launched. This gives you the opportunity to then launch the next module that you may need in the editing process. In any case, launching and then returning to the Easy Media Creator Home gives you a much better sense of how all its diverse components come together to make almost any type of media editing possible. See Chapter 1 for more on using the Easy Media Creator Home module.

Napster at Your Service

I'm definitely no rapster, but when it comes to downloading and streaming audio from the Internet it just has to be Napster. This Napster is not the much maligned pirates' cove of free music downloads but has been reborn as a great online music service where you can sample and then purchase almost any genre of music. Best yet is the Napster Premium Service. For $9.95 a month, this subscriber service (which I'm using to listen a favorite playlist even as I write this paean) enables you to stream and download almost any tune in its enormous music database to your computer for your listening enjoyment (you have to purchase the tracks if you want to be able to burn them to audio CDs using Easy Media Creator's Creator Classic program).

If you have a MP3 portable player, you can download the Napster tunes you purchase directly to your player already organized in playlists. If you want to make an audio CD out of the tunes you buy, you can burn the CD directly from Napster without having to bother with returning to the Easy Media Creator Home and launching its Creator Classic program (both Napster and Creator Classic share the same burn engine).

Easy Media Creator Home gives you easy access to the Napster program through either its Download and Stream Music or Napster link. It also enables you to download and install the Napster program through a single click of the Napster button in the lower-right corner of the Easy Media Creator window. I just don't see how they could make it any easier for you to have and enjoy your favorite music.

Videos, Slideshows, and Playlists to Go with QuickShow

One of my most favorite features in Easy Media Creator 7 is quietly tucked away in the Media Manager module. This is the QuickShow feature that enables you to instantly turn a group of video clips, photos, or audio tracks into impromptu movies, slideshows, or playlists, respectively. All you do to put on any of these instant shows is open the folder or collection file that contains the media you want to use. Then select the thumbnails of all the same media type (video, still image, or audio files) in the Contents area of Media Manager window and click the Send Selected Items To drop-down list button on the Contents pane's toolbar and then click QuickShow.

Media Manager then arranges the selected media files into a show that Windows displays full screen on your computer. This screen contains a simple playback controller that you can then use to pause the show, advance to its next element, or even close to return to the Media Manager window. QuickShow is not only fun to use but is a great way to put together quick-and-dirty video sequences to create a kind of instant storyboarding. See the sidebar in Chapter 4 for more on this cool feature.

Simple to Create Music and Themed Videos

CineMagic and StoryBuilder are two new fun and easy ways to convert your digital video into finished productions in no time at all. With CineMagic you can turn the digital photos or video clips of your favorite vacation into a music video set to a music track of your own choice. All you have to do is select the media files and the background music to use in your production and CineMagic does the rest (making all the editing decisions for you).

With StoryBuilder you can quickly turn the digital photos or video clips of your child's last birthday party or your parents' 25th wedding anniversary into a themed video. All you have to do is select the digital photos and videos to include and the category and particular template of video theme you want to use and StoryBuilder does the rest. Like CineMagic, StoryBuilder makes all the editing decisions, including what background music to use.

See Chapter 10 for details on creating your own video productions with CineMagic and StoryBuilder.

More Complex Video Editing in Timeline Mode

VideoWave 7 adds a new editing mode known as Timeline to its already tried-and-true Storyline editing mode. When editing your video productions in Timeline mode, you have more control over your production, including the ability to add multiple elements (such as background audio, narration, text, special effects, and overlays) to either the entire video production or just one of its elements such as a particular video clip or still image that you've added to one of its panels.

In addition, editing in Timeline mode gives you a view of each of the elements in your video production as they relate to the Timeline ruler. This ruler gives you the time code for any point in the production and can be instantly expanded from the current position by simply dragging one its indicators with the mouse.

Combined with the intuitive Storyline mode, editing in Timeline mode gives you much finer control over video productions where you want to time and overlay different elements with great precision. See Chapter 10 for details on editing your video production in Timeline mode.

Scene Stealing with SmartScan

SmartScan is a real dream come true when it comes to capturing digital video from your camcorder. Instead of forcing you to manually scan and then capture each and every scene on your videotape, with SmartScan you can have VideoWave do all the work. SmartScan will scan your entire videotape for scene breaks. It then presents each scene with its own thumbnail and time code, enabling you to pick and choose the scenes that you actually want captured as video clips on your hard drive.

After selecting the scenes to capture, SmartScan will then automatically locate these scenes in the videotape and copy them to your hard disk without your having to click another button. For more on this timesaving feature, see Chapter 9.

Direct From Tape to Disc with Plug & Burn

Plug & Burn is another one of those wonderful features that you didn't know you missed until you got it and then you wondered how you ever did without it. This little wonder enables you to go directly from videotape to DVD disc without having to bother with the intermediate step of using a DVD editor such as DVD Builder. This is perfect for transferring finished video cassettes to the more durable disc media or for immediately creating DVD discs from digital videotape that doesn't need any type editing such as recordings of live events (for which you have the right to copy, of course!).

All you need to do to use Plug & Burn convert videotape into DVD disc is connect the videotape player or camcorder to your computer, put the DVD disc in your computer's DVD drive, and then cue up the place in the tape where you want to start the recording. If you want to record the entire tape to disc, all you have to do is click the Capture Entire Tape button in the Plug & Burn dialog box. For more on using this nifty feature to go from tape to disc in one step, see Chapter 11.

Easy DVD Disc Copies

In addition to making copies of your audio CDs, you can use Roxio Disc Copier to make copies of any unencrypted DVD disc (which, of course, includes all the DVD projects that you burn to DVD disc with DVD Builder). Because Disc Copier visually displays the video and audio contents of your DVD disc, you can easily remove any unwanted content from the copy. If you want to make a duplicate disc, all you have to do to make the copy is switch the original and blank DVD disc when Disc Copier prompts you to do so. Duplicate discs make it possible to keep one set on the business site and another off-site just in case anything goes wrong at the office.

Direct Editing of Your DVD Discs

Last but not least of the coolest Easy Media Creator features is the ability to edit the contents of rewritable DVD discs or discs that you didn't finalize when originally burning them in DVD Builder. Editing DVD discs enables you to delete video content that you no longer want as well as add updated video content. This feature is perfect for editing DVDs created by capturing TV content through a set-top DVD recorder attached to your set. You, of course, can also use it to edit DVD discs that you've burned from DVD projects created in DVD Builder. For more on editing DVD discs, see Chapter 11.

Index

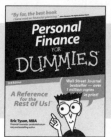

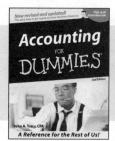

FOR DUMMIES®

A world of resources to help you grow

HOME, GARDEN & HOBBIES

0-7645-5295-3

0-7645-5130-2

0-7645-5106-X

Also available:

Auto Repair For Dummies
(0-7645-5089-6)

Chess For Dummies
(0-7645-5003-9)

Home Maintenance For
Dummies
(0-7645-5215-5)

Organizing For Dummies
(0-7645-5300-3)

Piano For Dummies
(0-7645-5105-1)

Poker For Dummies
(0-7645-5232-5)

Quilting For Dummies
(0-7645-5118-3)

Rock Guitar For Dummies
(0-7645-5356-9)

Roses For Dummies
(0-7645-5202-3)

Sewing For Dummies
(0-7645-5137-X)

FOOD & WINE

0-7645-5250-3

0-7645-5390-9

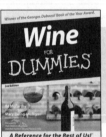

0-7645-5114-0

Also available:

Bartending For Dummies
(0-7645-5051-9)

Chinese Cooking For
Dummies
(0-7645-5247-3)

Christmas Cooking For
Dummies
(0-7645-5407-7)

Diabetes Cookbook For
Dummies
(0-7645-5230-9)

Grilling For Dummies
(0-7645-5076-4)

Low-Fat Cooking For
Dummies
(0-7645-5035-7)

Slow Cookers For Dummies
(0-7645-5240-6)

TRAVEL

0-7645-5453-0

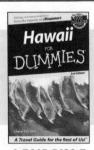

0-7645-5438-7

0-7645-5448-4

Also available:

America's National Parks For
Dummies
(0-7645-6204-5)

Caribbean For Dummies
(0-7645-5445-X)

Cruise Vacations For
Dummies 2003
(0-7645-5459-X)

Europe For Dummies
(0-7645-5456-5)

Ireland For Dummies
(0-7645-6199-5)

France For Dummies
(0-7645-6292-4)

London For Dummies
(0-7645-5416-6)

Mexico's Beach Resorts For
Dummies
(0-7645-6262-2)

Paris For Dummies
(0-7645-5494-8)

RV Vacations For Dummies
(0-7645-5443-3)

Walt Disney World & Orlando
For Dummies
(0-7645-5444-1)

Available wherever books are sold. Go to www.dummies.com or call 1-877-762-2974 to order direct.

FOR DUMMIES®

Plain-English solutions for everyday challenges

COMPUTER BASICS

0-7645-0838-5

0-7645-1663-9

0-7645-1548-9

Also available:

PCs All-in-One Desk Reference For Dummies (0-7645-0791-5)

Pocket PC For Dummies (0-7645-1640-X)

Treo and Visor For Dummies (0-7645-1673-6)

Troubleshooting Your PC For Dummies (0-7645-1669-8)

Upgrading & Fixing PCs For Dummies (0-7645-1665-5)

Windows XP For Dummies (0-7645-0893-8)

Windows XP For Dummies Quick Reference (0-7645-0897-0)

BUSINESS SOFTWARE

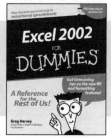
0-7645-0822-9

0-7645-0839-3

0-7645-0819-9

Also available:

Excel Data Analysis For Dummies (0-7645-1661-2)

Excel 2002 All-in-One Desk Reference For Dummies (0-7645-1794-5)

Excel 2002 For Dummies Quick Reference (0-7645-0829-6)

GoldMine "X" For Dummies (0-7645-0845-8)

Microsoft CRM For Dummies (0-7645-1698-1)

Microsoft Project 2002 For Dummies (0-7645-1628-0)

Office XP For Dummies (0-7645-0830-X)

Outlook 2002 For Dummies (0-7645-0828-8)

Get smart! Visit www.dummies.com

- **Find listings of even more** *For Dummies* **titles**
- **Browse online articles**
- **Sign up for Dummies eTips™**
- **Check out** *For Dummies* **fitness videos and other products**
- **Order from our online bookstore**

Available wherever books are sold. Go to www.dummies.com or call 1-877-762-2974 to order direct.

FOR DUMMIES®

Helping you expand your horizons and realize your potential

INTERNET

0-7645-0894-6

0-7645-1659-0

0-7645-1642-6

Also available:

America Online 7.0 For Dummies
(0-7645-1624-8)

Genealogy Online For Dummies
(0-7645-0807-5)

The Internet All-in-One Desk Reference For Dummies
(0-7645-1659-0)

Internet Explorer 6 For Dummies
(0-7645-1344-3)

The Internet For Dummies Quick Reference
(0-7645-1645-0)

Internet Privacy For Dummies
(0-7645-0846-6)

Researching Online For Dummies
(0-7645-0546-7)

Starting an Online Business For Dummies
(0-7645-1655-8)

DIGITAL MEDIA

0-7645-1664-7

0-7645-1675-2

0-7645-0806-7

Also available:

CD and DVD Recording For Dummies
(0-7645-1627-2)

Digital Photography All-in-One Desk Reference For Dummies
(0-7645-1800-3)

Digital Photography For Dummies Quick Reference
(0-7645-0750-8)

Home Recording for Musicians For Dummies
(0-7645-1634-5)

MP3 For Dummies
(0-7645-0858-X)

Paint Shop Pro "X" For Dummies
(0-7645-2440-2)

Photo Retouching & Restoration For Dummies
(0-7645-1662-0)

Scanners For Dummies
(0-7645-0783-4)

GRAPHICS

0-7645-0817-2

0-7645-1651-5

0-7645-0895-4

Also available:

Adobe Acrobat 5 PDF For Dummies
(0-7645-1652-3)

Fireworks 4 For Dummies
(0-7645-0804-0)

Illustrator 10 For Dummies
(0-7645-3636-2)

QuarkXPress 5 For Dummies
(0-7645-0643-9)

Visio 2000 For Dummies
(0-7645-0635-8)

Available wherever books are sold. Go to www.dummies.com or call 1-877-762-2974 to order direct.

FOR DUMMIES®

The advice and explanations you need to succeed

SELF-HELP, SPIRITUALITY & RELIGION

0-7645-5302-X

0-7645-5418-2

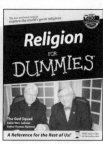

0-7645-5264-3

Also available:

The Bible For Dummies
(0-7645-5296-1)

Buddhism For Dummies
(0-7645-5359-3)

Christian Prayer For Dummies
(0-7645-5500-6)

Dating For Dummies
(0-7645-5072-1)

Judaism For Dummies
(0-7645-5299-6)

Potty Training For Dummies
(0-7645-5417-4)

Pregnancy For Dummies
(0-7645-5074-8)

Rekindling Romance For Dummies
(0-7645-5303-8)

Spirituality For Dummies
(0-7645-5298-8)

Weddings For Dummies
(0-7645-5055-1)

PETS

0-7645-5255-4

0-7645-5286-4

0-7645-5275-9

Also available:

Labrador Retrievers For Dummies
(0-7645-5281-3)

Aquariums For Dummies
(0-7645-5156-6)

Birds For Dummies
(0-7645-5139-6)

Dogs For Dummies
(0-7645-5274-0)

Ferrets For Dummies
(0-7645-5259-7)

German Shepherds For Dummies
(0-7645-5280-5)

Golden Retrievers For Dummies
(0-7645-5267-8)

Horses For Dummies
(0-7645-5138-8)

Jack Russell Terriers For Dummies
(0-7645-5268-6)

Puppies Raising & Training Diary For Dummies
(0-7645-0876-8)

EDUCATION & TEST PREPARATION

0-7645-5194-9

0-7645-5325-9

0-7645-5210-4

Also available:

Chemistry For Dummies
(0-7645-5430-1)

English Grammar For Dummies
(0-7645-5322-4)

French For Dummies
(0-7645-5193-0)

The GMAT For Dummies
(0-7645-5251-1)

Inglés Para Dummies
(0-7645-5427-1)

Italian For Dummies
(0-7645-5196-5)

Research Papers For Dummies
(0-7645-5426-3)

The SAT I For Dummies
(0-7645-5472-7)

U.S. History For Dummies
(0-7645-5249-X)

World History For Dummies
(0-7645-5242-2)

Available wherever books are sold. Go to www.dummies.com or call 1-877-762-2974 to order direct.

FOR DUMMIES

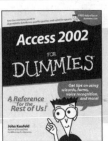